Deconstructing
Twilight

This book is part of the Peter Lang Education list.
Every volume is peer reviewed and meets
the highest quality standards for content and production.

PETER LANG
New York • Washington, D.C./Baltimore • Bern
Frankfurt • Berlin • Brussels • Vienna • Oxford

DONNA M. ASHCRAFT

Deconstructing Twilight

Psychological and Feminist Perspectives on the Series

PETER LANG
New York • Washington, D.C./Baltimore • Bern
Frankfurt • Berlin • Brussels • Vienna • Oxford

Library of Congress Cataloging-in-Publication Data

Ashcraft, Donna Musialowski.
Deconstructing Twilight: psychological and feminist perspectives
on the series / Donna M. Ashcraft.
p. cm.
Includes bibliographical references and index.
1. Meyer, Stephenie, 1973– Twilight saga.
2. Feminist literary criticism—United States. 3. Sex role in literature.
4. Psychology and literature. I. Title.
PS3613.E979Z57   813'.6—dc23   2012000746
ISBN 978-1-4331-1638-4 (paperback)
ISBN 978-1-4539-0538-8 (e-book)

Bibliographic information published by **Die Deutsche Nationalbibliothek**.
Die Deutsche Nationalbibliothek lists this publication in the "Deutsche
Nationalbibliografie"; detailed bibliographic data is available
on the Internet at http://dnb.d-nb.de/.

To Morgan and the rest of my feminist family

Table of Contents

List of Figures and Tables

Acknowledgments

No book can be completed without the help of many people and this book is no exception. *Deconstructing* Twilight was definitely a "family affair" and would not have been written and published were it not for my spouse and children, but friends, students and (obviously) the staff at Peter Lang publishing were also instrumental in its development and completion. Thanks go to my husband, Paul Ashcraft especially. It was he who pushed me to begin writing and to start the process of looking for a publisher, telling me, "You have something to say." He also was the one who kept pushing me to continue writing when I doubted that I could finish it, and he reviewed the entire manuscript, correcting formatting errors. My daughter, Morgan, was also extremely significant in the development and completion of *Deconstructing* Twilight. She helped me brainstorm about ideas to be included in the book, found examples of concepts I was looking for in the novels, organized my data and typed out notes. She was, in many ways, a personal assistant, despite her being still in high school while this book was being written, and her enthusiasm kept me going. My other children, Sam and Ryan, also helped me by typing up notes, relieving me of other responsibilities so that I could write, and enduring my repetitive discussions of the *Twilight* series. Thanks also to everyone at Peter Lang Publishing for their hard work, including, among many others, Caitlin Lavelle, who gave me extensive feedback on the first draft of *Deconstructing* Twilight that I sent in to Peter Lang Publishing. My students were also certainly influential in the development of *Deconstructing* Twilight. Their interest and enthusiasm was encouraging, and discussions we had in class provided additional ideas for some of the content of this book. My colleagues, especially Mark Mitchell, were also supportive as this project progressed through the long, bumpy road to publication. Finally, thanks need to also go to Clarion University and the Pennsylvania State System of Higher Education (PASSHE) for granting me a sabbatical to complete this manuscript.

CHAPTER ONE

Introduction

Like many mothers, I began reading the *Twilight* novels because my preteen daughters were reading them and because I kept hearing about them in the media. I was interested in what my daughters were reading and hopeful that this series was something that I, too, could enjoy and share with them. After all, who doesn't like vampire and werewolf stories! But unlike many mothers who applauded the books for their ability to encourage discussion with their daughters about such topics as boys, love relationships, sex, and violence (Leogrande, 2010), as I read through them I was disturbed by the traditional gender roles in the storylines. In fact, even though many readers are aware of the (feminist) criticisms of the series and are able to dismiss them in order to enjoy the series (Leogrande, 2010), I was unable to do so. I was further disturbed by just how much hype the novels were getting despite these traditional roles. The books were often praised for their message of sexual abstinence, but the troublesome inherent messages about the power differential in the sexual relationship between Bella and Edward were ignored. The gentlemanly manners of Edward Cullen were commended, but his controlling behaviors were disregarded even though they were often referred to by both Edward's and Bella's friends and family in the first books. Bella's protection of the Cullen family and friends was applauded, but her need to be repeatedly rescued was overlooked. Considering the popularity of the series, it was evident that many readers either interpreted the books differently than I or they did not see a problem with the depiction of the traditional roles. Thus, disparity in interpretations of the series created the seeds of *Deconstructing* Twilight, the goal of which is to provide an alternate view of the novels and movies.

Mirroring contradictory individual reactions of readers of the series are public reactions. The popularity of the series is evidenced by the enormous consumption of the *Twilight* franchise: At the end of 2009 more than 85 million copies of the *Twilight* series books were sold (Adams & Akbar, 2009). They have been translated into more than 38 languages, have received numerous awards (Adams & Akbar, 2009), and have been turned into vastly popular movies, the fifth, and last, of which was released November 2012 (Weintraub, 2010). But numerous blogs and magazine articles (e.g., Miller, 2008; Seifert, 2008) have pointed out problems with the sex-typed behaviors depicted in the books and movies. Unfortunately, those discussions have been dismissed as being antifeminine and as being feminist, as if that is a bad thing. Some have suggested that the series has been criticized unfairly, claiming the feminists who object to the series are elitist (Zach, 2009), that the criticism stems from a "rhetoric of superiority" (Sheffield & Merlo, 2010, p. 220), implying that such an analysis of the saga is unwarranted and sexist instead of vice versa. But the criticisms lodged against the *Twilight* saga are not antifeminine. Rather, they are anti-maladjustment. They consider problems that develop because of inequitable power in relationships, differentiate between dysfunctional and true love relationships, and encourage readers to contemplate limitations of traditionally feminine behaviors.

Certainly the *Twilight* books contain scenes and behaviors that are constructive. For example, although there has been an extensive amount of criticism launched against the characters of the series, Bella's and Edward's devotion to each other is admirable. Jake's loyalty and patience toward Bella are praiseworthy. And Carlisle's kindness and concern for humans are inspiring. The fact is that fans of characters in books and other media have always embraced characters and storylines that are less than ideal. Fans find action-movie heroes such as Laura Croft and James Bond appealing, despite their arrogance. They like television characters such as Dexter despite the fact that he is a serial killer. They like the story of *Wuthering Heights* despite the fact that neither Heathcliff nor Catherine is very likeable. Fans are able to focus on the positive aspects of these characters and stories while still being aware of their flaws, just as in real life, we are able to love and like our friends and family members despite the fact that they have flaws. But such commendable characteristics must not be the sole focus of the interpretation of the series. Concentrating on the series' supportive messages about love and friendship, ignoring other less admirable, more dysfunctional, behavior also depicted in the storylines, is akin to seeing the world through rose-colored glasses; it is pleasant and yet unrealistic. Thus, this book examines the *Twilight* series in more depth, noting the unhealthy, maladjusted behaviors of the characters, as well as the more inspiring actions, in the hope that if book lovers want to read the *Twilight* series, and other similar titles, despite their depiction of traditional gender roles, they (or we) are aware of the subtle, troublesome messages that are found in the saga, as well as the more overt positive ones.

Popularity of the *Twilight* Series

The popularity of the *Twilight* series has led to an extensive examination of the reasons for its appeal. Although there are other readers, the primary readership of the romance genre is heterosexual females (Romance Writers of America, 2011). Numerous literary scholars have suggested that the reason this genre is attractive to so many women is because, in addition to their entertainment value, such novels provide an opportunity to vicariously experience romance that readers might not ever have experienced or that they experienced in the past and are trying to relive and recapture (Juhasz, 1988). Romance novels allow (primarily female) readers to imagine experiencing the feeling of being pursued passionately by an attractive male partner, to dream about being the center of another's universe. From a psychological perspective, romance novels such as *Twilight* can be viewed as fulfilling needs, love needs especially. Many personality theorists have suggested that humans have a psychological need for love. For example, Abraham Maslow (1970) suggested that the need for love and feelings of belonging is the third level of a need hierarchy that motivates humans. Erich Fromm (1955) suggested that humans attempt to fulfill a series of existential needs in order to reunite with nature, one of which is a need for relatedness, that is, the need to form relationships with others. And Julian Rotter (1982) discussed six categories of needs, including one that encompassed the need for love and affection. Thus, romance novels can help readers to fulfill these needs, albeit only vicariously. Similarly, the appeal of romance novels can also be attributed to the possibility that they assist readers in their understanding of love relationships (Behm-Morawitz, Click, & Aubrey, 2010), an explanation that is also consistent with psychological theory: Notable psychologist Erik Erikson (1968), for instance, did not discuss the notion of psychological needs but did suggest that humans develop a certain aspect of personality as they go through stages and as they mature. During each of these stages we encounter a crisis, the resolution of which determines the aspect of our personality that is developed. In the sixth stage, young adulthood, which takes place during the approximate ages of 19–40, the crisis is one of intimacy versus isolation. It is during this stage that we learn to develop genuine, healthy love relationships. We learn to commit to another in an intimate way. Accordingly, reading romance novels might assist readers in the development of ideas on how to form a long-lasting love relationship and what are the characteristics of such relationships (Behm-Morawitz, et al., 2010).

Literary scholars have also suggested that romance novels help to shape the identities and self-concepts of their readers. For example, Radway (1991) suggests that the romance novel influences readers' thoughts and beliefs and allows them to take on the role of the protagonist. This notion can explain the popularity of the *Twilight* saga among tweens and teens in particular. The *Twilight* novels are not romance novels geared toward adult women as so many books in this genre are. They are considered to be young adult literature and so widely appeal to, and are written for, readers aged 14–21—although they are very popular among adult women as well (Leogrande, 2010)—and it is during this age that teens develop their sense of unique identity. Erikson's theory is again useful in the understanding of this process. According to Erikson (1968), it is during the fifth stage, adolescence, which takes place from about the age of 12 to about the age of 18, that children experience the conflict of identity versus role confusion. It is during this stage that adolescents figure out who they are, form their own identities, and romance novels might assist them in doing so. Feminist critiques of the genre, however, point out that the messages in romance novels that allow for the further development of identity, and ideas about what romantic relationships should be like, are unhealthy. Romance novels, for example, indicate that true love relationships adhere to traditional gender stereotypes, that conventional gender roles are appropriate, that the love of a woman can change a man, that love completes or fulfills a person (e.g., Sterk, 1986), all notions that are inaccurate and that will be discussed in later chapters. Thus, *Deconstructing* Twilight examines the *Twilight* series as part of the romance genre and applies similar feminist analysis to it, pointing out problems with these sex-typed portrayals and noting their dysfunctional qualities from a psychological perspective.

It should be noted, however, that while there is a substantial amount of feminist criticism lodged against the romance genre in general, other literary analysts contradict these opinions suggesting instead that "[r]omance novels are feminist documents. They're written almost exclusively by women, for women, and are concerned with women: their relations in family, love and marriage, their place in society, and the world, and their dreams for the future" (Bustillos, 2012, para. 5). In fact Dixon (1999) suggests that the underlying philosophy of romance novels is that "love is omnipotent . . . It is the solution to all problems, and it is peculiarly feminine" (p. 177). Moreover,

> the romance heroine draws her man into the domestic sphere, the realm of women, of home, in order to resolve their differences and establish sex with love as the central principle in their lives. . . . Men must be transformed by love and enter into the woman's realm in order to emerge as fully-realized human beings: this is the core message of romance fiction, Dixon argues. We need one another; embrace this idea and everything will magically work out. (Bustillos, 2012, para. 11–12)

Readers see this in the *Twilight* series as Edward slowly evolves, that is, transforms, becoming less paternalistic and controlling throughout the four novels (McClimans & Wisnewski, 2009), and as Bella adamantly believes that everything will work out, especially that she will magically survive her difficult pregnancy, and she ultimately does. She tells Jake, who is worried about her health, "'I'm not saying things will work out *easily* Jake. But how could I have lived through all that I've lived through and not believe in magic by this point?'"

(*Breaking Dawn*, p. 189). But, although romance fiction certainly is primarily written by women and for women, and although its content focuses primarily on what has been traditionally feminine concerns (family, love, marriage), such exclusivity does not necessarily imply feminist tendencies, especially considering that many (although not all) the male protagonists in such novels initially treat the female heroine with disrespect (Bustillos, 2012; Sterk, 1986), just as Edward initially treats Bella with contempt. Furthermore, feminism, by definition, implies progression toward gender equality. By tolerating initial power differentials between the male and female protagonists and by continuing to relegate female protagonists to traditional concerns of family, love, and marriage, equality is not advanced. Feminine is not feminist. Furthermore, as Bustillos notes, early romance novels were "rife with the sociopolitical limitations of their period" (Bustillos, 2012, para. 5)—they involve primarily heterosexual, Caucasian couples—and consequently are sex-typed. Those written today need not embrace traditional gender roles because today's sociopolitical culture is quite different, embracing extensive advancement toward gender equality. But the sex-typed behaviors in the *Twilight* series are often excused because the characters, such as Edward, were born in more traditional times and, therefore, learned more traditional behavior. As such, they continue to demonstrate attitudes and behaviors more appropriate to years gone by. In any case, the popularity of the *Twilight* series is at least partially due to the same reasons the romance genre in general has remained popular for centuries.

Natalie Wilson (2011a), author of *Seduced by* Twilight, speaks more specifically about the popularity of the *Twilight* series rather than the romance genre in general. She suggests that the series is so popular because the novels are written in a simple, open style that permits readers to interpret the storylines in multiple ways. This writing style allows the stories to essentially be all things to all people. Similarly, Granger (2010) suggests that the combination of the genres present in the novels (romance, horror, action) allow for fans of many types of stories to enjoy the series. Thus, some readers interpret the novels from a religious Christian lens (Felker-Jones, 2009; Gravett, 2010). Others interpret the novels from a Mormon perspective (Granger, 2010; Toscano, 2010) or a historical perspective (Reagin, 2010) or a philosophical perspective (Housel & Wisnewski, 2009), and still others from a feminist perspective (Ames, 2010). The books, therefore, appeal to so many because they allow readers to use and confirm their own frames of reference. Whether the open writing style that allows for these multiple perspectives is the reason for the series' popularity or not, contrasting interpretations of the novels will be discussed throughout this book.

Others have suggested that the *Twilight* series is popular because of the extensive social networking Meyer used to discuss the novels with her fans (Click, Aubrey, Behm-Morawitz, 2010) and because of the merchandising and clever consumerism and commodification of the series (Martens, 2010). Still others suggest that the novels fulfill other psychological needs than those noted for readers of romance novels. McMahon (2009) describes the novels as wish fulfillment, suggesting that their popularity is evidence of anxiety over our mortality and our fear of death. Zach (2009) and Buttsworth (2010) indicate that the novels are popular because they reflect what young women want: marriage into an upper-class family, a child, beauty, the epitome of success for Western women. Still others note that their popularity is due in part to the books allowing mothers and tween and teen daughters to bond and connect over their stories and appealing male characters (Leogrande, 2010). And author Stephen King (cited in Granger, 2010) credits the popularity of the novels to the fact that they are sexually appealing to adolescent girls but not in an overtly explicit way. While we may never know what ultimately made the *Twilight* franchise so immensely popular, it is certainly safe to say that most likely there were many factors involved, creating a "perfect storm," so to speak, which includes the majority of those noted here.

Deconstruction

The title of this book, *Deconstructing* Twilight, is loosely based on the literary usage of the term *deconstruction* and loosely based on postmodernist feminist philosophy. The goal of postmodernism, as is the goal of deconstruction in literature, is to separate myth from reality, to examine the subtle messages in literature, and in society, for accuracy. Deconstruction allows for a distinction between explicit and implicit messages in literature and other media. Explicit messages are those that are obvious. Implicit messages are not as obvious and are perceived only through deeper examination of storylines and the behavior of characters. These implicit meanings can be thought of as what is "read between the lines." Deconstruction, then, encourages "reading between the lines." It encourages examination of not only the obvious messages in a novel but also the less obvious, more subtle assumptions of those explicit messages that can be missed if one does not look closely or does not think deeply about them.

Thus, you can think of postmodernism as a theory and deconstruction as a tool that those theorists use. Consequently, a postmodernist feminist would use deconstruction to examine societal assumptions about gender and gender roles. For example, a postmodernist might examine the assumption that women are more nurturing than men and are, therefore, best to care for children. They might question the assumption that when couples have children, one parent should give up their career to stay home and care for the children. They could question the assumption that such a sacrifice is beneficial to children when compared to daycare. The same is true for literary criticism. Literary critics would examine a manuscript, evaluate it, and possibly determine the subtle messages in the manuscript. They could challenge alternate interpretations of the work. The goal of this book is to do just that, to challenge the acceptability of the traditional roles depicted in these novels and movies and expose problematic themes in them. In other words, the objective of *Deconstructing* Twilight is to examine the behaviors portrayed by the characters in the novels in a deeper way, to look beyond the overt and obvious in order to expose more subtle themes.

Support

As I deconstruct the *Twilight* series I rely on a number of different types of data, one of which is informal survey data I collected from a small number (roughly 100) of my undergraduate students, the majority of whom fell into the age range for which the *Twilight* series is written, that is, 14- to 21-year-olds. In an effort to better understand the popularity of the novels and movies and to better understand the vastly different impressions people have of the stories, I developed a questionnaire that asked respondents their impressions of the characters and stories, as well as their thoughts on feminism and whether they thought the books were feminist in nature or not. The majority of the questions were open-ended so that respondents would not feel compelled to provide answers that did not completely reflect their true feelings. Rather, the open-ended questions allowed respondents to write down their opinions as accurately as possible. Clearly, this is not an exhaustive survey of *Twilight* readers nor is it a representative sample of *Twilight* readers, but the comments students wrote are useful in further illustrating points that are already supported by other research projects as well as by the books themselves. Thus, when I refer to surveyed readers, it is this to which I am referring. Furthermore, I also refer to Web sites and blogs that discuss the *Twilight* series and, of course, the books themselves, which present ample evidence of the assertions I make and that I readily quote. Finally, I make extensive use of research and theory in the area of psychology, along with feminist writings. As such, *Deconstructing Twilight* is a logical examination of the *Twilight* series whose assertions and conclusions are supported also by scientific evidence described in understandable terms.

Common Themes

Behaviors in the Novels Are Sex-Typed

As numerous points are made through this book you will notice common themes, the first of which is that the gender roles in the novels are very sex-typed and traditional. Traditional persons behave in ways that typify conventional male and female roles: A man might be a breadwinner and his wife might be a stay-at-home mother, for example. There is considerable debate about whether the novels depict traditional gender roles or are examples of more modern gender roles (Seltzer, 2008) because, as Wilson (2011a) notes, the behaviors of the characters are inconsistent and often contradictory. Certainly, the characters in the *Twilight* series do sometimes display nontraditional (more modern) gender-role behaviors: Rosalie is exemplary at fixing cars; Alice and Bella are instrumental in saving the Cullen clan at the end of the series; Bella repeatedly attempts to assert herself in Edward's presence, trying to maintain control over her own body as she repetitively asks him to change her into a vampire. But, as Wilson (2011a) also notes, even though female characters do sometimes act nontraditionally, the main premise of the stories is that the primary focus of women is (and should be) men, love, marriage, having children, and family life. In fact, author Stephenie Meyer herself indicates that Bella values her love relationship with Edward above everything else (Meyer, n.d.a). Consequently, the portrayal of nontraditional behavior is subordinate to more traditional concerns. Mann (2009) comments on this concern as she describes her reaction to reading the series. She notes a sense "of having gone back in time to an old-fashioned world where women were seen as empty conduits of masculine desire and valued for the propensity for self-sacrifice" (p. 134). Further she describes Bella "as a representative of the idealized womanhood of my mother's generation" (p. 132).

Moreover, it could be argued that although the conduct of both the male and female characters is nontraditional on occasion, it is conventional the overwhelming majority of the time. From a psychological perspective just because a man engages in traditionally feminine behavior occasionally—let us say he cooks for his family—does not mean that he is feminine. Likewise, just because a woman acts masculine occasionally—perhaps she fixes the plumbing in her house—does not mean that she is masculine. When psychologists study masculinity and femininity in people, they measure the proportion of masculine to feminine behaviors. The Bem Sex Role Inventory (Bem, 1974), for example, requires a respondent to indicate, on a scale of one to seven, how characteristic a list of 60 adjectives are about themselves. Some of these items are masculine characteristics; others are feminine characteristics and still others do not fall into either category. Masculinity and femininity scores are then determined. If someone scores above a certain level on masculinity *and* below a certain level on femininity, s/he is considered masculine. If someone scores above a certain level on femininity *and* below a certain level on masculinity, s/he is considered feminine. Note then, that the amount of *both* femininity and masculinity is important in determining gender roles. Note also that if a respondent who usually acts in a feminine way engages in some masculine behavior, but not in a significant amount, s/he would still be considered feminine. Conversely, if a respondent who usually acts in a masculine way engages in some feminine behavior, but not in a significant amount, s/he would still be considered masculine. Thus, just because someone acts nontraditional occasionally, it does not mean that they *are* nontraditional. A certain level of cross-gender behavior is necessary to be placed in a different gender role category. If that level is not met, then that person is still considered traditional even with occasional episodes of nontraditional behavior. The point is that in the *Twilight* novels female characters occasionally act in traditionally masculine ways (and male characters occasionally act in traditionally feminine ways) but not enough so that they can be considered nontraditional.

The next five chapters demonstrate that the *Twilight* characters display primarily traditional gender roles: Chapter 2, *Feminist or Feminine?*, provides extensive evidence that the series heroine, Bella, especially engages in traditionally feminine roles, as do the majority of supporting female characters. Chapter 3, *The Motherhood Mystique*, further demonstrates the traditional feminine sex role by discussing the obsession the women characters in the novels have with motherhood, and chapter 4 discusses the debate about whether mothers should sacrifice careers in order to care for their children, noting the lack of career interest in the female *Twilight* characters. Chapter 5, *The Damsel in Distress*, details Bella's need to be rescued by her prince charmings, Edward and Jacob. Similarly, it is not just traditionally feminine behavior that is described in the *Twilight* series; the men in the novels also display many traditionally masculine behaviors. This is examined in chapter 6, *The Embodiment of Patriarchy*, which demonstrates that the behaviors of Edward and Jacob are paternalistic, sometimes bordering on abusive.

Again, it should be noted that there are readers who view the *Twilight* series as feminist in nature and see Bella as nontraditional. In fact, author Stephenie Meyer views Bella as a modern-day feminist (Meyer, n.d.a). Certainly Bella evolves from the beginning of the series to the end, from an insecure love-sick adolescent, to a wife and mother with supernatural powers that allow her to save her daughter and the entire Cullen clan. Indeed, the cover of the last book of the series, *Breaking Dawn*, depicts a crown, a metaphor for Bella's evolution during the saga, from being the physically weakest link, a pawn, to becoming the strongest, a queen (Meyer, n.d.a). Thus, at the end of the series Bella is stronger and much more independent than she is at the beginning, but while there is some indication of feminism on Bella's part, there is substantial evidence that she is traditional. This debate is discussed more fully in chapter 2, but it should also be noted that deconstruction is about getting past the obvious messages of (in this case) novels in order to examine the deeper messages in them. And sometimes these deeper messages do not match the superficial or obvious ones. It can be compared with knowing how to detect when someone is lying or covering something up. The words that that person says are the superficial, obvious, surface messages and the nonverbal cues to which we pay more attention are the deeper messages. We can determine "truth" by paying closer attention to the nonverbal cues or the deeper messages than we can by paying attention to the surface messages, that is, the words. Thus, although the *Twilight* novels do occasionally depict nontraditional gender roles, if one looks deeper at the behaviors of the characters in the novels, it is evident that the overwhelming majority of the time they behave in ways typical of conventional gender roles.

While the novels are certainly sex-typed and traditional, that is not to say that they are antifeminist, as they are often described (Wilson, 2011a). Certainly there is a difference between the two ideologies. If someone is traditional, she or he behaves in ways that typify conventional gender roles, but someone who is antifeminist is uncomfortable with feminist ideology, with equality between the sexes. In both cases people might embrace conventional behaviors, but in the former case, the person may be supportive of feminist ideology despite traditional behavior. In the latter they most definitely are not supportive of feminist ideals. Consider, for example, the antifeminists of the 1970s when the women's movement was relatively young. Recall the defeat of the Equal Rights Amendment, the derision that feminists faced, the attitudes that suggested that women were not equal to men or capable of the same types of jobs and activities. Certainly, these types of antifeminist attitudes (and behaviors) are different, both qualitatively and quantitatively, to simply traditional gender stereotypic attitudes and behaviors. The antifeminist attitudes represent a need to prevent social change that encourages gender equity whereas traditional attitudes are much more passive and apathetic about such social change. As such, *Deconstructing* Twilight argues that the *Twilight* novels are sex-typed and traditional but not that they are antifeminist. Consequently, the focus is on demonstrating the sex-typed roles in the novels and on discussing the problems inherent to those roles.

Social Learning

The second theme in *Deconstructing* Twilight notes that we learn traditional roles from media sources such as novels like *Twilight* through a process known as *social learning* (also called observational learning, vicarious learning, and modeling). It is widely accepted and documented that one of the ways that humans (and possibly other animals) learn is through observation of (role) models (Bandura, Ross, & Ross, 1961). Consider, for example, how someone might learn to cook. While, in theory, they could pick up a book and follow the instructions in a recipe, in reality the instructions in recipes can be unclear. What does it mean to dice an onion and how does that differ from mincing an onion? How does frying differ from sautéing? What does it mean to knead bread dough? More likely, people learn to cook from seeing other people cook. They watched their parents or grandparents as children or they watched people on television prepare dishes. Seeing how to do something is sometimes a more effective learning method than simply reading instructions about how to do something. Note that these models can be either real-life people, such as teachers, family members, or friends, or they can be symbolic models, for instance, characters in books, television programs, or movies. A child running, waving a stick as though it is a wand, pretending to cast spells, most likely is imitating behavior she has read about in books or seen in movies, such as those of the *Harry Potter* series. Certainly, she did not learn such behavior from real-life models! The same is true for a child who ties a towel around his neck, as if it were a cape, and jumps off a chair pretending to fly like

Superman. Thus, we learn from both real models and symbolic models.

For decades psychologists have studied the socializing effects of the media on children, adolescents, and adults. Some of this research has focused on the relationship between viewing violence in television programming and levels of aggressive behavior displayed. Other research has focused on the effect of the portrayal of gender stereotypic roles on viewers (Bussey & Bandura, 1999). In both cases, numerous researchers have found substantial evidence that seeing symbolic models in television programs, movies, and so on creates similar behaviors in viewers. That is, viewing portrayals of aggressive behavior is related to increased levels of aggression in children (Bushman & Huesmann, 2001; Tobin, 2006). And seeing sex-typed images is related to more sex-typed attitudes in viewers. In fact, there is growing concern that television might be contributing to a growing ambivalence about gender equality in our society (Signorielli, 1989). Studies indicate that women have fewer career aspirations after being presented with gender stereotypic images in the media, in comparison to women who are presented with nontraditional images of gender in the media (Geis, Brown, Jennings, & Porter, 1984; Yoder, Christopher, & Holmes, 2008). Conversely, other research has found that children exposed to nontraditional (reversed) gender roles on television are more likely to perceive traditionally masculine careers as appropriate for women than children exposed to only traditional roles on television programming (Atkin & Miller, 1975). In still other studies, researchers found that the more television that children watched, the more likely they were to have sex-typed attitudes and engage in sex-typed behaviors, presumably because so much television programming still depicts traditional gender roles (Barner, 1999; Brown, 1998; Jennings, Geis, & Brown, 1980; Lauzen, Dozier, & Horan, 2008). While these studies do focus on the effects of television programming, the same argument could be made for other types of media because they also reflect traditional gender roles (Diekman & Murnen, 2004). In other words, this research suggests that when people are presented with gender stereotypic portrayals of men and women in such media as books like those of the *Twilight* series, readers are more likely to develop gender stereotypic attitudes and behaviors. In fact, people often learn sex-typed behaviors from symbolic models, without necessarily being aware of their influence, because they identify with the characters demonstrating the traditional behavior (Radway, 1991). In books we can see the storyline images in our mind's eye, and sometimes we place ourselves in the role of one of the characters. As one respondent noted in the informal survey I conducted on perceptions of the *Twilight* series: "I like the books because it takes me out of reality. I'm able to imagine a world where I'm the main character."

One might argue that these are just stories, that most adults are able to distinguish between the fantasy of these stories and real life. Even author Stephenie Meyer has dismissed the possibility that her novels can influence ideas of gender-appropriate behaviors in her readers (Click, et al., 2010). She states about Bella, "I never meant for her fictional choices to be a model for anyone else's real life choices. She is a character in a story, nothing more or less" (Meyer, n.d.a, para. 18). But whether Meyer intended Bella to be a role model or not, and even though readers can distinguish between fantasy and reality, these stories have had considerable influence on "Twihards," fans of the series: A 2010 article in the travel section of *USA Today* (Bly, 2010) noted that tourism to Forks, Washington, home to the Bella and Cullens characters in the *Twilight* novels, jumped 600% since the first novel was published in 2005. Approximately 70,000 fans visited the vampire Mecca in 2009 even though *no real* events took place there. Relatedly, the names of the main characters in the series have made their way into the mainstream. According to the U.S. Social Security Administration and the BabyCenter Web site (Lassiter, 2010; 100 Most, n.d.a), Isabella, the name of the female protagonist in the novels, was reported to be the most popular name for girls in 2009 and the second most popular name in 2010. Jacob, one of the main male characters in the novels, was also the most popular name in 2009 and second most popular in 2010. And Cullen, Edward's family name, leaped toward the top of the list in 2010 according to the *New York Times* even though it was not very popular previously (McKinley, 2010). Consider, also, some of the comments of readers of the *Twilight* series as indicated in their responses to my informal survey about the stories. One 20-year-old woman wrote that Edward Cullen "is Bella's prince charming. One day I hope to find love like they have for one another." Another 20-year-old woman wrote that since Bella is just an average woman, "if she can find someone like Edward, so can I." Still another reader notes that Edward and Bella's relationship "is so passionate. It seems very real." Finally, a 21-year-old woman indicated that she likes the Edward Cullen character and that she "doesn't like that Edward Cullen isn't real." Additionally consider the fact that there is a Facebook page titled, "I put glitter on my boyfriend so that he sparkles like Edward Cullen" (I put glitter on my boyfriend, n.d.a). It's a fan club site for "every girl who wants her own Edward Cullen." Similarly, on the FMyLife.com Web site, where people post a few sentences describing humorous and sometimes painful events that really wrecked their day, one person wrote, "Today, my girlfriend dumped me proclaiming she wanted someone more like her 'Edward.' I asked her who Edward was. She held up a copy of her '*Twilight*' book. She was talking about a fictional vampire" (Today my, 2010). This posting may or may not be factual, but if it is, certainly one can see the sway that characters in stories can have on us.

While all these examples of the way the *Twilight* series has affected us might seem anecdotal, research in a variety of disciplines, although it is in its infancy, also indicates long-lasting influences of literature, especially on adolescents. Maria Nikolajeva, Cambridge University professor and director of the Cambridge Hornerton Research and Training Center for Children's Literature, discusses this influence by summarizing some of the findings presented at an interdisciplinary conference called The Emergent Adult: Adolescent Literature and Culture, held in 2010. She notes that a significant amount of research is emerging that indicates that teen literature, such as the *Twilight* series, can affect the workings of the teenage brain. Drawing on research in diverse disciplines such as psychology, anthropology, and neuroscience, she notes that while we do not know exactly how literature affects the brain, we do know that certain areas in the brain respond specifically to literature (Moskowitz, 2010; Strauss, 2010). And although there is limited research that examines the effect that the *Twilight* novels have had specifically on reader's expectations of, and behavior in, relationships, this, combined with the substantial amount of evidence supportive of social learning theory noted earlier, indicates that the *Twilight* novels can and do affect readers. As Click et al. (2010) note, "the stories media tell both reflect and create reality" (p. 9). Teens and tweens are especially susceptible to the effects of the media because they have not necessarily developed the critical thinking abilities that adults have (Coates, cited in Moskowitz, 2010; Nikolajeva cited in Strauss, 2010; Piaget, 1952). They are still developing physically, psychologically, emotionally, and cognitively. It is during childhood and adolescence that children and teens form their ideas of gender roles, their ideas of what it means to be a man and a woman. They are also forming ideas about what adult relationships should be like. Nikolajeva, as well as others (e.g., Saedi, 2011), is especially concerned because trends in young adult literature have been dark in recent years. She notes,

> Writers who address young audience[s] should, in an ideal world, be very careful about what they say. Exactly because teenage brains lack the ability to make judgments. In plain words, they may get wrong ideas. Not because they are stupid, but because their brains are wired like that. Because they are socially and emotionally unstable. The so-called social brain is under development during adolescence. (Strauss, 2010, para. 10)

Thus, social learning theory is discussed throughout this book by noting the messages our teens and tweens can learn through their observations of the behaviors of the characters in the *Twilight* novels.

Problems with Traditional Gender Roles

The third theme of *Deconstructing* Twilight is that there are problems with traditional gender roles for both men and women. As noted, *Deconstructing* Twilight argues that the characters in the *Twilight* novels typically act in traditional ways, and throughout this book problems inherent to those traditional gender roles are pointed out. Specifically, chapters 2–5 discuss problems fundamental to the traditional feminine role. For example, chapter 2 discusses the restrictive nature of traditional gender roles; chapter 3 discusses concern about overemphasizing the motherhood role for women; and chapter 4 discusses the financial dilemma related to sacrificing career for family life. Chapter 5 focuses on the difficulties with women being repeatedly portrayed as needing rescue and men being consistently portrayed as being rescuers. Chapter 6 changes focus by concentrating on Edward and traditionally masculine behaviors instead of the traditionally feminine behavior of Bella and the other female characters in the *Twilight* novels. Specifically, the chapter concentrates on problems with men being portrayed as arrogant, forceful, and controlling, as is typical of the romance genre the *Twilight* series exemplifies, noting that such behavior is illustrative of early stages of relationship abuse. Relatedly, chapter 7 discusses the relationship between Bella and Edward (and Jacob) from a psychological perspective, noting that it is not the ideal that so many fans covet. Rather the chapter demonstrates that the relationship is maladjusted and explains the maladjustment through the use of psychological theory. Finally, chapter 8 distinguishes between healthy and unhealthy characteristics of relationships and between the healthy and unhealthy behaviors displayed by the main characters of the novels and movies.

Feminist or Feminine?

The last theme of *Deconstructing* Twilight addresses the issue of whether feminist behavior is synonymous with feminine behavior. As was previously mentioned, Stephenie Meyer sees her character Bella as a feminist (Meyer, n.d.a; Siering, 2010) although, as I demonstrate later, she exhibits traditional behaviors and concerns. For some, these traditional roles are evidence that gender equity has been achieved. To illustrate, note that Susan Douglas (2010), whose work will be discussed in later chapters, describes *enlightened sexism*, an illogical belief that sex-typed behavior is evidence that gender equity is realized. It is the notion that because people believe that gender equality has been achieved, it is now acceptable for women and men to behave in ways that reflect traditional gender roles, to behave in ways that were typical of men and women before equality was achieved. As such, in the *Twilight* series, the fact that Bella makes so many traditional choices (marries at an early age, has a child immediately after marrying, is not interested in a career) can be cited as evidence that she is a feminist. She has *chosen* to make these choices instead of being forced into these choices, which indicates her feminist tendencies even though she behaves traditionally. Interestingly, Stephenie Meyer objects to the idea that Bella is a traditional, or in her words "antifeminist," character precisely because of this type of reasoning (Meyer, n.d.a, para. 18).

> It's as if you can't choose a family on your own terms and still be considered a strong woman. How is that empowering? Are there rules about if, when, and how we love or marry and if, when, and how we have kids? Are there jobs we can and can't have in order to be a "real" feminist? To me, those limitations seem anti-feminist in basic principle. (Meyer, n.d.a, para. 18)

Clearly, Meyer views even traditional choices as being feminist. But feminism is not just about choices (Williams, cited in Luscombe, 2010). It ultimately is about pursuing equality between men and women (Ashcraft, 1998; Baumgardner & Richards, 2000), and if women keep making traditional choices (or if they are forced to make these traditional choices) then political, economic, and social equality of the sexes never will be realized. The main reason that many feminists object to traditional choices is that such choices typically result in inequitable situations and relationships. Certainly, Bella evolves over the course of the four novels in the series—she is clearly stronger and more empowered at the end of *Breaking Dawn* than at the beginning of *Twilight*—but the problem with this storyline is that Bella evolves into a stronger, more empowered woman at the end of the series, in response to repetitively making *traditional* choices. In real life this is much less likely to happen, and if readers use Bella's choices as models for their own, they can sabotage their own growth, their own empowerment, and potentially their access to nontraditional choices. Thus, the fourth and final theme in this book focuses on noting that adhering to traditional roles is not evidence for gender equity. Consequently, *Deconstructing* Twilight notes inconsistencies in logic in multiple interpretations of the *Twilight* novels, demonstrating that the *Twilight* saga subtly encourages readers to interpret patriarchal culture as feminist. In fact, some would suggest that the extensive popularity of *Twilight* reflects a returned interest in traditional roles, especially feminine roles for women, which could be due to an increasingly conservative political climate in the United States (Ames, 2010). This, accompanied by apathy about equality for women, helped to create the perfect storm mentioned earlier that contributed to the saga's popularity. As noted, Zach (2009), for example, suggests that the success and popularity of *Twilight* is due to its depiction of the "Western ideal of romantic love" (p. 122): a heterosexual woman marrying into an upper-class family. She further suggests that since this is a primary concern for a majority of American women, intellectual and scholarly feminists need to minimize the differences in their thinking with those of the rest of the population by embracing "heterosexual objectified beauty and male-identified power" (p. 125). In other words, she suggests that feminists should embrace the conventional roles for women that they have been working to alter for decades! *Deconstructing* Twilight dispels the myths that suggest that women are and should be satisfied with heterosexual marriage, looking good, and the power women can attain in the world as it is today, that is, as defined by men. In sum, *Deconstructing* Twilight encourages you, the reader, to examine your own assumptions about gender roles, as well as relationships between men and women, as it provides new ideas to ponder.

CHAPTER TWO

Feminist or Feminine?

Modern Feminism?

*F*eminism is a complex, often misunderstood, term. It is a term that evokes a wide range of emotions: feelings of sisterhood, empowerment, resentment, loathing. People sometimes mistakenly believe that feminists work to undermine the power of men and want to dominate or control men (Rockler-Gladen, 2008). Some believe that feminists hate men (Faludi, 1991; Goldner, 1994; Kanner & Anderson, 2010; Rosen, 2000). Others believe that all feminists are lesbians (Kanner & Anderson, 2010). And yet a feminist, simply stated, is just a person (male or female) who believes that men and women should be politically, socially, and economically equal. What makes the term confusing, however, is that what is meant by the term *equal* can vary from one person to the next, even from one feminist to the next (Ashcraft, 1998; Evans, 1995; Kanner & Anderson, 2010). For some, *equality* means equality of opportunity. They want men and women to have equal chances to be hired for a job in the workforce or to get an education or to participate in sports. This equality of opportunity will eventually lead to a type of financial and social equality between the sexes. For others, equality means that men and women should have identical wealth or income. This is called equality of condition. Such latter ideas can be found in the economic theories of communism and socialism and so there are some who can be considered socialist feminists. But there are also liberal feminists, radical feminists, and cultural feminists, among others. The differences between these types of feminists revolve around how they define equality but also revolve around thoughts on what is the cause of gender inequality and how equality between the sexes can be achieved. While people often believe that there is only one type of feminist, nothing could be farther from the truth.

Author Stephenie Meyer believes that feminism is about women having a choice between career and family life. As noted in chapter 1 she states that "the foundation of feminism . . . is being able to choose" (Meyer, n.d.a, para. 18). As such, Meyer sees Bella as a modern feminist (Meyer, n.d.a). She sees the fact that Bella made her own choices as being indicative of feminism, even if these choices were traditional. For example, Meyer notes that Bella "chooses romantic love over everything else . . . she chooses to marry at an early age and . . . to keep an unexpected and dangerous baby" (Meyer, n.d.a, para. 18), implying that this is evidence for Bella's feminist tendencies, even though those choices are traditional. The problem with this definition, however, and therefore Meyer's assessment of Bella as a modern feminist (Meyer, n.d.a), is that it inaccurately describes feminism. Certainly, the women's movement resulted in a greater variety of opportunities for women, but refusing to take advantage of those new opportunities is not evidence for feminism, because, as noted in chapter 1, the traditional roles they maintain still encourage a power differential between the sexes. Meyer clearly disagrees with this interpretation of feminist choices. She notes, "... some feminists seem to be putting their own limits on women's choices" (Meyer, n.d.a, para. 18), referring to feminists who object to women sacrificing careers in favor of family life. But while some feminists might object to this choice, they are not necessarily trying to *limit* women's choices. Rather, this is a definitional issue: What these feminists object to is the contradiction involved in calling traditional sex-typed behavior, feminist behavior.

Consistent with Meyer's definition of feminism and her perception of Bella as a feminist, some readers agree that the *Twilight* novels are feminist in nature. On this side of the debate are those readers who suggest that the novels are feminist because a portion of the storyline revolves around Bella's right to choose to become a vampire and Edward's refusal to change her. It is about her right to make decisions about her own body rather than have a man make that decision for her. To illustrate, note that one of my survey respondents stated, "The book promoted women's rights such as Bella choosing to become a vampire." In fact, Stephenie Meyer suggests that the most pivotal moment in *Eclipse* is when Bella finally understands what the cost of becoming a vampire is and still decides that that is what she wants (Meyer, n.d.b). Similarly, some suggest that the novels—and Bella in particular—are feminist because Bella is perceived as adventurous and independent as she learns to ride a motorcycle and cliff dive. Other arguments that support the notion that the novels represent feminist ideology include the fact that both Bella and Alice are instrumental in saving the Cullen clan from the Volturi at the end of the series in *Breaking Dawn*. Still other readers use examples of nontraditional behavior in the female characters as evidence of feminism. They note that Rosalie is very adept at working on cars and that there is a female werewolf, Leah, who is able to hold her own with the rest of the pack who are all males (Mann, 2009; Myers, 2009). They also draw attention to the fact that the female vampires are just as aggressive as the male vampires. One of my survey respondents, for example, stated about the books, "It puts women in power. The books make the women vampires look just as vicious as the males."

But while many agree with Meyer's interpretation of Bella and the novels as feminist, others adamantly protest that they are not (Mann, 2009). Indeed, some readers have suggested that the series is not just traditional but, as noted earlier, is antifeminist (Wilson, 2011a). Those readers of the novels who disagree that Bella or the novels are feminist, despite Meyer's opinion of the character, also disagree with the perception that Bella is independent. Instead, they note Bella's dependence on male characters and her repetitive need to be rescued. They note her childlike behavior in the presence of Edward, her insecurity, and her compulsive need for her love interests, Edward and Jacob. One 34-year-old female surveyed did not think the series is feminist because "Bella is unable to live her life without Edward." A 25-year-old female indicated, "Bella is always having the men in her life protect her. She fails at trying to portray a strong independent woman because she cannot live without a man in her life. Once Edward left she replaced him with Jacob and then back to Edward." Other reasons for not perceiving the series as being feminist address the concern that Edward is paternalistic and controlling. "No feminist would put up with Edward's possessive behavior," wrote one 23-

year-old female. "Bella is easily controlled by Edward's actions," wrote another woman. Still another indicated, "I don't really see the book addressing problems that feminists fight for."

Clearly there are contrasting views of the series and the series' heroine, but interestingly, the overwhelming majority of the readers of the *Twilight* novels I surveyed indicated that they did not perceive the series as feminist in nature. When asked whether they thought the *Twilight* series is feminist in nature, 70% of the respondents indicated no; only 28% said yes. (The other 2–3% either did not answer or were unsure.) Similarly, the Bella character also was not perceived as a feminist in the survey: Only 24% of the respondents indicated that they thought Bella was a feminist; 74% did not agree that Bella was a feminist. Certainly these results might be due to the limited sample of the survey (students in college classes), but the reasoning behind these responses is similar to those noted in the more public debates on these topics: Consistent with the opening discussion of this chapter is the fact that a number of survey respondents seemed confused about what feminism is or seemed to misunderstand what feminism means. As an illustration note that one respondent wrote, "I don't really understand this question." Another wrote, "I'm not a good judge of feminism." And similar to our earlier discussion about whether traditional behavior can be considered feminist, other respondents who thought the series was feminist seem to have mistaken the term *feminist* for *feminine*. One 27-year-old respondent explained why she thought the series was feminist: "Bella seems weak and helpless—all of the guys fall over themselves to help her." Clearly this does not demonstrate feminist qualities but it does demonstrate feminine qualities. Other respondents to the survey about the series also misunderstood what the term *feminist* means but in a different way. They implied that the term *feminist* meant something of interest to women only. They implied that if women are interested in something, men would not be interested in it. For example, one respondent said the series was feminist because it "appeals to more women than men." A 19-year-old male respondent stated the series was feminist because "it is geared more toward girls [sic]." And a 20-year-old male stated, "It really appeals to women because it's a romance novel/movie and most men don't like that."

Still other respondents seem to retain the stereotype that feminists are men-haters who want not just equal power with men but power *over* men. For example, one respondent stated that the novels were not feminist because "it deals with men to [sic] and doesn't cut down men." Another wrote, "It isn't showing any kind of women over men." Still another indicated that she did not think that Bella was a feminist because "I didn't find any indications that she is prejudiced towards males." This lack of understanding of the definition of *feminism* is especially disturbing given that the women's movement is 50 years old, but it is certainly understandable given the various types of feminists and the misunderstanding the term can engender.

Some interpretations of the series suggest that it contains elements of both traditional and feminist attitudes. Wilson (2011a) suggests that both the male and female characters act in both traditional and nontraditional ways. The main male characters, Edward and Jacob, for example, are controlling and paternalistic toward Bella, but they also demonstrate emotion, show interest in Bella's needs and thoughts, have no trouble with commitment, and engage in other behaviors that can be viewed as being traditionally feminine. Likewise, the female characters demonstrate both feminist and conventional qualities: Bella is repeatedly in need of rescue at the beginning of the series but is instrumental in saving the Cullen clan at the end of the series. Rosalie is overly concerned with her appearance but also works on cars. Leah is a werewolf but concerned with not being able to reproduce. Wilson further suggests that such contradictory behaviors mirror the real-life experiences of women (and men). That is, men and women in real life engage in both traditional and nontraditional behavior. And in some cases, men and women might have feminist attitudes even though their behavior reflects traditional sex-typed attitudes. However, as is argued in this chapter, traditional gender roles are much more readily depicted and emphasized in the *Twilight* series than nontraditional roles. And, as noted in the previous chapter, unless nontraditional behavior reaches a certain threshold, a person's gender role is still categorized as traditional or conventional (Bem, 1974). Therefore, even though there are examples of nontraditional behavior in the series, the novels can be categorized as traditional. That is not to say that the series is antifeminist; as noted, the term *antifeminist* is not equivalent to the term *traditional* because the term *antifeminist* suggests hostility toward feminism whereas the term *traditional* does not—although it might suggest apathy toward feminism.

Feminist or Feminine?

In any case there is not enough data to know with any certainty whether Bella (and the other characters) have feminist attitudes or not because there is little to no discussion about gender equality in the *Twilight* series. What we do know is that although Bella displays some nontraditional behaviors, she demonstrates many more behaviors that are very traditionally feminine. Bella, for example, is the prototypical damsel in distress; she repeatedly requires rescuing, and this quality will be discussed in detail in another chapter. But her feminine qualities go beyond just that characteristic. As is discussed in the following sections, there is ample evidence that Bella is a caretaker, as many women are, that she has little to no career aspirations, and that she places her romantic relationships above any other interests (Meyer, n.d.a).

The Nurturer-Caretaker

Evidence for Bella's nurturer-caretaker role is plentiful. The series begins with Bella moving to Forks to live with Charlie, her father, in order to give her mother, Renée, who was her original custodial guardian, more freedom to travel with her new husband. Note that Bella is making sacrifices to take care of her mother, indicating a caretaker role. In *Twilight*, Bella thinks to herself, "'How could I leave my loving, erratic, harebrained mother to fend for herself?'" (p. 4), as she is about to board the plane to fly to Forks to live with her father. In *Eclipse*, Bella responds to an e-mail her mother sent informing her that she had tried skydiving even though Renée is afraid of heights, noting that she would have done a better job caring for her mother than Phil, Renée's husband, who supported Renée in this new experience. Edward even remarks to himself about Bella's caretaking role in *Midnight Sun*, Stephenie Meyer's retelling of *Twilight* from Edward's (instead of Bella's) perspective, noting that Bella's maturity is due to the fact that she became her mother's caretaker. Regardless of whether this type of mothering of her mother is appropriate or not, it certainly indicates the traditional nurturing qualities of the female caretaker.

Other evidence for Bella's caretaker role comes from the fact that Bella takes on several traditionally "wifely duties" immediately upon settling into her new home with her father. She begins caring for her father by taking over the cooking, food shopping, and much of the housecleaning duties. To illustrate, note that Bella asks to be in charge of cooking:

> I'd discovered that Charlie couldn't cook much besides fried eggs and bacon. So I requested that I be assigned kitchen detail for the duration of my stay. He was willing enough to hand over the keys to the banquet hall. I also found out that he had no food in the house. So . . . I was on my way to Thriftway. (*Twilight*, p. 31)

In another illustration note that in *Eclipse* Bella is described as not only doing her own laundry but also doing Charlie's laundry. She strips his bed, as well as hers, in order to throw the sheets into the washer. The roles that Bella takes on are the housekeeping chores that are typical in the traditional housewife role, a role that again indicates caregiving. Note once more that Bella is taking care of a parent, in this case Charlie, rather than her father taking care of her. Again, this might be inappropriate in a parent-child relationship, just as taking care of her mother is a role reversal, but it is even more notable that in taking care of her father, Bella assumes the traditional female role. In fact, when asked if Bella had any other interests besides Edward, author Stephenie Meyer noted very few beyond housekeeping chores and taking care of her parents. She replied, "Bella is first and foremost a bookworm. She also likes to cook. She enjoys drawing . . . She takes care of her parents—bookkeeping, housekeeping, shopping, etc. She likes the house run just right, ha ha" (Meyer, 2006a, para. 35).

There also is a plentiful amount of evidence that Bella thinks the caretaker role is completely appropriate for her. In *New Moon*, Bella makes lasagna "to atone for all the pizza" (p. 167) she and Charlie had been eating, implying that she has been slack in the completion of her duties. In *Eclipse*, Bella places a plate of food in front of Charlie, just as the stereotyped 1950s wife would have done after her husband came home from a long day at the office. In another scene in *Eclipse*, she thinks about making something special for dinner for Charlie in order to "butter him up," again just as a stereotyped 1950s wife would have done if she wanted something from her husband or if she wanted to avoid an argument with him. Bella makes stroganoff and specifically indicates that she did so in order to make Charlie happy. In fact, this traditional role of cooking and cleaning is not only embraced by Bella, it is also accepted by Charlie. He quickly assumes that it is natural and takes for granted that Bella will complete these traditional tasks. For example, in *Eclipse* Bella notices the smell of smoke. "In another house, the fact that someone besides myself was cooking might not be a cause for panicking" (p. 5), thus suggesting that they do not share this task but rather that it is Bella's chore. Later, after Bella's initial alarm about Charlie's cooking, she finds out that her father cooked for her only because he wanted to talk to her about something he knew she would find irksome. He indicates that he has an ulterior motive for taking over her chore on that particular day. Similarly, in *New Moon*, Charlie brings home a pizza for supper on another occasion, saying to Bella, "'I thought you'd like a break from cooking and washing dishes for your birthday'" (p. 21). Note the implication from both of these examples that the cooking and dishwashing chores are Bella's responsibility and that Charlie is just being nice by giving her a break. As noted in the last chapter, Mann (2009) agrees that Bella exemplifies the traditional nurturer-caretaker role, noting that when she first read the novels she was taken aback by the gender stereotypes in the novel because of these (and other) scenes. She describes feeling that she was reading about the behavior of earlier generations.

Other female characters are also portrayed in this traditional manner. Emily, the girlfriend of Sam who is one of the werewolves in the packs depicted in *New Moon*, *Eclipse*, and *Breaking Dawn*, is frequently described as being in the kitchen cooking not only for her fiancé but for all the boys who are part of the werewolf pack: In *New Moon* she pulls muffins out of a tin asking the boys if they are hungry. Rosalie, Edward's adoptive sister, also notes the traditional feminine tasks completed by her mother as she describes her history to Bella.

She says, "'It was my mother's job to keep our house—and myself and my two younger brothers—in spotless order'" (*Eclipse*, p. 154). Arguably, this is due to the sociopolitical time in which her mother lived, and yet it still is another example of traditional roles. Interestingly, as Rosalie tells Bella her story, it becomes evident that Rosalie had no interest in completing these types of chores herself. She hoped to marry into affluence so that she could hire someone else to complete them for her. While this might seem contradictory to the caretaker-nurturer role, it should be noted that marrying into a family that allows for upward financial mobility is often seen as the dream of many (traditional) women (Buttsworth, 2010; Zach, 2009). In this case, keeping house would still be considered the woman's responsibility, but she could fulfill that responsibility by hiring someone else to complete the necessary tasks. As such, the behaviors in all these scenes are indicative of the feminine caretaker role.

Absence of Career

Also consistent with the traditional female role is the fact that the main female characters in the *Twilight* series have no careers. Consistent with Meyer's description of Bella choosing "romantic love over everything else" (Meyer, n.d.a, para. 18), careers are inconsequential for them, in comparison to relationships and having children. Note, for example, that Bella has no clear career path and, unlike many real-life high school students, does not seem to consider or discuss possible careers or college majors with anyone. Although Bella makes tentative plans for college, she does so half-heartedly in order to please others, her parents and Edward in particular. In fact, Bella's lack of enthusiasm for attending college is evidenced as she repeatedly refers to attending college as an alternate plan to being changed into a vampire and spending time with Edward. To illustrate, note that in *New Moon* Bella states, "College was Plan B. I was still hoping for Plan A, but Edward was just so stubborn about leaving me human . . ." (p. 13). In the epilogue of *New Moon* Bella confirms that college is still "Plan B." She states, "Many deadlines had passed me by . . . thanks to my procrastination, we might both end up at Peninsula Community College next year" (pp. 548–549), indicating that Bella's priority is certainly not college and a career. In fact, it is really Edward who repeatedly encourages her to have that human experience before she is turned into a vampire. In *Eclipse* Edward wants Bella to apply to Dartmouth, but she resists, telling him, "'You're going way overboard with this, you know. . . . I really don't need to apply anywhere else. . . . There's no need to throw away a bunch of money, no matter whose it is'" (p. 23). Obviously, her priority is not college, nor is it a career. College is seen merely as a means to disguise the fact that she will be a vampire. But Edward's persuasive appeal continues as he describes the potential pride her parents would experience at her college graduation. She describes the experience: "His velvet voice painted a picture in my head before I could block it. Of course Charlie would explode with pride . . . And Renee would be hysterical with joy at my triumph" (*Eclipse*, p. 226). At a later point in the saga Bella does express interest in attending Dartmouth, but it is not because of interest in growth or development or learning or career preparation. Instead, she makes this suggestion to Edward because she wants to remain human for a while longer. She tells Edward,

> "Well, I was thinking . . . I know that the whole Dartmouth thing was just supposed to be a cover story, but honestly, one semester of college probably wouldn't kill me," I said, echoing his words from long ago, when he'd tried to persuade me to put off becoming a vampire. . . . "Still . . . eighteen, nineteen. It's really not such a big difference. It's not like I'm going to get crow's feet in the next year. . . . But I *do* want to go. Well, it's not college as much as it's that I want—I want to be human a little longer." (*Breaking Dawn*, pp. 102–103)

What is especially interesting about Bella's lack of career interest is her resistance to it despite encouragement from others. As just noted, Edward repetitively tries to persuade Bella to attend college, a step to career advancement, but although she ultimately agrees, it appears that she is going through the motions of the experience rather than embracing and owning it. In fact, although Edward is old-fashioned in many regards—because of the period he was born and lived as a human—he does assume that Bella, at least as a human, will have a career. This is evident because Stephenie Meyer allows readers a greater understanding of Edward's thought processes through her partial draft of *Midnight Sun*, located on her Web site. An exercise in character development that became extensive, *Midnight Sun* has one scene in which Edward is considering a conversation he had with Carlisle about his attraction to Bella and whether he should leave Forks. Carlisle has told him that Bella would leave Forks in a couple of years and that if Edward needed to leave so as not to kill her (Bella's blood smells especially sweet), he should and that the entire clan could move with him. Edward thinks about Bella leaving in a few years and considers that she would then attend college, start a career, get married. He clearly sees that as an acceptable human path despite the absence of interest in it on Bella's part. Although pushing Bella to go to college—and possibly start a career—is clearly in her best interest, it should be noted that it is Edward who is making these decisions for Bella rather than Bella herself. And again, although Bella does plan to attend college after her wedding and honeymoon, she makes these plans to please her family and to remain human rather than because of any interest in education, growth, or career prepara-tion. Ultimately this plan is derailed because she becomes pregnant on her honeymoon, resulting in a life-threatening pregnancy and conflict with the Volturi. Possibly, in Bella's long vampiric life, she will attend college as the other Cullens have repeatedly, but it is unfortunate, from a social learning perspective, that Bella, as a role model, is not more achievement oriented. It is also unfortunate that Edward seems to be molding Bella into an image that he thinks is appropriate for her.

Many other characters in the novels are also not career oriented. In the Cullen clan, although Carlisle is a medical doctor, the rest of the family members do not have jobs. Esme, Carlisle's wife, for example, can only be described as a stay-at-home mom, and Carlisle's "children," Edward, Alice, Jasper, Rosalie, and Emmett, also do not have careers. In fact, the Cullen clan does not seem interested in beginning any career despite their vampiric longevity and despite the fact that at least some of them look old enough to pass for college-aged adults, who could conceivably begin some type of career. Certainly many of the Cullen clan (both males and females) have repeatedly attended college but these college degrees have not resulted in any career aspirations except for Carlisle. The members of the Cullen clan have interests and hobbies, some of which have assisted them in amassing a fortune that allows them to be self-sufficient, but none other than Carlisle are in the labor force. Alice, for example, sees the future and is, therefore, useful to the financial advancement of the Cullens through her stock market predictions, but she is certainly not a stockbroker; and Esme does renovate houses, but she seems to do so as a hobby, for pleasure, rather than for profit. In fact, when asked about how the Cullens acquired their wealth, Meyer only indicates three characters as being instrumental, two of them male. She answers,

> Long term investments, heh heh. Carlisle originally got some financial help from his Italian friends (remember the painting? They've got an astronomi-cal amount of funds) and then was earning a doctor's salary all those years without really having normal expenses to worry about. Edward inherited a lot of property from his parents (he did pretend to "survive" to claim that later, along with his "uncle," because he wanted his mother's things. He still owns the house in Chicago). All this was invested shrewdly (both Carlisle and Edward are good with finances). And then Alice came along. Ha ha. She loves the stock market. (Meyer, 2006b, para. 3)

Clearly, because of their affluence the Cullens do not need to partici-pate in the workforce, but the males in the Cullen clan were achieve-ment oriented before they were changed into vampires. However, consistent with the sociopolitical culture of the times at which they lived as humans, the females in the Cullen clan were not. Edward expressed interest in a military career when he was human as did Jasper, for example, but Esme and Rosalie's primary interests were marriage and family. But after being changed into vampires, the males, except for Carlisle, seemed to have lost interest in careers. Edward has two medical degrees and yet no career of his own. And Jasper, although he rose through the ranks of the Confederate Army as a human, does not have a career as a vampire, despite his being "scholarly" (Meyer, 2006c, para. 9). In fact, the Cullens have repeat-edly attended college but have not taken any advantage of this career preparation. Meyer notes,

> ...they've all been through college several times, and they've studied a wide array of subjects. They don't always finish a degree—it doesn't take them four years to master a subject, so they usually learn what they want and then move on. Edward has studied many languages, and he's been through

medical school twice—this helps Carlisle keep current without having to neglect his practice. (Meyer, 2006d, para. 2)

Thus, in their vampire state, the Cullen clan is an example of the prototypical nuclear family where the father (Carlisle) works to take financial care of his family and the mother (Esme) does not have a career.

Although the deficiency in achievement orientation in male characters can be interpreted as problematic also, the lack of career interest in female characters is especially troublesome because depicting men as uninterested in careers is a nontraditional representation; they typically are portrayed as breadwinners in the media. However, the lack of career interest in the female characters in the *Twilight* novels just adds to an endless list of examples of traditional women who are not career or achievement oriented. Esme's representation is worrisome in particular because in addition to her not being career oriented, she is very family oriented due to the fact that, as noted in the novels, her loving spirit was magnified when she became a vampire. She, therefore, is the nucleus of her family. Some might argue that Esme is a stay-at-home mom because *someone* needs to stay home and take care of these traditionally feminine duties but note, however, that in this case, Esme does not need to cook for her vampire family, nor does she really need to care for any young children. We could assume as well that since all the "children" are way beyond human adult age, they can also clean up after themselves and assist in cleaning the house. Consequently, Esme is clearly indicating a preference for family life over career.

Other, more minor characters in the novels also avoid career aspirations. For example, there is a small reference in *New Moon* (p. 175) to one of Jacob's sisters who turned down a partial college scholarship in order to get married. This scene, although small, is especially important to note because Bella and Jake express confusion as to why his sister would not take advantage of the scholarship and why the tribal Elders would try to push her to go to college when they did not do so for Sam. Scenes such as these are especially troublesome because they imply that the novels are supportive of women's career goals but the support is actually superficial. The scenes noted earlier, those that demonstrate Edward's pressure on Bella to attend college throughout the series and his early assumption that Bella would have a career, are also indicative of support toward women's career goals, at least on the surface. But note that in each of these cases neither female character actually pursues these opportunities. From a social learning perspective, the message that readers can take away from these storylines is for women to not pursue their career aspirations but rather to resist pressure to become career oriented and pursue traditional roles instead.

Many of the male characters also do not have careers. For example, Billy, Jacob's father, is unemployed, and Jacob also seems to have no clear career path, but Charlie is chief of police in Forks, and Carlisle, the Cullen family patriarch, as noted is a medical doctor. On the other hand, none of the female characters are career oriented. As such, although there are minimal career role models for boys who read the series or see the movies, there are essentially no career role models for girls. The one exception to this lack of interest in careers is Renée, Bella's mother, whose occupation is only mentioned in passing, and who is described not as working but as following her new husband around as he plays minor league baseball. Thus, although the *Twilight* series is marketed toward the young adult population (ages 14–21), a time when young people are making career and college decisions, they do not provide role models that encourage career aspiration for girls—or for boys for that matter—and this is problematic because, as noted in the previous chapter, children, teenagers, and adults all learn through their observation of role models. Furthermore, children and teenagers are especially susceptible to the influence of attractive role models because their cognitive abilities have not yet fully developed (Coates, cited in Moskowitz, 2010; Nikolajeva, cited in Strauss, 2010; Piaget, 1952). Thus, tweens and teens are especially likely to be influenced by characters in such popular novels as the *Twilight* series, although as noted in the previous chapter, Meyer never meant for Bella to be a role model for anyone's real-life choices. As such, whether Meyer intended to or not, it is likely that many readers will, and do, see Bella as a role model. Consequently, because some readers—and Meyer herself—view Bella as empowered and as a modern feminist, her lack of career aspiration can be interpreted as indicative of feminism, but in fact, it is not. Such behavior does not allow for the financial independence that develops from participation in the labor force, nor does it encourage gender equity.

Emphasis on Relationships

Another aspect of the traditional female role is the emphasis on relationships, especially on romantic (heterosexual) relationships. Meyer freely admits this is the case with Bella; as mentioned earlier, Meyer notes that Bella allows romance to overshadow any other life experience (Meyer, n.d.a). And clearly, Bella's whole world revolves around the love of her life, Edward (and vice versa). This is noted by Bella's mother when Bella and Edward go to visit Renée in *Eclipse*. Renée notes to Bella, "'I wish you could see how you move around him . . . When he moves, even a little bit, you adjust your position at the same time'" (p. 68). This sentiment is also asserted by Bella's father in *Eclipse*. Charlie tells Bella, "'I don't think you should dump all your other friends for your boyfriend, Bella . . . If you'd had more of a life outside of Edward Cullen, it might not have been like that'" (p. 12), speaking of how debilitated she was after Edward left her in *New Moon*, and indicating her fixation with her romantic relationship. Such parental concern is legitimate given that in one scene in *Eclipse*, Edward goes hunting, and Bella feels as though she has nothing to do on a Saturday besides working at her part-time job at Newton's Outfitters. Clearly, Edward is the center of Bella's universe, typical of old-fashioned roles for women. Consider that Bella chooses to change completely in order to be with Edward. One example of this can be found in the first book of the series: We learn that Bella loves the sun, but as a vampire she will need to avoid it in order to evade detection by humans, and she learns to love Forks despite its cloudy, rainy climate. In fact, Bella emphatically wants to stay in Forks in order to be with Edward even though at one point she described Forks as her "personal hell on Earth" (p. 26 of *Twilight*). Specifically note that in *New Moon* when Charlie threatens to send her back to Renée because she is so depressed after Edward leaves her, Bella convinces Charlie not to so that she can stay in Forks *just in case* Edward returns. More significantly, however, Bella changes physically to become a vampire in the last book of the series, *Breaking Dawn*. She gives up her human life to be with Edward. Certainly Edward does not force her into these choices. Although he pressures her to get married, he repeatedly encourages her to remain human and live a normal human life, but Bella chooses to live her life revolving around Edward, just as her mother indicated her body movement did.

Bella's marriage to Edward at an early age is also certainly illustrative of the importance of her relationship with him and the emphasis it has in her life. She marries him right after high school although her mother cautioned her against such an early marriage numerous times before she moved to Forks. Bella chooses to form her identity based upon her relationship with Edward, becoming what Edward is, a vampire, instead of remaining what she is, a human, just as the identity of countless women in decades past revolved around their relationships with boyfriends, husbands, and children. Such behavior is troubling considering that for decades feminists have warned against women's identities hinging upon another being. In fact, as is discussed in a later chapter, psychologists also caution people against love relationships that are too encompassing, noting that such relationships are unhealthy. Stephenie Meyer, however, responding to criticism about the storyline regarding Bella and Edward's early marriage, sees no problem with it. She states,

> It's as if you can't choose a family on your own terms and still be considered a strong woman. How is that empowering? Are there rules about if, when and how we love or marry and if, when and how we have kids . . . Do I think eighteen is a good age at which to get married? Personally—as in, for the person *I* was at eighteen—no. However, Bella is constrained by fantastic circumstances that I never had to deal with. The person she loves is physically seventeen, and he's not going to change. If she and he are going to be on a healthy relationship footing, she can't age too far beyond him. Also, marriage is really an insignificant commitment compared to giving up your mortality, so it's funny to me that some people are hung up on one and not the other. Is eighteen too young to give up your mortality? For me, any age is too young for that. For Bella, it was what she really wanted for her life, and it wasn't a phase she was going to grow out of. So I don't have issues with her choice. She's a strong person who goes after what she wants with persistence and determination. (Meyer, n.d.a, para. 18)

Clearly, Meyer has no issue with Bella's choices but the problem with them is that, as noted previously, whether Meyer intended or not,

Bella *is* potentially a role model for her readers. And while Meyer does not need to be concerned about whether her readers give up their mortality for immortality at the early age of eighteen, it is possible that they will see Bella's early marriage and motherhood as something to which they should aspire, especially given the fact that these traditional choices are often described in subtly appealing and desirable ways.

The depiction of romantic relationships in the *Twilight* series is also troubling because they demonstrate that such relationships assist women in the formation of their identities. As noted, Bella's identity is dependent upon Edward, but these types of storylines also illustrate how women can blossom and grow if they are in a romantic (heterosexual) relationship. Bella, for example, is essentially a blank slate prior to her relationships with Edward and Jacob. We know very little about her and her life prior to Forks. We know that she liked the sun, was a good student, did not date, took care of her mother, and was clumsy. But we know little else. There are no friends with whom she keeps in touch after her move to Forks, no real references to past experiences. As noted earlier, when asked whether Bella had any other interests besides Edward, Meyer only noted reading, drawing, and housekeeping chores such as cooking (Meyer, 2006a). Similarly, when she is asked if Bella keeps in touch with any friends from Phoenix after her move to Forks, Meyer answers,

> Bella's Phoenix existence was pretty much as her mother's best friend as Renee takes an awful lot of effort and time. Bella is shy too, so has no real close girlfriends she'd go shopping with or anything like that. She didn't leave strong ties behind her and it's easy to fall out of touch with people. (Meyer, 2007, Feb.)

But after Bella begins relationships with Edward and Jacob, she begins all sorts of activities. She learns to ride a motorcycle, cliff dive, she gets a part-time job, makes plans to attend college, gets married, has a baby, becomes a vampire, develops supernatural powers, travels to Italy, goes camping. Certainly the lack of backstory on Bella might be a literary omission but even if it is unintentional, the way the storyline is written still leaves the reader with an impression, as many romance novels do, that love is a source of identity and growth.

And although many would agree, psychologists included, that love can be a growth-enriching experience, it is not so to the extent that is implied. In fact, this aspect of the storyline is disquieting because if the heroine is a blank slate, she can become anyone the male protagonist wants her to be instead of becoming a person in her own right.

Emphasis on Motherhood

Also typical of the feminine role is the fact that the *Twilight* novels depict women as having a consuming need to bear children. Esme, distraught over the loss of a child, attempts to kill herself but is "saved" by Carlisle, who changes her into a vampire before she dies. She is the mother figure to all the other Cullens. Rosalie has regrets over being changed into a vampire, one of which is that she cannot have children—and she protects Bella and her baby while Bella is pregnant, making sure that no one aborts the pregnancy. Leah also indicates to Jacob that she would help Bella protect her child if she was asked, and she expresses concern that she might not be able to reproduce. And, of course, Bella risks her life to have a half-vampire/half-human child. The implication is that women have an innate drive to have children, and once they do so, they will feel satisfied, complete. This emphasis is more fully discussed in the next chapter but certainly this illustrates the feminine, as opposed to feminist, behavior of the female characters in the *Twilight* stories.

Cultural Feminism

Clearly Bella does engage in a substantial amount of traditional behavior, but even if she is a feminist, as Meyer (n.d.a) claims, it is unclear as to what type of feminist Meyer believes her character is. As noted earlier, a feminist is a person who believes in equality between the sexes. Also, as noted earlier, there are many types of feminists, with different ideas about what equality means and how to achieve it. Perhaps what Meyer meant by Bella being a modern-day feminist is that she is a cultural feminist. This certainly would be consistent with the multitude of traditional roles in which she engages. Cultural feminists believe in a "culture" of women (Ashcraft, 1998). They suggest that women all have similar experiences and that this similarity of experience constitutes a "culture" that unites them. Cultural feminists can be described as a "difference school," meaning that they view men and women as having different traits, abilities, and roles from each other, and they often believe that those differences are biologically based, innate. They do not encourage women to take on masculine roles or for men to take on feminine qualities in order to achieve equality, as other feminist schools do. In fact, they prefer that women retain their traditional roles, especially those of wife, mother, and caretaker, precisely because they believe that those roles are natural and biologically based. Certainly, the female characters in the *Twilight* series are quite concerned with these traditionally feminine concerns as has just been illustrated in this chapter. They do not concern themselves with masculine concerns such as careers and they are caretakers with a consuming need for children.

These common concerns of the female characters reflect the unity of female experience that typifies the cultural feminist ideology. While cultural feminists are not particularly concerned with working toward financial or social equality between the sexes, they do believe that that which is feminine should be valued as much as that which is masculine. To illustrate, note that cultural feminists believe that the traditionally feminine role of motherhood and childrearing should be valued as much as the traditionally masculine role of breadwinner. They believe that the traditionally feminine quality of nurturance should be valued as much as the traditionally masculine qualities of industry and independence. Cultural feminists only work toward equality in the sense that they try to reclaim that which is feminine and which has been devalued by society, noting the worth of those feminine experiences, the traditional female role. But as is a common theme discussed in this book, there are problems with the traditional female role, if not for vampires and werewolves, at least for mere mortals like us. Most notably, these traditional roles are restrictive. Cultural feminists assume that all women share similar psychological needs and, therefore, do not account for individual differences. Cultural feminists want society to value women's experiences, perspectives, roles, and so on, but they also want women to maintain those roles. They likewise relegate men to traditionally masculine roles. For example, cultural feminists believe that women are more nurturing than men and so are better at child rearing. It should, therefore, be women who raise children because of their skills. But cultural feminists ignore the possibilities that some women might not want children or that some women might want careers. They likewise ignore the possibilities that some men might be more nurturing than some women and might want to be the primary caretakers of their children. In fact, both Charlie, Bella's father, and Billy, Jacob's father, are the primary caretakers of the children during their teen years even if neither is very vigilant in his parenting. Charlie, especially, is happy that Bella decided to move to Forks to live with him, indicating tendencies contradictory to the cultural feminist view. Similarly, Bella's mother, Renée, is not an especially effective parent because, as noted earlier, Bella often takes care of her instead of vice versa—which is also contradictory to the cultural feminist notion that all women are competent mothers. Working toward the appreciation of women's experiences is certainly beneficial: For too long, women's experiences were devalued. But by only addressing that aspect of gender inequality, cultural feminists relegate women to the traditional roles that other feminists have long fought to alter. Thus, while Bella might be a cultural feminist because she and the majority of the other female characters embrace traditionally feminine roles, such roles do still relegate women—and men—to conventional behaviors, and such restrictions carry with them the same problems they did before the women's movement of the 1960s and 1970s.

Some might disagree that Bella is a cultural feminist. Certainly she initially resists the possibility that she will want children at some point in her life, a key feature of cultural feminism, and certainly Bella pursued the option of becoming a vampire even though she initially thought she would not be able to have children after she was changed. This would seem counterintuitive to describing Bella as a cultural feminist, but Bella does ultimately have a child while she is still human, one whom she fervently protects even though the pregnancy is dangerous and could potentially kill her. And, as further discussed in a later chapter, Bella does eventually embrace motherhood, noting that she was shortsighted not to have done so earlier. As such, these attitudes and behaviors *are* certainly consistent with this type of feminism. Likewise, even if she had not become a mother, the fact that her life, her world, revolves around Edward is also indicative of this feminist perspective, as the traditional female role has always hinged on women's relationships with others, especially with their boyfriends or husbands. It is interesting that Edward's world revolves around Bella as well, a depiction that is contradictory to the cultural feminist view that indicates that the realms of males and females are separate with men's interests being found in the world outside home and family.

Although cultural feminists embrace the traditional female role, Bella seems most happy when she begins to act in a more masculine rather than feminine fashion. Her empowerment is most evident in *Breaking Dawn* when she is turned into a vampire. As a newborn vampire Bella is no longer fragile, breakable. She is able to take care of herself, defend herself. She no longer needs Edward (or Jacob or other vampires) to protect her. She has superhuman strength and speed. In fact, she is stronger than the male vampires in the series, at least temporarily. Consider, chapter 21 of *Breaking Dawn* when Bella goes on her first hunt after being completely changed into a vampire. She describes her joy at her new-found strength and agility. "As I ran, I couldn't help laughing quietly at the thrill of it . . . I laughed again, exultant, when I heard him falling behind" (p. 413), referring to Edward, who up until then had always been bigger, stronger, and faster than Bella and who often carried her on his back as he quickly ran. Bella describes her feeling of being "stronger than the strongest vampire" (p. 521) she'd known after she defeats Emmett in arm-wrestling. She is thrilled and elated. She notes, "I was having too much fun" (p. 521). Consider also chapter 38, which is titled "Power." In it the Volturi attempt to attack the Cullen clan through Chelsea, who can break emotional bonds between others, and Jane, who can cause others incredible pain, but Bella is able to protect the other vampires from these experiences through some sort of shield that she uses to envelope them. Edward asks Bella about the Volturi's inability to affect them, and Bella replies, "'I am *all* over this'" (p. 725). With that simple phrase, readers get a sense of Bella feeling confident, powerful, strong, and satisfied at being able to protect her loved ones and constructively contribute to resolving the situation at hand.

Compare this to a description she gives of her human existence in which her roles were much more traditional and sex-typed: "After eighteen years of mediocrity, I was pretty used to being average. I realized now that I'd long ago given up any aspirations of shining at anything" (p. 523). Clearly, the more masculine, empowering role is preferable to her than the more feminine human role.

In any case, labeling Bella a cultural feminist just adds to the substantial evidence that Bella engages in primarily feminine behaviors even though, as noted, there are examples of nontraditional behaviors in the series as well. This further indicates that the novels are traditional, not feminist (and not antifeminist). Some might argue that the prevalence of nontraditional behaviors does not differ substantially from that of sex-typed behaviors, but the evidence in this chapter suggests otherwise. And while the sex-typed behaviors seem to be not just more prevalent but also of greater importance in the series, others might argue that the importance of Bella wanting control over her own body (to become a vampire) and that she is instrumental in saving the Cullen clan from the Volturi should not be downplayed. But even with these arguments supporting the idea that Bella and the series is feminist in nature, one cannot overlook the fact that the main storylines are about Bella's relationships with Edward and Jacob. Meyer, herself, indicates that the series is first and foremost a young adult romance (Granger, 2010; Meyer, n.d.a), and as such, it reflects the sex-typed notion that, for women, the primary emphases in life should be (romantic, heterosexual) relationships, marriage, and children. The secondary plots might depict nontraditional behaviors but there is no doubt that the primary plots in the series accentuate traditional gender roles: In the first novel of the series, *Twilight*, the main plot revolves around the romance between Edward and Bella. The primary plot of the second novel, *New Moon*, involves Bella's heartbreak over Edward leaving her and her relationship with Jacob. The primary plot of the third novel, *Eclipse*, emphasizes the competition for Bella between Edward and Jacob. And in the last novel of the series, *Breaking Dawn*, the principal storyline highlights Edward and Bella's marriage and honeymoon, Bella's pregnancy, and her protection of her child, Renesmee, from the Volturi. Thus, even if there were equal amounts of both sex-typed and non-sex-typed behaviors portrayed in the series, the fact that the novels emphasize the traditional feminine roles of marriage and motherhood overrides the argument that the series is feminist.

Deconstructing the Gender Roles in the Series

The messages about feminism and the traditional female role in the *Twilight* series are certainly contradictory. Many readers interpret the series as feminist, although, as just presented, there is substantial evidence that the female characters act in primarily feminine ways. Some of the confusion about whether the series is feminist stems from the fact that on the surface, the characters can seem nontraditional, but when one looks closer, when one deconstructs their behavior, it is evident that they behave in ways that are contradictory to feminism. The novels appear to pay lip service to gender equality but do not reflect behaviors that are consistent with gender equality. As was illustrated earlier, Jacob's sister was encouraged to take advantage of a partial scholarship to go to college, but Sam was not encouraged in a similar way. Such portrayals imply support for women, but because Jacob's sister did not actually take advantage of the scholarship and attend college, the storyline does not ultimately support female empowerment. Similarly, this lip service was also noted as Edward encourages Bella to attend college, although she resists. Again, although Edward seems supportive of women, it is he who is attempting to make the decision for Bella, instead of Bella herself, and, therefore, also does not demonstrate empowerment for women. In fact, Edward literally forges her signature on applications, assists her in writing her application essays, and bribes colleges with sizable financial donations to guarantee Bella's acceptance despite her lack of interest.

Still other examples of this lip service can be found throughout the series as Bella expresses reluctance to get married, especially at such an early age and directly out of high school. One of the reasons for her reluctance is that she is concerned about the gossip that will be said about her. When Edward asks Bella why she does not want to marry him in the *Eclipse* novel, she replies, "'I'm not *that girl* . . . The one who gets married right out of high school like some small-town hick who got knocked up by her boyfriend! Do you know what people would think?'" (pp. 275–276). Later in the novel, as Bella agrees to marry Edward, she is still concerned about what her friends will think and says to Edward, "'Can you imagine what Angela will think? Or Jessica? Ugh. I can hear the gossip now'" (p. 455). But ultimately Bella does embrace the traditional role and marries Edward, having *his* baby shortly afterward, just like her mother. This superficial support of women is further illustrated if other reasons for Bella's initial resistance to marriage are also examined closely: An additional reason that Bella is reluctant to get married to Edward is that her mother Renée married quickly after graduating from high school and gave birth to Bella a year later. Dissatisfied with her life, she divorced Bella's father shortly afterward. Renée did not want Bella to make the same mistakes she made. She, therefore, repeatedly warned Bella to take marriage seriously and that "[m]ature people went to college and started careers before they got deeply involved in a relationship" (*Eclipse*, pp. 45–46). The fact that Bella is thinking about this consideration implies that Bella is interested in college and a career and yet she repeatedly refers to college as "Plan B." Consequently, on the surface it appears as though Bella is nontraditional and yet her behavior again indicates otherwise. In fact, although, as noted earlier, Bella tells Edward in *Breaking Dawn* that she is actually interested in attending Dartmouth, and they clearly make plans for doing so, she also indicates that this is not so much because she wants to attend college but that she wants to remain human for a while longer. She is doing what she has been told mature people *should* do rather than choose her own path (which might or might not include college). Bella is certainly influenced by her mother's perspective, and she is pressured even more by Edward, who is making the decision that she should go to college rather than Bella herself. Thus, although Bella's behavior might seem feminist on the surface, she is not the person making decisions about her own life. She is not empowered, at least initially, and at least in this regard. Instead, she relies on her mother and on her boyfriend to direct her as she tries to please them both. Neither Renée nor Edward encourage her empowerment, preferring instead to dictate what they perceive as best for her instead of assisting her in her own decision-making processes—nor does she empower herself. Some might suggest that Bella *is* actually in charge of her own life, that she is working and moving toward what she ultimately wants—to be changed into a vampire—and that her acquiescence to Edward's wishes move her that much closer to her final goal. Meyer certainly maintains this perspective. As noted earlier, she describes Bella as a "strong person who goes after what she wants with persistence and determination" (Meyer, n.d.a, para. 18). But the reason for her ultimate goal of becoming a vampire is so that Bella can spend eternity with her love interest, Edward—a goal that is traditionally feminine.

Likewise, cursory support of feminism can be found when Edward notes before his proposal to Bella in *Eclipse*, "'Do you get the feeling that everything is backward? . . . Traditionally, shouldn't you be arguing my side, and I yours?'" (p. 451), referring to the fact that he is trying to get Bella to marry him before having sex and Bella is trying to get Edward to have sex with her before marriage, again the implication being that this storyline in the novel is modern, nontraditional, and feminist. Certainly, the dialogue between these two characters implies that this is true. But when one looks deeper at the storyline, one can see evidence that is contrary to these conclusions because later in the novel Bella becomes convinced that the traditional role that she is resisting, and that Edward is encouraging, is really acceptable. Bella's change from nontraditional attitudes to more traditional ones is illustrated at the very end of *Eclipse*, when Edward offers to change Bella into a vampire without the need to marry him. Edward has this change of heart, is willing to back out of the deal he made with Bella—to have sex with her while she is human and to change her into a vampire, provided she marry him—because he realizes that he has been pressuring Bella to live her life according to his standards rather than hers, as has been indicated throughout this chapter, and that his controlling behavior has only caused her pain as he has just witnessed in her break-up with Jacob. Consequently, Edward decides to give Bella what she has always wanted—sex while she is still human and to be changed into a vampire so that they could live together throughout eternity—with no strings attached, no marriage necessary. Bella, in direct contrast to Edward, initially views being changed into a vampire as more of a sign of commitment than marriage and has been reluctant to marry, but in this scene she refuses Edward's offer to renege on their marriage plans and argues with him about going ahead with them instead. Edward even offers to have sex with Bella then and there, something that she has been begging to do for an extensive period of time but Bella stops him, explaining to him that she wants to wait until they are married after all, to "'do this right . . . Responsibly. . . . in the right order'" (*Eclipse*, p. 619). Bella is persuaded away from any feminist leanings and toward more traditional behavior, from her own initial opinions to opinions that are more representative of Edward. She becomes convinced that traditional behavior is desirable.

Additionally, notice Bella's thinking as she realizes that she will be married in the upcoming summer, just after graduating from high school: "... maybe it wouldn't bug me so much if I hadn't been raised to shudder at the thought of marriage" (*Eclipse*, p. 456). In fact, after Bella reluctantly tries on her engagement ring in order to make Edward happy, she looks at it on her finger and thinks, "It wasn't quite as awful as I'd feared, having it there" (p. 458). Certainly, her thoughts on marriage have again changed but, additionally, note the implication that society, including our parents perhaps (or feminists?), has told young women that marriage, especially at an early age, is unacceptable, that they should go to college and perhaps start careers at the expense of marriage. Note also Bella's rejection of this cautionary message. Clearly, some feminists did caution women against starting families at an early age and before establishing their careers: Radical feminists suggested that gender inequality was partially due to patriarchy and to certain aspects of sexuality. They noted that marriage, and women's childbearing abilities, kept women in subordinate roles. Similarly, early liberal feminists did suggest that women become more like men, that they should enter the workforce and delay marriage and children in order to achieve in their careers, thereby promoting at least financial gender equity (Ashcraft, 1998; Evans, 1995). But later in the women's movement second stage, liberal feminists noted concerns with this approach to achieving equality (Ashcraft, 1998; Evans, 1995). They especially noted concerns that some women expressed who delayed marriage and childbearing and who then experienced problems with age-related infertility. But women are well aware of these issues today, and although young women might be warned off marrying at an early age, certainly today's feminists are much more concerned about how to combine marriage and family life with a career as opposed to avoiding marriage completely. As such, implicit messages in novels such as the ones just noted here in the *Twilight* series, messages that encourage readers to dismiss feminist concerns, are unfortunate and somewhat dated.

Confusion about the gender roles in the *Twilight* series also results from the fact that the novels subtly suggest in a variety of scenes that the traditional feminine role is more than acceptable; it is enviable. The traditional roles are portrayed in especially appealing ways. Note when Bella does get married in *Breaking Dawn*, the scene depicted is a prototypical wedding fantasy complete with wedding march fanfare, white dress, and flowers. The ceremony ends and the reception begins just as the sun sets and the decorative lights in the trees begin to twinkle. The beauty of the scene is certainly appealing to many women, young and old, and can be especially charming to impressionable tweens and teens, for whom the series is marketed, thereby encouraging interest in this traditional role without thought as to what comes after the wedding. Beyond this, despite all Bella's protests about getting married, as Bella walks down the aisle to Edward,

> it was only the pressure of Charlie's hand on mine that kept [her] from sprinting headlong down the aisle. The march was too slow . . . And then, at last, at last, [she] was there [by Edward's side.] (*Breaking Dawn*, pp. 48–49)

Although Bella resists getting married again and again, this scene, and her actions, certainly do not support that sentiment. Her verbal and nonverbal messages are not consistent. In other words, just because Bella says that she is reluctant to get married does not mean that she does not want to. Ultimately she does get married, and actions speak louder than words. Certainly, Bella willingly participated in the marriage ceremony. She had the free will to refuse and, as just noted, when Edward gives her the option to not marry, Bella is the one who insists on it. However, readers receive two messages: Resist marrying at an early age but it is perfectly acceptable, even beautiful and romantic, when you do.

Another example illustrating how scenes from the novels can persuade *Twilight* readers that traditional roles are acceptable, even desirable, can be seen as Bella and Edward discuss marriage in *Eclipse*. Edward asks Bella to understand that he is old-fashioned and Bella notes,

> And for one second, I could. I saw myself in a long skirt and a high-necked lace blouse with my hair piled up on my head. I saw Edward looking dashing in a light suit with a bouquet of wildflowers in his hand, sitting beside me on a porch swing. (p. 277)

This scenario is charming and romantic but, disturbingly, Bella's thinking about marriage slowly changes, and so can the thinking of the readership of the series. Despite her reluctance, Bella gets married at an early age.

There are a number of concerns that should be noted regarding the contradictory messages in the scenes described in this section. The first concern is that these types of scenes in the novels persuade readers into thinking that the traditional roles they portray are actually desirable. This typifies one of the noted themes of this book: that we learn from these traditional characters. In other words, the characters serve as role models. Consider the messages that adolescents (and possibly adults) come away with from these storylines. The novels encourage (young) women to embrace their femininity. And while there is nothing wrong with that, it is problematic that no other aspect of their personality is encouraged. In fact, the storylines encourage women to ignore the importance of college or careers, and they encourage women to overvalue their love relationships.

A second problem with these settings and dialogues is that they create confusion about feminism and traditional gender roles. They encourage readers to believe that the characters and storylines in the books are feminist when in actuality they are not. Because readers of such novels are looking primarily for entertainment, they often do not look past the superficial messages in novels and, hence, do not notice the inconsistency between the settings in the novels—or character discourse—and the reality of the characters' behaviors. They do not recognize that just because the novels *appear* to be feminist on the surface does not mean that they are. In fact, such contradictory portrayals of sex-typed behavior can lead to misinterpretations of that behavior as nontraditional behavior, as is noted by Susan Douglas (2010), author of *Enlightened Sexism: The Seductive Message That Feminism's Work Is Done*. She states that sex-typed media "takes the gains of the women's movement and uses them as permission to resurrect retrograde images of girls and women" (p. 10). In the case of the *Twilight* saga, the gains of the women's movement are used to resurrect traditional roles. The stories freely portray women engaging in traditionally feminine roles (and men engaging in traditionally masculine roles), but they also portray some non-sex-typed behaviors, and because there is the public perception that equality has been achieved, they encourage women to believe that feminine roles can now freely be chosen, that there is no longer a need to work toward gender equity. As feminist scholar Rosalind Gill observes, "The extreme of sexism is evidence that there is no sexism" (cited in Douglas, 2010, p. 13). In other words, some seem to think that the freedom to behave in feminine ways is evidence that equality has been achieved, as was discussed earlier. The traditional roles, behaviors, and storylines in the *Twilight* novels are used as evidence for their feminism!

A third problem with portrayals of the gender roles typified by these scenes is the fact that readers who use them as role models, who, perhaps unwittingly, adopt traditional roles, risk experiencing the same issues that women had with these roles 50 years ago. The problems with traditional gender roles, those discussed in the book that really started the women's movement of the 1960s, Betty Friedan's (1963) *The Feminine Mystique*, still apply today. Traditional choices are likely to result in social, political, and economic inequity between the sexes. Clearly, women's life choices should not be dictated by feminists or traditionalists, but the reason that feminists have discouraged traditional behavior stems from concern from a humanist viewpoint: If women make life choices that sacrifice careers for family life, they sacrifice financial independence. If women make life choices based upon the direction of others (such as boyfriends or husbands), they sacrifice their own needs and potentially their own growth and development. Women potentially risk being left alone due to divorce, death, and an empty nest if they mold their world solely around their love relationships (with boyfriends, husbands, children). As discussed, Meyer disagrees that these traditional choices are problematic, she disagrees that Bella is traditional, and she makes the traditional, old-fashioned roles sound romantic, but she also does not discuss the mystique surrounding those roles. Traditional gender roles are restrictive and prescriptive. They have financial repercussions. And they generally discourage psychological growth.

Summary and Implications

In sum, although there is extensive debate about whether the *Twilight* series and its characters are feminist in nature, there is substantial evidence that they are not. This is true even if one considers the examples of nontraditional behavior exhibited by the characters and the possibility that characters such as Bella might be cultural feminists. Such differences in opinion are likely due to multiple definitions of *feminism* and confusion as to what the term means in addition to the fact that Stephenie Meyer's use of the term *feminist* ignores vital implications of the word, that is, that feminists work toward gender equity. But recall that, from a psychological perspective, the ratio of feminine to masculine behavior is important in the determination of gender roles. Thus, because there are so many examples of traditional behavior in the *Twilight* novels and such a limited number of nontraditional behaviors, because the examples of sex-typed behavior far outnumber the examples of non-sex-typed behavior, it can be concluded that the novels are sex-typed, that is, traditional.

The fact that the *Twilight* novels are so popular indicates a renewed interest in traditional gender roles, perhaps, as noted in the last chapter, due to an increasingly conservative sociopolitical climate (Ames, 2010). The acceptance of a minimal amount of nontraditional behavior as indicative of feminist leanings indicates an apathy toward advancing gender equity in any meaningful way. This apathy toward feminism is reflected in an especially insightful response by a man who did not think that the novels were feminist in nature in the previously described informal survey about the *Twilight* series. He wrote that Bella "just wants to be happy with Edward, not necessarily his equal." Maybe the popularity of these novels, and their accompanying traditional gender roles, reflects this notion that the readers just want to be happy, and equality is subordinate to that experience. As Susan Douglas (2010) notes, "women today have a choice between feminism and antifeminism, they just naturally and happily choose the latter because, well, antifeminism has become cool, even hip" (p. 12). In fact, some writers suggest that feminists should embrace the (traditional) ideals of many American young women in order to interest today's women in feminism, that is, heterosexuality, marriage, children, objectified beauty, and power for women that has been defined by men (Zach, 2009). In other words feminists should return to traditional ideals in order to reduce apathy toward feminism!

While the *Twilight* saga places the importance of romantic relationships over all other experiences (Meyer, n.d.a), feminists have long noted that inequity will undermine relationships (McClimans & Wisnewski, 2009). Consequently, being apathetic toward feminism, ignoring the importance of working toward gender equity, can actually interfere with happiness in more traditional romantic (heterosexual) relationships, can interfere with the happily-ever-after promised by romance novels like those in the *Twilight* saga. Even Bella notes the importance of relationship equity when she discusses with Edward why she wants to be turned into a vampire. She tells Edward, "'I can't always be Lois Lane. I want to be Superman too'" (*Twilight*, p. 474).

CHAPTER THREE

The Motherhood Mystique

Motherhood is a role that evokes an almost reverential reaction in our society (Ganong & Coleman, 1995; Johnston & Swanson, 2008) and, considering societal perceptions of the role, rightly so: Mothers are viewed as altruistic, concerned only for the well-being of their families, consistently putting aside their own needs for the needs of their children. They are incredibly patient, taking in stride spilled milk and last-minute runs to the store for supplies needed to complete a school project due the next day. They diaper, they bathe, they cook, they clean, they nurse, they chauffeur, and they shop, without resentment of their obligations and without pay for these time-consuming duties. With assumptions about motherhood such as these, it is no wonder that the word takes on devotional meaning! But are these expectations consistent with the actual experience of motherhood, and what impact do these assumptions have on women who are considering becoming mothers or who are already mothers? It is these assumptions, their implications, and their influence on women that will be examined in this chapter. More specifically, this chapter considers how the *Twilight* series depicts motherhood and the implicit and explicit messages those depictions can have for readers.

The Motherhood Mystique

These worshipful attitudes revolving around motherhood are best understood through an examination of a feminist concept known as the motherhood mystique. The *motherhood mystique* is a term that refers to society's devotional attitudes toward mothers and mothering. It places mothers and mothering on a pedestal, encouraging the glorification of this role and this experience. In particular, the motherhood mystique consists of excessively flattering assumptions and attitudes about motherhood (Hays, 1996; Hoffnung, 1995; Johnston-Robledo, 2000; Oakley, 1974). This admiration of motherhood is exemplified in the fact that in 2011 the Museum of Motherhood was opened, its purpose being to educate the public about the role of the mother (Cohen, 2011). The museum boasts "virtue boxes" that are "paintings of words such as 'hard work' and 'courage' that remind visitors that mothers invest in human capital instead of their own economic capital when raising children" (para. 12). Additional evidence comes from Mamapalooza, a growing online organization whose mission is "serving, promoting, celebrating, encouraging, inspiring, and awakening ALL mothers through Media, Commerce, Connection, and Performing Fine Arts" [sic] (Mamapalooza, 2011, para. 13). And certainly, the societal devotion to motherhood is typified in the media, in particular in the *Twilight* series, especially in the fourth novel, *Breaking Dawn*, in which the primary storyline revolves around Bella becoming pregnant, risking her life to continue the pregnancy, almost dying in the process of giving birth, and then protecting her newborn from the Volturi, who see the newborn—and the other Cullens—as a threat. But this veneration comes at a cost. It is accompanied by numerous unrealistic expectations and stringent standards by which mothers are judged (Hays, 1996; Hoffnung, 1995; Johnston-Robledo, 2000; Oakley, 1974). Susan Douglas and Meredith Michaels (2004), authors of *The Mommy Myth*, also discuss the unrealistic expectations and assumptions of the motherhood mystique, including "the insistence that no woman is truly complete or fulfilled unless she has kids, that women remain the best primary caretakers of children, and that to be a remotely decent mother, a woman has to devote her entire physical, psychological, emotional, and intellectual being, 24/7, to her children" (p. 4). Let us examine each of these assumptions in more depth.

The Motherhood Mandate

One of the assumptions that is an essential part of the motherhood mystique is that motherhood is the epitome of the female experience (Douglas & Michaels, 2004; Hoffnung, 1995; Johnston & Swanson,

2003). It is the ultimate fulfillment of women. And because of this, all women desire children, an idea that is sometimes referred to as the *motherhood mandate* or *compulsory motherhood* (Russo, 1979). Taking this supposition one step further, the implication is that women who claim not to want children are misguided or misinformed or will change their minds about having children later, when they get older or when they accidentally get pregnant. *Breaking Dawn* explicitly demonstrates this motherhood mandate through the behaviors and thoughts of a number of characters. For example, Rosalie initially resents Bella for a number of reasons but especially because, as a human, Bella is able to bear children. Rosalie, as a vampire, is unable to reproduce and desperately wishes she could have a child; she envies Bella's ability to do so. Note, for example, that in *New Moon*, when Bella asks the Cullens to vote on whether she should be allowed to be changed into a vampire, Rosalie votes against it because she believes that Bella is squandering her chance at this human experience. When Bella does get pregnant in the fourth book in the series, *Breaking Dawn*, Rosalie protects Bella from others who believe that the pregnancy should be aborted. Moreover, note Jacob's observation of Rosalie as she protects Bella. He thinks, "The baby, the baby. Like that was all that mattered. Bella's life was a minor detail to her— easy to blow off" (p. 303). Clearly Rosalie's storyline is consistent with this aspect of the motherhood mystique: her behavior demonstrates that not only does she desperately want children, but that she believes that Bella will eventually regret not having children if she becomes a vampire before doing so.

It is interesting that, and yet unclear why, Rosalie does not "adopt" children as Esme did (young vampires who were taken "under wing"), despite her yearning for children. Perhaps it is because they would not be her biological children or perhaps because the adoption might not be an authentic motherhood experience for her. If she adopted other humans that had been changed into vampires she would not experience their growing from an infant into an adult. Instead, most likely due to ethical considerations the person turned into a vampire would be at the youngest, a young adult, just as Edward suggested to Bella the possibility that they "adopt" a teen vampire in *Eclipse*. Therefore, Rosalie still might not experience the nurturing aspect of motherhood, the experience of watching a being develop and evolve from a small child to an adult. Instead, her "child" would be another companion. While this seems to be satisfying for Esme, it might not be for Rosalie.

Bella, on the other hand, does not express any concern to Rosalie about her possible childless future in response to Rosalie's story, but the depiction of her character demonstrates the aspect of the motherhood mandate that suggests that women who have no interest in motherhood are misguided and misinformed, that they will want children eventually even if they claim otherwise. Notice Bella's change in attitudes about motherhood in *Breaking Dawn*: She notes, "I'd never imagined myself a mother, never wanted that. . . . Children, in the abstract, had never appealed to me" (p. 132). But her opinion changes completely once she is pregnant. She observes, "I wanted him like I wanted air to breathe. Not a choice—a necessity" (p. 132), referring to her unborn baby. It is unclear what prompts this change in opinion; possibly it is due to the telepathic (and therefore emotional) bond she has with her unborn baby. Alternatively, it might be due to perceiving the baby as an extension of Edward since Bella rejected the possibility of human children with Jacob. In either case, however, the change in opinion is consistent with the motherhood mystique and the reader is alerted to Bella's need for the child, even though she previously indicated no interest in becoming a mother. This aspect of the motherhood mandate is even better exemplified as Bella further thinks to herself, "Maybe I just had a really bad imagination. Maybe that was why I'd been . . . unable to see that I would want a baby until after one was already coming" (p. 132), the implication being that even when women think they do not want children, later they will find out that they actually do.

Even minor female characters in *Breaking Dawn* demonstrate this overwhelming yearning for children. For example, Jacob observes Kate and Carmen with Renesmee, both from the Denali vampire clan who are like an extended family of the Cullens, and both of whom have traveled to visit the Cullens to possibly assist them in a fight against the Volturi. Jake notes, "...it was easy to read the longing in them" (p. 595), indicating that both wanted to hold the child and, to be more specific, that they both coveted a child. Similarly, some of the male characters demonstrate an assumption that all women want children. Edward, for example, is concerned about changing Bella into a vampire because he does not want Bella to sacrifice her ability to have children. He says, "'I *hate* taking that away from you,'" referring to her potential to have children (*Breaking Dawn*, p. 28). As noted, however, Bella is initially unconcerned about her ability to reproduce being eliminated once she is a vampire. She replies, "'I know what I'm doing.'" Edward responds, "'How could you know that, Bella? Look at my mother, look at my sister. It's not as easy a sacrifice as you imagine'" (p. 28), which typifies societal reactions to women, regardless of their age, who indicate that they do not want children.

Clearly the repetitiveness of these storylines suggests a subtle implication that women have an all-consuming drive to have children and those who want to remain childless just do not know any better. Obviously, there is nothing wrong with wanting children, and most women do become mothers (Etaugh, 1993), but about 3% of women want to remain voluntarily childless (Jacobson & Heaton, 1991). Unfortunately, these women are often viewed condescendingly: They are perceived as less fulfilled, less happy, and as having a less rewarding life than those women with children (Mueller & Yoder, 1997). And such perceptions are mirrored in novels and other media sources that depict the motherhood mystique. To illustrate, note Bella's reaction to Kate, another vampire who visits the Cullens in *Breaking Dawn* when they are preparing to meet the Volturi and who does not always show the same reverential devotion to Renesmee as the majority of the other characters. Bella thinks, "Kate probably didn't understand, never having known for herself the passion of a mother for her child" (p. 620). These societal attitudes and these implicit (and explicit) messages in the media ignore the advantages of being childless, for example, more flexible lifestyles and less drain on financial resources (Boston Women's Health Book Collective, 2005; Ceballo, Lansford, Abbey & Stewart; 2004; Megan, 2000; Warren & Tyagi, 2003). They also can make readers who are not interested in motherhood roles wonder what is wrong with them, can make women believe that they should want children, and pressure them into becoming mothers when they would rather follow other paths through life. This is especially problematic because the adolescents who read young adult novels with these themes are provided narrow and inaccurate images of what it means to be female, images that they might not have the critical thinking abilities to decipher and invalidate. As indicated throughout this book, it is not a particular storyline, in this case the glorified portrayal of motherhood, that is problematic, but rather it is the repetitiveness of the theme that is depicted in the media. In other words, because readers are only given one view of motherhood, it becomes difficult to develop alternate views. The repetitive depictions do not allow for an alternate view of women's lives, one that does not include children.

Effortless Mothering

A second assumption of the motherhood mystique is that women are innately good at mothering, that it is instinctive (Johnston & Swanson, 2003; Johnston-Robledo, 2000). Thus, women are perceived as naturally patient and nurturing. Consequently, society believes that mothers—as opposed to fathers—should be the primary caregivers of children because they are perceived as being better at parenting (Hoffnung, 1995). As such, the motherhood mystique promotes different standards for men and women, encouraging women to be primary caretakers of children despite feminist attempts to deinstitutionalize this mandate. This aspect of the motherhood mystique can be found as Bella describes her experience in holding her daughter. She says, "'She fit so easily in my arms, like they'd been shaped just for her'" (*Breaking Dawn*, p. 462). Clearly the implication in this scene is that Bella and Renesmee are made for each other and that Bella naturally knows how to hold her daughter. Such depictions suggest that motherhood is effortless. Certainly Bella repeatedly observes that just about anything vampires do seems effortless in comparison to humans, but Renesmee, who is half human and half vampire, does, in fact, require little parenting in comparison to human babies: She can communicate telepathically with her caretakers, eliminating the need to decipher what she needs as parents must do when an infant cries. She starts to talk just a few days after being born, saying "Momma" at one week. She begins to walk at three weeks. And she has multiple caregivers, most of whom have no need of sleep. In fact, Edward remarks on how little caretaking Renesmee requires. He comments to Bella, "'The only parents in the world who don't need sleep, and our child already sleeps through the night'" (*Breaking Dawn*, p. 429).

But mothering (parenting) for humans is typically not this easy and is a learned skill. Mothers and fathers often need to learn how to do such seemingly simple tasks as bathing a baby, feeding a baby, and burping a baby. Evidence for the need for education on parenting can be found merely by looking at the number of pregnancy and parenting books available and sold at local bookstores and the number of parenting magazines available for purchase and perusal! In fact, mothers often describe feeling incompetent (Fuligni & Brooks-Gunn, 2002; Gager, McLanahan, & Glei, 2002; Warner, 2005). But again, from a social learning perspective, because the media portrays one repetitive perspective on motherhood, readers of such novels as *Breaking Dawn* can have difficulty imagining other scenarios, for instance, imagining the difficulties and uncertainty that can also typify motherhood. Certainly Bella faces some difficulties after she becomes a mother: She is faced with the possibility that Renesmee will die prematurely because she ages so rapidly in childhood, and Renesmee, along with the other Cullens, is threatened by the Volturi. But these scenarios are not typical of humans, and while human parents are sometimes challenged by life-threatening childhood illness, these extraordinary circumstances are not relevant to the motherhood mystique which applies primarily to typical mothering experiences. Thus, readers of such descriptions of the mothering experience can be left with the impression that mothering is a blissful, effortless experience, and those adults who might be feeling less than confident in their mothering abilities can be left wondering what is wrong with them.

Love, Adoration, and Devotion

Another set of assumptions intrinsic to the motherhood mystique is that motherhood is a universally positive experience despite the amount of work it entails (Hoffnung, 1995) and that mothers love everything about their children and about mothering (Douglas & Michaels, 2004). In other words, good mothers love mothering! This perspective is exemplified in a number of scenes in *Breaking Dawn*.

For example, Bella is described as she experiences some type of telepathy with her unborn child: "Her breath caught, and it was impossible not to see the fanatical gleam in her eyes. The adoration and devotion" (p. 326). And after almost losing her life during the pregnancy and birth of Renesmee (and some could argue that she did actually lose her life because she was turned into a vampire!), Bella remarks that she misses having Renesmee inside her. After recovering from her being changed into a vampire Bella notes, "'It was so odd, so wrong not to have her inside me still. Abruptly, I felt empty and uneasy'" (p. 426). Her enjoyment of the pregnancy experience is evident despite the fact that she was slowly withering away during the experience, that her pregnancy was often painful (resulting occasionally in broken bones), and that she needed to drink blood in order to stay alive long enough for her baby to develop adequately to survive after birth. While many women do enjoy the experience of pregnancy, many others do not because of the physical discomfort involved (morning sickness, weight gain, body aches) (Feeny, Hohaus, Noller, & Alexander, 2001; Melender, 2002; Philipp & Carr, 2001). And in the weeks immediately following childbirth women often feel pain from the birth itself and experience a menstrual type discharge, as well as leaking breasts if they are nursing. Many report unpleasant reactions to these physical experiences, such as feeling dirty (Thompson, Roberts, Currie, & Ellwood, 2002). Unfortunately, the media does not often depict less pleasant motherhood experiences, leaving readers whose experiences do not match those of such characters in novels wondering why they do not feel the same.

Subtle messages implying that parenting is a blissful experience can be found in a variety of other scenes in *Breaking Dawn*. When Bella does finally meet Renesmee, after having been changed into a vampire, she thinks, "I was staring at the most beautiful face in the world" (p. 446). She later notes, "The days were not long enough for me to get my fill of adoring my daughter" (p. 527). Numerous scenes describe other characters' positive reactions to Renesmee also, thereby suggesting that not only is Renesmee loved but that she provides pleasurable experiences for others as well. For example, when Edward describes Renesmee to Bella, Bella notices, "He said her name with an understated fervor. A reverence. The way devout people talked about their gods" (p. 396). In fact, Edward says, "'She's like nothing else in the world,'" and Bella again notices that there was "an almost religious devotion . . . in his voice" (p. 428). And it is not just Renesmee's parents that are mesmerized by her. In one scene Jacob and Rosalie bicker about whose turn it is to feed Renesmee, and in another scene Carmen, a friend of the Cullens, is described as charmed by her. Her grandfather, Charlie, is also captivated by Renesmee. Bella notes, "Charlie was just as helpless against her magic as the rest of us. Two seconds in his arms and already she owned him" (p. 515). And in still another example, other members of the Cullen clan observe Renesmee: "Alice, Jasper, Esme, and Carlisle were sitting on the couch, watching her as if she were the most engrossing film" (p. 489). Clearly these scenes depict unmitigated joy in experiencing children, the implicit message being that parenting only provides happiness. But while many parents want to believe this, as well as give this impression to others, these ideas that exemplify the motherhood mystique neglect to acknowledge that parenting can also be frustrating and stressful (Bergman, Ahmad, & Stewart, 2003; Crosby & Sabattini, 2006; Stern & Bruschweiler-Stern, 1998). Because the negative experiences of mothering are not discussed, women whose experiences are other than enjoyable can be led to believe that, again, there is something wrong with them. From a social learning perspective, describing the positive experiences of sweet baby smiles and unconditional baby love but not addressing the less positive experiences of physical exhaustion, worry, and dirty diapers, in novels such as *Breaking Dawn*, can lead to a belief that mothering is uncomplicated and trouble-free. Subsequently, when mothers do run into difficult times, they are ill prepared to deal with them. In fact, women often underestimate the amount of crying a baby does (Feeney et al., 2001), which exemplifies the distorted view of motherhood our society (and the media) promotes. This is not to say that motherhood is an unpleasant experience. On the contrary, most mothers say that the positive outweighs the negative (Feeny et al., 2001). But a well-balanced view of what is required for this role is necessary to develop the skills needed to perform this responsibility successfully.

Not only does the motherhood mystique suggest that mothering is an unadulterated joyous experience, it further implies that women must selflessly, and happily, devote themselves to their children's best interests in order to be considered good mothers (de las Fuentes, Baron, & Vasquez, 2003; Douglas & Michaels, 2004; Ex & Janssens, 2000; Hoffnung, 1995; Hurtado, 2003; Johnston & Swanson, 2003). This aspect of the motherhood mystique is dramatically exemplified by Bella's self-sacrificing behavior as she struggles to stay alive long enough so that her child will develop enough to survive after birth. Bella, who has a difficult time with her pregnancy in *Breaking Dawn* because the fetus is half vampire and half human, becomes increasingly weaker throughout the pregnancy because of the complications involved in bearing this hybrid species and, in fact, almost dies. The people who love her best look on, practically helpless, as Rosalie continues to protect Bella from would-be abortionists and as Bella continues the pregnancy. In fact, Bella never once thinks of aborting the pregnancy in order to save her life and spare others the pain of losing her; she immediately rejects this possibility when it is presented to her. And it is clear that Bella thinks nothing of her potential (some would argue impending) death. She is willing to make the ultimate sacrifice for her unborn child. Although we could discuss the pro-life/pro-choice debate here, that is not the issue at hand. The issue is that Bella is willing to sacrifice everything to give birth to her child, even her coveted relationship with Edward, the focus of the first three novels. She is willing to give her life in order to give birth. Certainly Bella's self-sacrifice is found in other aspects of the *Twilight* saga storylines also: She is willing to sacrifice herself to save her mother in Arizona and to save Edward in Italy, for example. This self-sacrifice is definitely part of Bella's personality, but from a psychological perspective it is not healthy, and numerous characters in the novel do remark on Bella's martyrdom in general. Jacob, for example, refers to her behavior as "sickening" in *Breaking Dawn*, when he visits her and there is discussion of whether Jacob could be left alone with the pregnant Bella, the implication being that there might be an attempt to abort the pregnancy if Rosalie left her side. Jacob thinks Bella is a martyr and that she would have been perfectly comfortable having lived in an earlier time where she could have been fed to the lions. It is not my intention to imply that Bella's behavior is wrong or unreasonable. Rather, it is my intention to use this storyline to exemplify this self-sacrificing aspect of the motherhood mystique. However, while many readers will view Bella's behavior as admirable, one must be cautious in the interpretation of this story line in *Breaking Dawn*: As will be further discussed, there is nothing wrong with placing the needs of children before the needs of adults and parents some of the time. In fact, it is often warranted. But there is a problem with being completely self-sacrificing in order to fulfill the needs or wants of children. As will be discussed later, such intensive and extensive parenting is not healthy for the child or the adult (Bernstein & Triger, 2011; Leupp, 2011). But also consider that Bella's decision to maintain the pregnancy comes at a substantial cost to many around her. She (and her baby) put the entire Cullen clan in danger from the Volturi, as well as placing the humans in Forks at risk. As such, numerous characters disagree with Bella's decision to continue the pregnancy, at least initially. Edward's initial reaction to finding out that Bella is pregnant is to terminate the pregnancy, and Jacob has difficulty understanding why Bella does not. Sam's pack also believes that the baby or Bella need to be sacrificed for the greater good of the community.

The excessive self-sacrificing parenting standards that are reflective of the motherhood mystique are sometimes referred to as the *new momism* or as the *mommy myth* (Douglas & Michaels, 2004). Others refer to it as overparenting or intensive parenting (or mothering) (Arendell, 2000) or helicopter parenting, so called because parents "hover" over their children (Gibbs, 2009). In any case, intensive parents (mothers) perceive their children as vulnerable and helpless and, therefore, are motivated to continuously monitor their children in order to control them and keep them safe (Bernstein & Triger, 2011). And while this seems a natural concern for parents, the monitoring and protection of children in intensive mothering is excessive to the point that mothers feel the need to be doing something for their children constantly, and to believe that community or institutionally organized activities are inferior to anything mothers could do for their own children (Warner, 2005). As such, intensive mothers tend to take over tasks that beforehand had been taken care of by the government, the school system, or community organizations. For example, intensive parenting can be found in such time-consuming trends as homeschooling children so as to control the quality and content of a child's education (D'Arcy, 2011). Minor examples can be seen as parents drive their children to school everyday instead of having them take the bus, or as they organize social activities for their children instead of allowing their children to determine their own social life. Because mothers, and society in general, perceive the extra effort these activities entail for the parent as beneficial for the child, these rigid standards are used to judge mothers. Those who meet these expectations and engage in intensive parenting are viewed as good mothers (or judge themselves as good mothers), and those who cannot (or will not) meet these standards are perceived as neglectful (Hays, 1996; Hoffnung, 1995; Johnston-Robledo, 2000; Oakley, 1974). Therefore, the motherhood mystique encourages women to devote an extraordinary amount of time to the raising of their children, a task that even without these lofty standards is time-consuming. As such, even good mothers are sometimes judged poorly because they do not meet these unreasonable demands for self-sacrifice.

Other examples of excessive parenting standards, beyond Bella's self-sacrificing behavior during her pregnancy, can be found in the behaviors of other characters in *Breaking Dawn*. Consider that in one scene when Renesmee cries *all* the Cullens drop what they are doing to comfort her and find out what is wrong. All she wanted was her mother. In another scene we find that Jake has not left Renesmee's side since she was born (a total of about 3 days) except once to talk to his friend Sam. And in an even more telling example, we find that Renesmee always sleeps in someone's arms. Alice tells Bella that Renesmee has never been put down, that she has been held her entire life thus far, when Bella asks where Renesmee sleeps. Some of the excessive attention lavished on Renesmee is due to the fact that the Cullens are concerned that her unexpected rapid growth and development will result in her premature death, and clearly under similar circumstances such behavior by human parents might be warranted. But due to societal expectations—the motherhood mystique—mothers can feel the pressure to engage in intensive parenting even when it is uncalled for, partly because other mothers are engaging in it and imply that mothers who do not are neglectful (Bernstein & Triger, 2011). Note that a 2012 *Time* magazine cover featured a mother breastfeeding her 3-year-old (Harpaz, 2012). In the cover story, the mother indicates that she hopes to normalize such behavior. Clearly, most mothers in the human world do not have the time (or energy) to give their children similar care, nor should they feel as though they ought to. But because women feel pressure to be perceived as good mothers, they can fall victim to adhering to unreasonable mothering demands. In other words the motherhood mystique encourages people to perceive excessive parenting demands as reasonable, and media depictions such as those in *Breaking Dawn* add to and confirm these expectations, making it difficult to perceive these standards as unfounded. Unfortunately, these excessive standards are difficult, in some cases impossible, to meet, especially for women who are trying to combine motherhood with careers. And this is part of the reason that career women (who can also be good mothers!) are sometimes perceived as being neglectful of their children (Brescoll & Uhlmann, 2005; Johnston & Swanson, 2007; Newcomb, 2007; Riggs, 2005). The motherhood mystique implies that careers and motherhood cannot be combined in an effective way and that those mothers who also have careers are selfish, depriving their children of more intensive parenting, which is perceived as ideal. As discussed at length in chapter 2, this is seen in *Breaking Dawn* in that Bella is not career oriented and neither are any of the secondary female characters, although some of the female characters, such as Esme and Alice, do have hobbies, and some of these hobbies, such as Alice's stock market predictions, result in financial gain. But none of the main female characters are in the labor force, the possible exception, as noted, being Renée, Bella's mother, who is described as following her new husband around as he plays minor league baseball instead of working at her job as a teacher. Thus, sacrificing career for family is just another example of the differential standards our society places on men and women as parents: Sacrificing career for motherhood is permissible, optimal even, because the motherhood mystique implies that full-time mothers are best for children, but men are not pressured to be full-time fathers. Furthermore, because mothers are typically portrayed as careerless in the media, female role models combining both experiences are minimal. Hence, adolescent girls can have difficulty imagining and pursuing the combination of the two.

Summary

In sum, the motherhood mystique suggests that all women want to be mothers, that women enjoy all aspects of motherhood, and that women's single-minded devotion to their children is beneficial to them. It encourages an exaggerated admiration of motherhood because of its unreasonable expectations for women, requiring them to mother above and beyond the call of duty. The depiction of motherhood in *Breaking Dawn* illustrates the assumptions inherent to the motherhood mystique and sustains them through the social learning process. This is problematic because the mystique's assumptions about women's experiences of motherhood—which are often generated from media depictions such as those in *Breaking Dawn*—are often different from the actual experiences of women. Consequently, women can wonder whether they are deficient in some way when they find that motherhood is not the ideal experience they have been led to believe. In fact, research suggests that women often feel inadequate about their mothering skills because they are unable to live up to the excessive societal standards required of mothers (Caplan, 2000; Quindlen, 2005). Similarly, data indicate that mothers who attempt to meet these excessive societal parenting standards are likely to experience frustration, depression, and guilt (Leupp, 2011). Additional problems with the motherhood mystique are examined next.

Problems with the Motherhood Mystique

Detrimental to Children's Growth

Although the motherhood mystique implies that full-time mothers are better for children than mothers who work outside the home (Johnston & Swanson, 2007; Pew Research Center, 2007), research does not support this assumption: According to the National Institute of Child Health and Human Development (NICHD; 2005, 2006), the cognitive development of children who attend daycare is similar to that of children who remain with their full-time mothers, and in some cases is even better. Likewise, infants who spend time in daycare are just as emotionally close to their mothers as those who do not (NICHD, 2001, 2005). And children who attend daycare are often more cooperative and have fewer behavioral problems than their stay-at-home peers (NICHD, 2004, 2005, 2006). While there are exceptions to these generalizations, they seem to be dependent primarily upon the quality of the daycare experience rather than on whether the child attends daycare or not; children can actually benefit from daycare attendance, as long as it is a high-quality setting (NICHD, 2005, 2006). Furthermore, women who work outside the home also tend to encourage independence in their children (Johnston & Swanson, 2002) and serve as role models of competent career women (Casad, 2008). Thus, the assumption that full-time mothers are best for children is not supported by research. Unfortunately, the media, including novels such as *Breaking Dawn*, do not reflect or encourage these facts. Rather, they encourage myths typifying the motherhood mystique.

While the well-being of children of stay-at-home mothers does not differ significantly from the children of mothers who work outside the home as long as quality childcare is available and as long as the mother engages in competent parenting practices, it should be noted that not all parents utilize effective parenting techniques. An example of a potentially damaging parenting practice is the overprotective and overly invested parenting style typifying the mother mystique discussed previously. Although some intensive parenting practices can have positive effects, including making it less likely that children are injured (Schwebel, Brezausek, Ramey, & Ramey, 2004) and increasing academic achievement (Bernstein & Triger, 2011), there is also significant data that indicates that this new momism can have detrimental effects on children. Specifically, it prevents or delays children from becoming independent from the parent (Marano, 2004) and encourages them to become more self-centered (Twenge, 2006). Further research indicates that children raised with intensive parenting techniques have more difficulty with coping skills, time management, study skills, and general organization (Hofer & Moore, 2010) in comparison to children who are not raised this way. And there is still more data that suggest that they are less likely to show enjoyment, creativity, and spontaneity and are more likely to show signs of depression, anxiety, stress, and low self-esteem than other children (Twenge, 2006).

While intensive parenting is a recent societal trend, historically psychologists have warned against providing children with too much attention, suggesting that doing so will damage their ability to develop in a well-adjusted way. For example, Freud (1963), father of modern psychology, suggested that both neglect and overindulgence during early childhood could result in fixation at an early stage of development. Such fixation leads to unhealthy, rigid behavior that typifies the stage at which the fixation developed. Adler, best known for developing the concept of the inferiority complex (1972) and the notion that birth order influences the development of personality (1927, 1964), suggested also that too little and too much parental attention is detrimental to children. He theorized that, in either case, children will develop a low level of social interest, that is, a low level of concern for others and for their community, which is indicative of maladjustment (Adler, 1939). Conversely, he also suggested that only children who have experienced an intermediate level of parental attention can develop a higher level of social interest and behavior indicative of mental health. Similarly, Horney (1937, 1950), whose work on the neurotic personality will be discussed in more detail in a later chapter, also discussed the importance of parental practices, in this case on development of neurotic and well-adjusted relationships later in life. And more recently, attachment theorists have also noted the importance of parental style on the psychological adjustment and personality development of children (Baumrind, 1991). Consequently, the excessive parental attention indicative of the motherhood mystique is contrary to decades of advice from numerous, notable psychologists.

How is it possible for a parent to give a child too much attention? How can too much attention be detrimental to a child? The premise behind these ideas is that if children are given too much attention, they learn that they are the center of their family's universe, that their parents are present to fulfill their every need or desire. The extensive attention they receive does not allow them to discover that other people, such as their parents, also have needs and desires, does not allow them to develop the skill of being able to take another person's perspective, and does not allow them to develop empathy and sympathy for others because they learn to be concerned only about themselves. Furthermore, overparenting, as evidenced by the research noted above, does not allow children to develop other skills, including independence, because parents take care of so much for them. In sum, although the motherhood mystique suggests that giving a child extensive (and intensive) attention is ideal, the research indicates that this assumption is not supported. Instead there is extensive research that suggests that this parenting (mothering) style is detrimental to the child's psychological and cognitive development. Therefore, media portrayals of intensive mothering, or the new momism, such as those depicted in *Breaking Dawn*, are problematic because they encourage the continued unfounded belief in these motherhood stereotypes. Further because this parenting style is so time-consuming it is detrimental to mothers who employ it, as is indicated in the next section.

Detrimental to Women's Growth

Clearly the motherhood mystique exemplifies that at least certain aspects of the traditional female role still exists in our society. And clearly it idealizes and encourages the traditional motherhood role. Such thinking is typical of the cultural feminist philosophy discussed in the previous chapter. As noted, cultural feminists embrace the traditional feminine role (Ashcraft, 1998) and are most concerned with promoting that role and persuading society to value it. But while valuing roles that are feminine is vital in the pursuit of gender equity, the previous chapter also noted problems with this philosophy, notably that it still relegates women to traditional roles. As such, so does the motherhood mystique. It encourages women (and men) to think that all women want children, that motherhood is the epitome of the female experience, that women enjoy all aspects of motherhood, and that to be a good mother, women must willingly devote all their time and attention to their children (Douglas & Michaels, 2004; Ex & Janssens, 2000; Hoffnung, 1995; Johnston & Swanson, 2003; Russo, 1979), assumptions that are all typical of the traditional feminine role, which feminists have long argued is restrictive to women. Consider that Betty Friedan, the mother of the women's movement of the 1960s and 1970s, discussed this issue in her book, *The Feminine Mystique*, 50 years ago. Friedan (1963) described the emotional experiences of countless women who felt dissatisfied even though they were living the female American dream, a dream that ultimately included motherhood. These were women who had the nice house in the suburbs, the station wagon in the driveway, the husband who had a good job, and the children that they wanted and needed, or at least that society told them that they *should* want. And yet they felt incomplete and dissatisfied. They even felt guilty for feeling dissatisfied! Why? Friedan determined that women also have other needs, needs similar to those of men, that women could not live their lives through their husbands and their children, that women needed to fulfill their own potentials. Clearly, the storylines in the *Twilight* novels do not address these issues. Instead, they exemplify the traditional feminine role typical of the pre-women's movement era, without thought for feminist analysis of these roles. But author Stephenie Meyer herself indicated that she needed a creative outlet, needed to be something in addition to a stay-at-home mother. Referring to her stay-at-home mothering experience, she described her brain as oatmeal (Granger, 2010), a description similar to the experiences of women discussed in the *Feminist Mystique* 50 years ago. As such, the problem with portrayals of the motherhood mystique, like that in *Breaking Dawn*, is that not only are they unrealistic depictions of motherhood with unattainable standards, but they also do not address the other needs of mothers, thereby implying that women do not have other needs. As will be discussed in more detail in a later chapter, data indicate that women employed outside the home, including mothers, report better physical and psychological health (Fokkema, 2002; Klumb & Lambert, 2004), but the motherhood mystique discourages the combination of motherhood with careers. Therefore media, like *Breaking Dawn*, that depict the motherhood mystique not only discourage career aspirations of mothers but also encourage restrictive roles for women, roles that can ultimately contribute to feelings of dissatisfaction and can encourage behaviors in women that can be detrimental to their physical and mental well-being, roles that encourage them to live their lives through their children instead of living for themselves. Feminists have long argued that if women want to be well-rounded, well-adjusted people, if they want to feel whole, complete, and satisfied, they must reach beyond motherhood for additional experiences (Friedan, 1963). In other words, women cannot live fulfilling lives vicariously.

Radical Feminism

Although it is quite controversial, another feminist philosophy, radical feminism, has also discussed problems inherent to the motherhood mystique. As noted in the last chapter, there are many different types of feminists, and views of radical feminists differ significantly from views of the cultural feminists just discussed, especially their views on motherhood (Ashcraft, 1998). Whereas cultural feminists promote and value the motherhood role, radical feminists see the motherhood role as a source of gender inequality. According to radical feminists, it is women's motherhood role (and therefore the motherhood mystique) that has prevented women from achieving equality (Firestone, 1993). They suggest that women's reproductive abilities have contributed to their disempowerment, that because women bear children they are forced into traditional motherhood roles and into behaving in traditionally feminine (nurturing) ways. Consequently, motherhood has prevented women from taking positions of power in society, instead allowing men to do so. As such, radical feminists suggest that patriarchal society is responsible for gender inequality. In particular, they suggest that traditional implications of sex and gender are responsible for the inequity between men and women, that society encourages *compulsory heterosexuality*, which disempowers women (Evans, 1995; Rich, 1993). Compulsory heterosexuality reflects the idea that society pressures people into heterosexual roles, that society pressures men and women to marry and have children. These compulsory roles subsequently deprive women of power and place men in positions of power because they, like the assumptions of the motherhood mystique, endorse the value of stay-at-home mothering and intensive mothering, roles that do not allow for the development of other aspects of women's lives, such as careers. As such, it robs women (mothers) of power by making them financially dependent upon their husbands.

While the women of the *Twilight* saga might not be completely financially dependent upon their male partners, they certainly are motherhood oriented and not career oriented, which is noted as typical (and is objected to) by radical feminist arguments. But more telling, consistent with the radical feminist philosophy is the fact that Carlisle is the only Cullen in the labor force and also the family patriarch. He, although kind and benevolent, clearly is an authority figure and holds significantly more decision-making power than others in his family, who are not in the labor force. Illustration of Carlisle depicted as head of the family can be found as his family members look to him for advice and for finalizing decisions. We see this as Edward looks to Carlisle for advice in *Midnight Sun* as Edward finds himself irresistibly drawn to Bella's sweet-smelling blood. We also see this in scenes depicting the Cullen clan members gathering together as a family in their dining room to discuss decisions as a family. For example, note that in Meyer's partial draft of *Midnight Sun*, Carlisle sits at the head of the table when the Cullens have a family conference about the possibility that Edward might have exposed them as vampires by saving Bella from being crushed by a vehicle in the school parking lot. They clearly look to Carlisle in the decision-making process: Rosalie wants to kill Bella to keep their secret safe but Carlisle will not allow it. There is a similar dining room scene in *New Moon* when Bella asks the Cullens to vote on whether she should become a vampire. Carlisle starts the meeting by indicating to Bella that she should begin discussing her request. To further illustrate, note that Carlisle is responsible for negotiating peace between the Quileute and the "cold ones," as the vampires are referred to, for encouraging his family to be vegetarian and for managing to hide his family's vampirism from the outside world. Such subtle indicators demonstrate Carlisle's position of authority. Consequently, this storyline is consistent with the radical feminist notion that labor force participation is related to power.

Conceivably it could be argued that Carlisle's authority might not be due to his workforce participation but rather due to other reasons, like his longevity. Similarly it could be argued that although the

Cullen women do not participate in the workforce, they are also not financially dependent upon their male partners, as radical feminists suggest, but rather are financially independent, that they, as well as the Cullen men, are affluent. Certainly readers are given this impression through repeated descriptions of designer clothes purchased by Alice, and clearly Esme needs money to refurbish old houses. But note the lack of clarity about where this wealth originated. As noted earlier, Stephenie Meyer (2006) only describes three sources of the Cullen's wealth: (1) Edward, who inherited property from his parents; (2) Carlisle, who makes a good living as a medical doctor and who also acquired assets from his time with the Volturi; and (3) Alice, who can predict the stock market. This, combined with their vampiric longevity and lack of living expenses, allowed for the accumulation of assets. But note, first, that two out of the three characters responsible for the Cullen wealth are male and that only one (Carlisle) is currently in the labor force. Further note that one of these male characters, Carlisle, the family patriarch, "began" the Cullen clan, along with their wealth. Thus, even if the Cullen women are financially independent, the majority are not so because of their own devices but rather because Carlisle assisted them, at least initially. This is also likely given that Edward tells Bella in *Eclipse* that once they are married, his wealth is her wealth. He tells her, "'If you're my wife, then what's mine is yours...'" (p. 440). If Edward insists on such a benevolent financial arrangement, it is likely that Carlisle did also, and in fact, in *Breaking Dawn*, Bella wonders whether Edward learned his generosity from Carlisle. As such, the depiction of gender roles in the *Twilight* saga is consistent with the radical feminist notion that there is a relationship between labor force participation, wealth, and power or authority, complete with decision-making power.

Radical feminists also note that society ostracizes those who do not conform to these compulsory heterosexual roles (lesbians, gays, bisexuals, people who do not want to marry or have children). Such attitudes are reflected in the *Twilight* saga in that there are no characters that have a sexual orientation other than heterosexual. Likewise, as discussed earlier, *Breaking Dawn*, in particular, implies that women who claim to want to remain childless are simply misguided. It does not allow for the possibility that a woman might legitimately want to remain voluntarily childless. These alternate views and lifestyles are invisible in the series. But radical feminists readily promote reproductive technology, such as contraception, noting that such technology can free women from these traditional roles by preventing unwanted pregnancies and by allowing for painless labor if, and when, women did want to have children (Ashcraft, 1998). They also promote interest in lifestyles other than the traditional family, lifestyles in which gays, lesbians, and bisexuals could be comfortable, as well as lifestyles in which heterosexuals do not feel the need to conform to societal expectations. They might, for example, suggest communal living or that two heterosexual women share a house and share responsibilities of raising their children instead of expecting those women to marry and live with the fathers of their children (Firestone, 1993). It is interesting that some of the vampires in the *Twilight* series do demonstrate this approach to family life, especially the Denali clan and, of course, the Cullens. The Cullens consist of Esme and Carlisle, who act as parents to other vampires—Edward, Rosalie, Emmett, Alice, and Jasper—who are all young adults and, in the case of Rosalie and Emmett, and Alice and Jasper, who are in relationships with each other. Thus, although they appear to be a traditional nuclear family in some ways, in other ways the Cullens can also be described as having a nontraditional living arrangement in that their family consists of multiple adult couples living together communally.

In sum then, radical feminists suggest that the source of gender inequality and women's lack of societal power is their reproductive potential, that is, motherhood. While many will disagree with this analysis there are some legitimate points. As is discussed in more detail in the next chapter, the current structure of our society does not allow for easy integration of motherhood and employment for women: Affordable, quality daycare is not readily available, nor is adequate maternity and paternity leave (Heyman, Earle, & Hayes, 2007). Furthermore, society does not hold fathers to the same rigorous standards as mothers, continuing to view full-time mothers as being best for children (Johnston & Swanson, 2007; Pew Research Center, 2007). Such attitudes, then, encourage women to sacrifice financial independence for motherhood or to choose "mommy tracks" that are also less economically lucrative. As such, the lack of governmental, institutional, and employer policies that assist in the combination of work and motherhood, as well as the continued promotion of the motherhood mystique in books like *Breaking Dawn*, do discourage gender equity, even if motherhood, per se, does not.

Summary and Implications

It is certainly not my intention to suggest that mothering is anything but a deservedly praiseworthy role. As a mother of three I can conclusively state how much I have enjoyed raising my children. And generally speaking, parents, mothers especially, indicate that having children is an enriching, fulfilling, creative experience, that watching them grow and develop into independent beings is rewarding (Boston Women's Health Book Collective, 2005; Ceballo, et al., 2004). But, also as a mother, I, like other parents, can attest to the fact that raising children can also be time-consuming, exhausting, and exasperating (Cusk, 2002; Fulgini & Brooks-Gunn, 2002; Gager et al., 2002; Huston & Holmes, 2004; Thompson et al., 2002; Warner, 2005). Such experiences and research findings reflect the disparity between societal stereotypes of motherhood and its reality. The point is that mothering is not one-dimensional as it is often portrayed in books and other media sources. It involves both pleasurable and unpleasant experiences, but because the motherhood mystique addresses only the positive, it does not allow people to view parenting in a realistic light. It allows for only one perspective on mothering, discouraging and ignoring other views of motherhood. Such disparity can leave new mothers feeling disappointed and incompetent because their experience does not mirror the motherhood mystique (Caplan, 2000; Fuligni & Brooks-Gunn, 2002; Gager et al., 2002; Warner, 2005; Quindlen, 2005).

Furthermore, because research on social learning demonstrates that we all can learn from vicarious (or symbolic) models, for instance characters in television shows, movies, and novels (Bandura, et al., 1961; Bussey & Bandura, 1999), the media is an important source of gender role development, especially in children and adolescents. As such, depictions of the motherhood mystique in books like *Breaking Dawn* encourage traditional motherhood roles for women and discourage career aspirations in our young women (Geis, et al., 1984; Yoder, et al., 2008). Because the motherhood mystique is a repetitive theme in the media, it does not allow for alternate views of the experience, including the possibility that there are women who do not want children (Jacobson & Heaton, 1991). I am not suggesting that all media portrayals of motherhood should focus only on the negative aspects of parenting, and certainly I am not suggesting that only women who are voluntarily childless should be portrayed in the media, but a wider variety of perspectives on motherhood in novels such as *Breaking Dawn* could be beneficial to readers as they learn about this aspect of the feminine role.

Some might argue that the female characters in the *Twilight* novels do demonstrate a variety of motherhood experiences: As a human, Esme lost a child but as a vampire adopted a number of young adult children in their vampiric state. Rosalie regrets not having children as a human but has not adopted any children as a vampire, at least not by the end of the saga. Leah is concerned that she might be infertile as a werewolf. Renée gave birth to a biological child, Bella, but is not an attentive mother even though she claims not to regret becoming a mother at a young age. And Bella initially indicates that she does not want children but when she does unexpectedly become pregnant risks her life to maintain the pregnancy until the baby is able to live on its own. But even with this variety of experiences, the majority of these storylines are consistent with the motherhood mystique: The characters are all excessively interested in the motherhood role although in different ways. There are, however, some exceptions to this rule. Some characters, such as Alice for example, seem unconcerned about motherhood, both in her human and vampire states, although we do not know for sure whether she will never be interested in becoming a mother (the motherhood mystique would suggest she eventually will), and it is unclear whether this lack of interest is part of her character or simply an underdeveloped aspect of it. Nevertheless, it should be noted that just because an exception to a rule exists, does not mean that the rule is invalid. Instead, rules are representative of experiences most of the time. Rather than focusing on the exception, the rule is what needs to be focused on. As such, most of the depictions of motherhood in the *Twilight* saga are consistent with the overly simplified and inaccurate images of the mother-hood mystique.

Also consistent with the motherhood mystique are most of the images of fatherhood. While the motherhood mystique does focus primarily on mothers, fatherhood can also be examined through this stereotype in that if mothers are viewed as ultimate, nurturing caregivers for children, then fathers can only be viewed as less competent by comparison. And again, although there are exceptions in the depictions of fathers in the *Twilight* novels, many of them are portrayed in less-than-ideal ways. For example, although loving, Charlie, Bella's father, can be described as a neglectful parent: He is not very nurturing and, in fact, has difficulty expressing emotion or affection, especially toward Bella. He also does not spend a lot of time home with Bella who is often left to her own devices. Because of this Bella engages in numerous dangerous activities of which is he un-aware (dating vampires, befriending werewolves, riding motorcycles, diving off cliffs). Likewise, Charlie does very little caretaking in that he rarely is described as cooking or cleaning. Instead, Bella is repeti-tively described as completing these chores. Jacob's father Billy, although also loving, is likewise portrayed as utilizing a nonchalant approach to parenting in that Jacob is also often left to his own devices. Similarly it often appears that Jacob takes care of Billy instead of vice versa. Also consistent with the motherhood mystique, many of the male characters demonstrate less interest in parenting than the female characters: Jasper and Emmett do not indicate any interest in fatherhood, although, like Alice, it is unknown whether this is because of lack of character development or because this is truly one of their traits. Edward also demonstrates a lack of interest in parenting, at least initially. He expresses no regrets about not having had biological children and shows no interest in adopting vampire children until he discusses Bella's potential infertility with her. Additionally, his initial reaction to Bella's unexpected pregnancy is that she should abort the child. Later, after he is able to telepathically communicate with the unborn child and after Renesmee is born, he is much more nurturing, behavior that is much more likely to typify women's reactions to babies, children, and parenting than men's, at least according to the motherhood mystique. The other exception to portraying fathers as being inattentive parents is, of course, Carlisle, the Cullen family patriarch, who is very nurturing, understanding, and patient with all of his adopted children, Edward, Rosalie, Emmett, Alice, and Jasper. But note the number of examples demonstrating "the rule" outnumber the exceptions to "the rule." Because there are so many portrayals of traditional motherhood and fatherhood it is much more likely that readers will remember and use those as models for behavior rather than the exceptions.

CHAPTER FOUR

The Work-Family Dichotomy

T he previous chapter established that the majority of the female characters in the *Twilight* novels are uninterested in careers but are quite interested in motherhood roles. Such interests are consistent with the *work-family dichotomy*. The work-family (or bread-winner-homemaker) dichotomy is a widely accepted notion that the work world and the family world are separate spheres, the former a concern for men that revolves around the breadwinner role, the latter a concern for women that revolves around childbearing and family-caretaking roles. And while feminists have addressed a variety of issues over the decades, this assumption in particular has long been criticized. As Joan Williams (2010), University of California law professor and author of *Reshaping the Work-Family Debate: Why Men and Class Matter*, notes, "From the mid-1960s until the early 1980s, U.S. feminism focused primarily on deconstructing and deinstitutionaliz-ing the cultural mandate that women become homemakers and men breadwinners" (p. 111) and that women (but not necessarily men) must choose between careers and parenting because the two roles are incompatible. Consistent with this dichotomy is the fact that the majority of the women characters in the *Twilight* series are not career oriented. As noted in chapter 2, the heroine, Bella, does not show much interest in getting a college degree, describing it as "Plan B," despite the fact that she is portrayed as a good high school student in the novels and education is a step to career advancement. She shows even less interest in a career. Similarly, although the Cullen women have repeatedly attended college and are actively involved in a variety of pursuits, some of which make money (e.g., Alice predicts the stock market), none of these women are in the labor force. In fact, the only woman who does have a career in the novels is Bella's mother, who is a kindergarten teacher, a traditionally feminine occupation consistent with the family pole of the career-family dichotomy because it involves child-nurturing and care-taking roles. In contrast, we can find examples of male breadwinners, although many of the male *Twilight* characters are also unemployed. Bella's father, Charlie, is a police officer, and Carlisle, the Cullen family patriarch, is a well-respected doctor. Relatedly, the women in the novels, especially in *Breaking Dawn*, are excessively preoccupied with children: bearing them, raising them, and protecting them. For example, in *Breaking Dawn*, Jacob considers Rosalie's behavior, "The baby, the baby. Like that was all that mattered. Bella's life was a minor detail to her—easy to blow off" (p. 303). Likewise, Bella is described as she experiences some type of telepathy with her unborn child, "Her breath caught, and it was impossible not to see the fanatical gleam in her eyes. The adoration and devotion" (p. 326).

It is possible that the Cullen vampires in the *Twilight* novels do not have careers because they might not be able to fully integrate into the human world due to concerns about being unable to resist feeding off their coworkers. It is also likely that they do not participate in the labor force because of the extensive fortunes they accumulate over time. But it is interesting that the novels pay much more attention to motherhood (parenting) issues for women than for men and that they pay more attention to men's careers than women's. For example, Charlie's career as a police officer is frequently referred to whereas Renée's job as a kindergarten teacher is mentioned in passing. Motherhood is frequently discussed in the series but fatherhood is less frequently discussed, especially in *Breaking Dawn* in which the theme revolves around Bella's pregnancy and Renesmee's birth and protection from the Volturi. Such differential topics for storylines are certainly consistent with the work-family dichotomy. But the work-family dichotomy is not just a literary technique. It is present not just in novels such as those of the *Twilight* series but also in the real world. As such this chapter focuses specifically on this enduring model for determining gender roles and in the continued belief that women must still choose between motherhood and careers.

While women have increased their workforce participation significantly since the 1960s and the beginning of the feminist criticism of the career-family dichotomy, data also show that women have become increasingly dissatisfied with working full-time over the past decade, that there is a gender differential in attitudes about working full-time, and that women are still more likely than men to care for children. For example, a 2010 report on women in the labor force from the U.S. Bureau of Labor Statistics noted that from 1975 to 2000 the labor force participation rate of mothers with children under 18 years of age rose from 47% to almost 73%, but a 2007 survey of more than 2000 U.S. adults by the Pew Research Center indicated that only 32% of working mothers said that full-time work was ideal for them in 1997. Of even more concern is that this number had dropped to only 21% by 2007. In contrast, 72% of fathers surveyed indicated that working full-time is the ideal situation for them. Furthermore, the U.S. Bureau of Labor Statistics (2011a) indicated that in 2010 the percentage of families with children in which the mother was employed but the father was not was 7.4, but the percentage of families in which the father was employed but not the mother was 30.2. Thus, the traditional gender roles portrayed in the *Twilight* novels reflect current gender roles and attitudes found in society. It is important to note, however, that in addition to mirroring current societal trends, books such as the *Twilight* novels (in addition to other media sources) also help to perpetuate them through the social learning process.

Feminist Criticism

These data, and the fact that the *Twilight* novels are so popular despite their depiction of traditional gender roles, suggest that current society continues to view work and family through a lens of gender differences (Williams, 2010), a polarity of gender roles reflected in the work-family dichotomy. In other words, society still sees the caretaker role for women and the breadwinner role for men as appropriate and legitimate. Consistent with this view, Glass von der Osten (2010) notes that in some ways *Twilight* celebrates the nuclear family in which there is a mother, father, and children, whereby the father is the breadwinner and the mother is the stay-at-home child caretaker. And certainly, Carlisle is portrayed as the breadwinner of the Cullen family clan (although he really does not financially need to work because of his wealth) and Esme as the stay-at-home mother, reflecting societal assumptions that these roles are appropriate. Some would argue that the Cullens represent a nontraditional family, that is, a multigenerational, large family unit made up of six couples, not just one. But even considering this perspective, that the Cullens are an alternate family unit, there are clear indicators that Carlisle is still the father figure (patriarch) and Esme is still the mother figure, as noted in the previous chapter.

Expanding on the idea that the male breadwinner and female mother-caretaker roles are appropriate, there are some who take this dichotomy a step farther and suggest that it is natural, perhaps biologically based, that women be less concerned about careers and more concerned about motherhood roles. Lisa Belkin (2003), author of the *New York Times* article, "The Opt-Out Revolution," startled feminists and raised eyebrows when she suggested that women do not want careers, money, or power because they come at the expense of personal balance. She stated, "Why don't women run the world? Maybe it's because they don't want to." (p. 3). Belkin's article is sometimes interpreted as meaning that women prefer to choose motherhood over careers or that women are uninterested in career achievement. Some see opting out as a preference of cultural feminists, that is, as fulfilling women's needs and roles, which are substantially different from those of men. As noted in chapter 2, as a difference school, cultural feminists see men and women as being very different from each other, with different needs, abilities, and so forth. Thus, cultural feminists view women's opting out of the labor force in order to fulfill motherhood roles as being natural, as being biologically driven. Examples of this reasoning can be found in *Breaking Dawn* as Jacob discusses Bella's difficult pregnancy with Leah, who becomes part of Jacob's pack when he breaks off and forms a second pack apart from Sam's. Leah is worried about her inability to reproduce and also wonders if there is something wrong with her. Jacob wonders in response why Leah became the "'only female werewolf in the history of forever. Was that because she wasn't as female as she should be?'" (p. 318), referring to her disrupted menstrual cycle and her inability to imprint and get pregnant. Leah tells Jacob,

'There's something wrong with me. I don't have the ability to pass on the gene [for becoming a werewolf] . . . So I become a freak—the girlie-wolf—good for nothing else. I'm a genetic dead end and we both know it.' (p. 318)

This conversation indicates that Leah perceives becoming the first female werewolf as a curse, not as an exciting, groundbreaking experience, because she thinks it means that she cannot have children and that is her priority. Note the insinuation, by both Leah and Jacob, that if women do not reproduce there is something wrong with them; they are "freaks" and, consistent with the work-family dichotomy, and the motherhood mystique, the implication is that the primary role for women is bearing and raising children.

Others translate women's opting out as evidence that gender equality has been achieved, that now that women are able to freely enter the labor force, to freely choose careers, to freely achieve in nontraditional careers, they do not need to. Consistent with Stephenie Meyer's definition of feminism, they can *choose* not to work outside the home (Meyer, n.d.a). For example, in a 1998 *Time* magazine article on the (then) current state of feminism, 50% of women aged 18 to 34 surveyed indicated that they had feminist leanings, but that for them feminism meant choice, being able to choose a career, motherhood, or both (Bellafante, 1998). Thus, a significant portion of those surveyed perceived choosing traditional roles as a feminist choice. As noted earlier, this logic is flawed because such choices do not encourage gender equity. This type of reasoning, that women could now freely engage in traditional roles because gender equality has now been achieved, is just another example of what author Susan Douglas (2010) calls enlightened sexism, an illogical belief that sex-typed behavior is evidence that gender equity is realized.

But what is not discussed in these interpretations of opting out is Belkin's suggestion that women who opt to be stay-at-home moms or who give up full-time work for part-time work, do so because the work environment is not conducive to their combining motherhood with their careers. The current structure of employment in our society is not compatible with motherhood because women are still the primary caretakers of children and most places of employment are not accommodating toward this responsibility. Fathers, on the other hand seem to have fewer problems with combining work and family than do mothers because they are not the primary caretakers of children (U.S. Bureau of Labor Statistics, 2011b; Cawthorne, 2008). It is less relevant to them that their places of employment offer benefits that help them to juggle the demands of both career and family life because the mothers of their children are assisting them in that regard. In other words, it might not be that women's *needs* to combine parenthood and work life are different than those of men. It might just be that women's *experiences* with combining parenthood and work life are different from those of men, and different in such a way that it makes combining the two poles of the work-family behavioral dichotomy more problematic for women than for men.

Although men are increasingly involved in active parenting, data indicate that they typically are not the primary child caretakers. For example, census statistics indicate that the number of stay-at-home dads increased from 140,000 in 2008 to 158,000 in 2010, but even this increased prevalence of stay-at-home dads accounts for less than 1% of married couples (Yen, 2010). Likewise, the U.S. Census Bureau notes that in 2008 when the number of stay-at-home dads numbered 140,000 (U.S. Census Bureau, 2009a), the number of stay-at-home moms numbered 5.3 million (U.S. Census Bureau, 2009b). Subsequently, because men do not experience the physical toll of pregnancy and childbirth, their work life is less affected when they become parents than when women do. Because men are not the primary caretakers of children, their work life is less affected when they become parents than when women do. Because men have wives and girlfriends to care for their children, their work life is less affected than that of women. Women have different, more complex, more difficult experiences than men when they attempt to combine motherhood with their work world. Thus, as Belkin (2003) notes, women might opt out of combining the two poles of the work-family dichotomy because it is so difficult for them to do so. Men, on the other hand, continue to combine the two behavioral poles because it is not as difficult. The current societal structure reflects the work-family dichotomy, which favors men, allowing them more manageable ways of combining work and family life. Some might suggest that this is evidence that traditional gender roles are best, that women are not capable of combining the two roles as men do and, therefore, should not, but as will be discussed, combining work and family life has numerous financial, physical, and psychological benefits (Fokkema, 2002; Klumb & Lambert, 2004).

Clearly the female *Twilight* characters do not combine these two roles. Instead, they have opted out of the workforce (whether it be for lack of interest, need to protect their identity, or lack of financial requirement). Unfortunately, neglecting to depict characters struggling with combining work and family life is typical in most media portrayals of women. Similarly, there are few depictions of women successfully combining the two roles (e.g., Barner, 1999; Brown, 1998; Jacobs, 2004; Jennings, et al., 1980; Lauzen, et al., 2008). As such, the depictions of the women characters and their family experiences in the *Twilight* series, as well as other media portrayals, do not encourage discussion of the problems inherent to the work-family dichotomy, nor do they present possible solutions to them. For example, they do not illustrate possible ways to restructure society to better accommodate the needs of working mothers, making the work world more conducive to women combining family life and work life, nor do they exemplify coping techniques mothers in the workplace can utilize to maneuver the two roles successfully.

Accommodating Working Mothers

Unfortunately, our culture is very resistant to accommodating the differential needs of women in the work world. The assumption is that if women want to combine work and family they must do so following the same model as men. But this basic assumption is flawed. The problem with this assumption is that because men's and women's experiences combining the two roles are so different it is difficult, if not impossible, for women to use the male model. It is like fitting the proverbial round peg into a square hole. It doesn't work. But if society is really committed to gender equity, work structures that allow fathers to be successful could be altered so that they allow mothers to be successful also. As Williams (2010) notes, places of employment are required by law to make accommodations for their employees who are disabled in some way. They must install ramps or elevators for those in wheelchairs to make buildings accessible and post Braille symbols next to text lists of floors in elevators, as well as make other accommodations that allow the physically disabled to complete their jobs. Additionally, employers allow employees to use sick time when they have the flu or to recover from surgery or other medical ailments with no apparent time limit. Accommodations for these physical experiences are made and yet employers (and society) assume that women should carry on with their usual work duties when they are experiencing morning sickness and fatigue due to pregnancy. They require women to recover from pregnancy and childbirth in a prescribed time frame that fits their employer's sick leave policy. They assume that women should be able to continue to be productive at work even though they are sleep deprived from nighttime feedings. And they assume that women should return to work even though they might still be breastfeeding and there is no on-site daycare for their newborn. Employers and society are reluctant to grant maternity (and paternity) leave or other policies that allow women accommodations for their physical experiences, accommodations that assist their combining work and family responsibilities successfully. As authors of *The Mommy Myth*, Susan Douglas and Meredith Michaels (2004) note, the United States has some of the worst maternity and paternity policies in Westernized society. In fact, a 2007 study conducted by the Institute for Health and Social Policy at McGill University found that the United States was one of only four other nations out of the 173 surveyed to not guarantee mothers paid maternity leave! The four other countries were Lesotho, Liberia, Papua New Guinea, and Swaziland. Beyond this, the study also found that 66 countries ensure paid *paternity* leave and 107 protect women's right to breastfeed, with 73 of the countries guaranteeing *paid* breastfeeding breaks. The fact that the United States does not live up to these standards is discouraging, but even more disheartening is the excessive standards our society places on mothering while at the same time not supporting mothers financially or institutionally.

Third-wave feminists often discuss concerns of juggling motherhood with the work world (Costain, 2003) as they also attempt to deinstitutionalize the work-family dichotomy and further move toward gender equity, but other countries seem to be several steps ahead of the United States in their resolution of this dilemma. Other countries seem to have realized that work life and family life intersect. Other countries understand that work experiences and family experiences influence each other. Unfortunately, the United States does not look to them as examples. And, unfortunately, the messages readers get from books such as *Breaking Dawn* just further encourage the survival of the work-family dichotomy, reinforce the motherhood mystique, and discourage the career aspirations of our young women. Stephenie Meyer objects to this type of feminist criticism of her series. As mentioned, she feels as though such criticism limits, rather than expands, women's choices (Meyer, n.d.a). Recall her response to a question regarding whether Bella is an antifeminist heroine. She states,

> One of the weird things about modern feminism is that some feminists seem to be putting their own limits on women's choices. That feels backward to me. It's as if you can't choose a family on your own terms and still be considered a strong woman. How is that empowering? Are there rules about if, when and how we love or marry and if when and how we have kids? Are there jobs we can and can't have in order to be a "real" feminist? To me, those limitations seem anti-feminist in basic principle. (Meyer, n.d.a, para. 18)

However, as noted in earlier chapters, when feminists criticize such choices they do so because such choices promote gender inequity. Consequently, criticism of the work-family dichotomy focuses on the power differential (financial and otherwise) between a stay-at-home mother and a father in the workforce, as well as other potentially negative implications for such a division in gender roles. Therefore, books—and other forms of media—such as *Breaking Dawn*, that strengthen the work-family dichotomy are problematic. Such media support the notion that women must choose between career and family for two reasons: (1) The characters in the novel(s) are not role models for doing otherwise; and (2) The description of motherhood and the experiences of the female characters encourage the motherhood mystique. Let us examine both reasons more closely.

Social Learning Theory

As has been discussed in previous chapters, one of the ways we learn is through social learning, that is, one of the mechanisms we use to understand what is appropriate behavior for our sex is through the observation of real people and fictional characters in books, movies, and television programs (Bandura, et al., 1961; Bussey & Bandura, 1999). Consider the behavior that readers "observe" as they read the *Twilight* novels. As is mentioned, the women characters in the *Twilight* novels, particularly *Breaking Dawn*, are not career oriented but they are very family oriented. Thus, there are two behaviors modeled by the women characters: (1) the lack of interest in careers and (2) excessive interest in having children. As noted previously the female characters do have some interests—Esme fixes up old houses; Rosalie works on cars; Alice plays the stock market—and some of these interests or hobbies do result in economic advancement for the Cullens, but none of these women are in the labor force and none juggle both motherhood and careers. Esme's children are grown vampires (Rosalie, Emmett, Jasper, Alice, and Edward) and neither Alice nor Rosalie has children. Likewise, as repeatedly noted, Bella shows no interest in a career either before or after becoming a mother. Certainly it could be argued that the Cullens have no need for labor force participation because of the material wealth they have been able to accumulate, but humans typically do need to participate in the labor force in order to survive and such models are necessary for teens to develop career interests. Unfortunately, as also noted, depictions of women juggling careers and family life successfully in the media are rare, as are depictions that demonstrate women choosing careers over family life (Barner, 1999; Brown, 1998; Jacobs, 2004; Jennings, et al., 1980; Lauzen, et al., 2008). Consequently, it is not just the *Twilight* series that is problematic in this regard. One novel depicting traditional roles would not necessarily hamper the career dreams of any one teen (or of an adult considering going back to school for career advancement). But what is problematic is that such depictions of female characters being uninterested in careers are prevalent. The sheer number of such characters is the issue. In fact, in much of young adult literature geared toward girls there is a tremendous amount of emphasis on what the female main protagonist looks like and on beginning a relationship, that is, attaining a boyfriend (Carpenter, 1998, Durham, 1998, McRobbie, 1991 all cited in Behm-Morawitz, et al., 2010; Jacobs, 2004), not on career aspirations. Moreover, Granger (2010) suggests that the difference between the young adult romance genre and other categories of the romance genre is that it is less realistic and more idealistic because it assumes its readers are less sophisticated. Therefore the romance aspect of it is even more extreme than in other types of love stories. And certainly one of the most important concerns of adolescent girls is being attractive to boys (Mann, 2009). In other words, readers are not given an adequate number of nontraditional role models from which to learn and encourage their vocational aspirations because many of the storylines in young adult literature geared toward females emphasizes romance. As such, when teens try on different roles during adolescence in an effort to figure out who they are, they encounter limited (and limiting) roles. And in the case of the *Twilight* series not only is the romance between Edward and Bella a primary focus but also, especially in *Breaking Dawn*, many of the female characters are very interested in motherhood, including Bella, who is still a teen herself. As such, readers can come away with the impression that in addition to a love relationship, motherhood is the one thing that all women should strive for and devote their lives to.

In sum, this discussion notes that in addition to modeling excessive interest in romance and motherhood, the *Twilight* novels also model a lack of interest in careers. But also consider other behaviors that the series does not model. The series does not demonstrate strategies that exemplify women breaking down the work-family dichotomy successfully. As such, the *Twilight* series, as well as other similar media, contributes to the persistence of the work-family dichotomy, and although Stephenie Meyer never intended the series to be a model for readers' choices (Meyer, n.d.a), social learning theory implies that it likely is.

Cultural Differences

Interestingly, the work-family dichotomy exemplified in the *Twilight* series is really only pertinent to women in the middle- to upper-

(typically Caucasian) socioeconomic class. Poorer women have never really had the "choice" to stay home with their children or to choose a career. Poorer women, and especially single mothers, are much more concerned about finding and maintaining jobs that pay enough and provide enough hours so that they can keep a roof over their children's heads, food on their table, and clothes on their backs. In fact, mother of the women's movement Betty Friedan (1963) was criticized for focusing on feelings of dissatisfaction that middle-class, white women experienced, and for initially ignoring the experiences of women of color, of lesbian and bisexual women, and of women from the lower socioeconomic levels. She was criticized for implying that the experiences of white middle-class women were the same experiences that women from other social groups also had. Supportive of this criticism are data from the Pew Research Center (2007) that notes that African American mothers are more likely to consider full-time working moms as ideal for their children's welfare than were Caucasian mothers or Hispanic mothers. They are also almost twice as likely to live in poverty as Caucasian women according to the Center for American Progress (Cawthorne, 2008). But consistent with Friedan's ethnocentric view is the fact that even though a few of the secondary characters in the *Twilight* novels are from different ethnic groups and cultures, the main characters in the novels are white and seem to be wealthy, with Carlisle belonging to the upper-class profession of medical doctor. In fact, the Cullens' wealth is often referred to in the *Twilight* novels, and Carlisle, in particular, is listed as the richest fictional character by *Forbes* magazine, worth an estimated $34 billion (Morran, 2010)! But women from diverse social groups and economic classes have different experiences and, therefore, different concerns and needs in the search for gender equality. These are important considerations and certainly the "choice" to become a stay-at-home mother is a luxury that many women cannot afford.

Beyond this, the work-family dichotomy also neglects two other cultural considerations. First, as is discussed in the previous chapter, there are women who do not want children and so do not see a choice between career and family life as necessary. Second, while some feminists have long suggested that women must have choices, that they should not be "forced" into traditional homemaker-motherhood roles, that they should be free to choose to be mothers or to enter careers (despite the fact that for many there is no choice because of financial need), in comparison there is little to no discussion of men choosing between careers and fatherhood. Joan Williams notes in an interview for an October 2010 article in *Time* magazine that "[t]he feminist argument has been that women should have choices. But that means fathers have no choice but to shoulder the burden of being the sole breadwinner" (Luscombe, 2010, para. 8). A large segment of the population assumes that men do not want to be full-time, stay-at-home dads, assumes that men should be the family breadwinners, and assumes that women should be the primary caretakers of children (Pew Research Center, 2007; Riggs, 2001). Certainly fathers are much less likely than mothers to be stay-at-home parents. As noted, the number of stay-at-home dads in the United States is minimal, even though there has been a recent increase in their number. And the vast majority of working fathers do indicate that they prefer to work full-time. According to the Pew Research Center (2007), 72% of fathers surveyed say the ideal situation for them is a full-time job (compared to just 24% of mothers). What is interesting about this report, though, is that one of the questions asked was "Is the increase in working mothers with young children generally a good thing for society, a bad thing for society or doesn't it make much difference?" The question "Are working fathers a bad thing for society?" is not asked. Again, the assumption is that mothers are the best caretakers of children. Again, the assumption is that mothers working outside the home might be problematic for children but that fathers working outside the home are not. The assumption is that one person needs to care for the children and that the other parent, assuming there is a two-parent household, needs to financially provide for the other family members. But what if both parents shared both jobs? What if both mothers and fathers were responsible for the financial, physical, and emotional well-being of the family?

The Cost of Choosing Motherhood Over Careers

There are a variety of scenarios from which women typically choose when deciding between career and family. In the first, women give up careers completely in order to (usually) get married and become stay-at-home moms. Other women interrupt careers to have children while they are younger and then reenter the workforce again after their children are grown. Still other women choose jobs or careers that are not as demanding—and are often lower status and lower pay—so as to accommodate motherhood better. These "mommy tracks" are sometimes discussed as a feminist strategy, a method to combine both work and family life, but such interruptions in and obstacles to employment come at a cost. There are problems with the pressure that society places on women to have children at the expense of pursuing careers. For example, from a practical standpoint giving up a career in order to have children can have a negative impact on a woman's financial security. When women take extensive time off to be stay-at-home moms or when they work part-time or when they choose lower-status, lower-pay careers, they contribute significantly less to the financial well-being of their households and to their retirement savings. In fact, according to the Center for American Progress, "poverty rates increase for women during their childbearing years and again in old age" (Cawthorne, 2008, p. 1). And generally, women are much more likely to live in poverty in the United States in comparison to men. Furthermore, the gap between the poverty rate of women and that of men is larger in the United States than in any other Westernized country. There are multiple reasons for this including those just mentioned, that is, that women spend more time on caregiving for children (and for other family members such as elderly parents) and that women are more likely to be segregated into lower-paying occupations, sometimes because of the necessity to care give. While this is certainly admirable and noble behavior, it is also problematic if a woman's husband who is a breadwinner dies or if the couple divorces. Nearly one quarter of people with incomes below the poverty line are single mothers. In approximately 80% of cases when couples divorce, women are granted custody of children. This means that they tend to take on the financial burden of raising children. In fact, "custodial mothers are twice as likely to be poor as custodial fathers," according to the Center for American Progress (Cawthorne, 2008, p. 2). And single mothers are more likely to be poor than any other social group (National Poverty Center, 2011). As one of my students said while I was talking about this issue in one of my classes, "But I don't want to go into a relationship thinking that it will breakup!" Of course not. Being concerned about potential future break-ups is not the point. The point is that men rarely sacrifice financial security in order to have children. Women often do, and women need to be financially self-sufficient, not just for themselves but for the sake of their children should tragedy strike and the father dies, or if the couple divorces.

Fortunately for the Cullen women in the *Twilight* series, including Bella, who marries into the family, money is not an issue: Stephenie Meyer (2006b) notes that the Cullens are wealthy because they were able to build up a fortune over the centuries that they have lived as vampires. Likewise, death of a spouse is not much of a concern for vampires, in general, for obvious reasons, although there is concern from the Cullens about angering the Volturi, which could potentially result in their elimination. Although not all vampires mate for life, because of the lifestyle they have chosen, the Cullens also do not need to be concerned about divorce. This is certainly convenient and promising for the Cullen women but does not reflect real-life possibilities. One might argue that novels do not reflect real life, nor is it necessary that they do, but again it must be noted that if there were an adequate number of novels that did not reflect stereotypic gender roles, where women did not routinely give up career aspirations in order to become self-sacrificing mother figures, such depictions would not be problematic. This would just be another storyline. The problem though is, again, that there are minimal nontraditional role models for teenage girls and because they are bombarded with images that glorify traditional roles, they have difficulty seeing through the fictional stories to possible real-life scenarios that do not reflect "happily ever after."

Psychological Benefits of Combining Career and Family

From a psychological viewpoint, this one-sided emphasis on women's childbearing and the de-emphasis on careers for women are not healthy. Conversely, the emphasis on men's breadwinner role and de-emphasis on fatherhood can also be viewed as unhealthy. Research on combining employment with family responsibilities indicates that those who combine the experiences are both psychologically and physically healthier and happier, although they are more likely to feel overwhelmed than those who do not combine the roles (Fokkema, 2002; Klumb & Lambert, 2004). In fact, research consistently shows that women who work outside the home experience less psychological distress than women who stay home full-time (Barnett & Hyde, 2001). Maternal employment has a positive impact on psychological health, most likely because the multiple roles allow for a variety of experiences, thereby, alleviating boredom and, possibly, the frustration and stress that are sometimes typical of raising young children. Similar results are also found for men who combine employment and family roles (Fokkema, 2002; Klumb & Lambert, 2004).

Relatedly, numerous humanists, some of them psychologists, have encouraged growth and well-being by promoting authentic living, endorsing new experiences, encouraging the development of a well-rounded personality, and persuading people to develop a sense of identity independent of societal pressure. Adhering to societal expectations for motherhood and ignoring career needs is not consistent with these recommendations. As Joan Williams (2010) notes, one of the goals of feminism has always been a matter of helping people, women especially, to explore and develop their own sense of personal identity, but she also notes that feminism typically does not discuss psychology as shapers of women's (and men's) identities. That notion is explored here.

Jung's Self-Realization

The importance of developing both the feminine and the masculine sides of our personality was discussed as far back as the early twentieth century with the writings of Swiss psychiatrist Carl Jung (1969), founder of analytical psychology. He discussed the importance of integrating all aspects of our personality in order to become well-adjusted, a process he called *self-realization*. While discussing the structure of personality, Jung suggested the existence of a collective unconscious that contains archetypes of primordial images passed on from generation to generation. Jung suggested that an extensive variety of archetypes that can influence our behavior without us being aware of their presence, the two most relevant to this discussion being the anima and the animus. The anima is the archetype of femininity, which predisposes us to act in traditionally feminine ways. The animus is the archetype of masculinity, which predisposes us to act in traditionally masculine ways. Bella's traditionally feminine behavior described in other chapters, including her housekeeping behaviors, her need to take care of others, and her need to have her child, can be interpreted as being motivated by the anima. Edward's masculine, even patriarchal, behavior, including his need to dominate Bella early in the series and his competitiveness with Jacob, can be attributed to the influence of the animus. According to Jung, it is vitally important to integrate these two aspects of our personality, and although one will be dominant over the other, the less influential archetype must also be developed in order to become a whole, well-adjusted person. As such, it follows that in order for women to become whole, they must not only pay attention to the anima influencing them to have children, but also to the animus influencing more masculine pursuits such as careers. And vice versa: In order for men to become well-rounded individuals they must not only pay attention to their careers but also to their family life. Therefore, the work-family dichotomy whereby men and women are relegated to different roles can be seen as preventing self-realization because it prevents them from experiencing both types of roles. It follows from this theory, then, that what is ideal for both men and women is for both to be financially responsible for the well-being of their families, as well as physically and emotionally responsible, but unfortunately, the characters in the *Twilight* novels do not integrate these two types of roles. Rather, they tend to focus primarily on maintaining traditionally sex-typed roles. Whether this is due to their nature—that it is difficult for vampires to completely integrate into the human world—or for other reasons, this role division is not consistent with Jung's interpretation of adjustment (of humans).

Erikson's Eight Stages of Psychosocial Development

Another notable psychologist, Erik Erikson (1950), also discussed the value of combining both work and family life. As mentioned in chapter 1, Erikson described eight stages that we go through as we progress through life. During each of these stages we experience a crisis, which can be resolved successfully or unsuccessfully. The resolution of the crises allows for the development of different aspects of our personality. The three stages most relevant to this discussion are the fifth, sixth, and seventh. Erikson suggested that in the fifth stage, called adolescence, teenagers (approximate ages 12–18 years) face the crisis of identity versus role confusion. They need to determine who they are, to develop a sense of their own identity. And this sense of identity must be separate from that of others, such as parents. It is during this developmental period, and a little beyond, that young people try on different roles in an effort to determine who they are. Hence, some try different styles (e.g., sexy clothing, body piercings, Goth clothing, different color hair, etc.), sometimes to the dismay of their parents. One factor that influences our sense of identity is career choice. Consequently, it is important that teenagers are provided with a variety of role models portraying an assortment of occupations because such diversity assists them in determining who they are and who they want to be. Unfortunately, a significant portion of young adult novels, like the *Twilight* saga, provide only one image or role model for young women especially: the teen overly concerned with establishing and maintaining a romantic relationship. Additionally, it should be noted that Erikson thought it was easier for men to develop a healthy sense of identity than it was for women because, at that time, men were more career oriented, again indicating the importance of career in the establishment of identity. As such, romance novels marketed toward tween and teen girls that do not provide a variety of career-oriented role models (Barner, 1999; Brown, 1998; Jacobs, 2004; Jennings, et al., 1980; Lauzen, et al., 2008) can hinder the development of a healthy sense of identity in young women. Erikson further suggested that such a lack of interest in a career could make it more likely that a woman's identity be dependent upon others, especially her husband (and his career). This is particularly troublesome because Erikson defined *identity* as a sense of individuality that is separate from others, including parents, boyfriends, and husbands, and Bella can certainly be seen as overly dependent upon Edward. (Similarly, Edward is obsessed with Bella.) Furthermore, of other importance is the fact that whether this stage is resolved successfully or not, that is, whether someone develops a true sense of who they are or emerges from this stage uncertain as to who they are, determines the likelihood of success at subsequent stages. Thus, if someone emerged from this stage without a strong sense of self, they would be less likely to emerge from the next stage, young adulthood, which is relevant to people aged 19 to about 35 or 40, having the ability to develop truly intimate relationships.

According to Erikson people in the young adulthood stage are faced with the crisis of intimacy versus isolation. Note that Erikson used the term *intimacy* to refer to genuine love relationships, which could be either sexual or nonsexual. As such, intimate loving relationships could refer to platonic relationships, such as best friends, or sexual relationships, such as that between lovers, as long as there was true attachment and concern between the individuals involved. It is the task of young adults to learn to develop these genuine love relationships and form these loving relationships at this stage. According to Erikson, if people do not develop a strong sense of self, that is, if they emerge from the adolescent stage with role confusion, they will find it difficult to develop intimate relationships in this young adulthood stage. Consider that if someone does not have a strong sense of self, if they do not know who they are, it makes it difficult for others to really know them and, therefore, truly love that person. Interestingly, in the *Twilight* saga, Bella does not demonstrate a true sense of identity. As noted, she is not interested in college, nor does she express any interest in a career or anything else, except her relationship with Edward, but she ultimately does love and marry Edward. While a successful resolution of the sixth stage is possible even if the resolution of the fifth stage has not been successful according to Erikson's theory, it is unlikely. That is, an intimate relationship can develop even in someone who has not developed a strong sense of identity but it is much more difficult to develop a genuine love relationship in that case. Hence, one can again see the importance that teens are provided a variety of role models that allow them to try on different identities, especially those that might be inconsistent with societal pressure to assume traditional gender roles. This is particularly true for young women because female characters in books and movies are often portrayed in limited and sex-typed ways (Barner, 1999; Brown, 1998; Jacobs, 2004; Jennings, et al., 1980; Lauzen, et al., 2008). Establishing a healthy sense of identity is crucial to establishing healthy love relationships.

An unsuccessful resolution of the young adulthood stage will also make it difficult for people to have a successful resolution of the seventh stage, middle adulthood. During middle adulthood, the crisis is one of generativity versus stagnation. *Generativity* is defined as a concern for future generations. Erikson thought that children were important in the continued psychological growth of adults, that adults need children (their own or others) in order to avoid routine living, of being caught in a rut. They encourage us to be creative and inventive because children themselves can be so unpredictable. Parents continuously struggle with developing new ways to meet the needs of their children and to encourage healthy, growth-enriching experiences for them. Teachers endlessly try new approaches for engaging their students and encouraging them to learn. Volunteers working with children regularly invent new activities that support the development of their young charges. Note, then, that Erikson did not just think that careers were important in continued adult psychological growth, but children were too, whether they are our own or others, because they make us concerned about the future for them. He viewed the combination of the two as being beneficial to adult adjustment. Thus, while it might be difficult for vampires, the Cullens in particular, to combine family life with careers, given the difficulty they have with fully integrating into the human world (and therefore potentially harming coworkers), a combination of family life and work life is a model for which humans can strive, and one that Erikson implied is beneficial to adult development and adjustment.

Maslow's Hierarchy of Needs

More recently, Abraham Maslow and Carl Rogers wrote of ideas also consistent with the belief that combining career and family is healthy. Abraham Maslow (1954, 1970) is best known for his hierarchy of needs. He suggested that we are always motivated by one need or another, with lower-level needs taking precedent over higher-level needs. The following pyramid depicts the hierarchy. At the bottom of the hierarchy are the physiological needs. These are the needs for food, water, sex, sleep, and so on. The next level consists of safety needs. These are the needs we have to feel safe and free from physical harm, but it would also include the need to feel secure financially and personally, about our income, about our jobs, that we will continue to be able to pay our bills, and so forth. Next on the hierarchy are the love and belongingness needs, that is, the need to love others and to be loved in return. The fourth level includes the esteem needs, which consist of both reputation needs (the need for others to like us and respect us) and the need for self-esteem (the need to feel good about ourselves). The final level of the pyramid is the need for actualization, which are needs to grow, to develop, to move toward the completion of our potential.

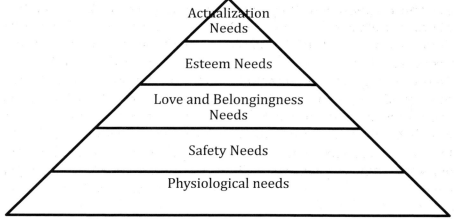

Figure 1: Maslow's Hierarchy of Needs

There are numerous examples of the characters in the *Twilight* novels fulfilling their needs. If vampires have the same physiological needs as humans (and they might not considering that they do not need to breath or sleep as humans do!), then the depictions of them feeding off blood exemplifies the fulfillment of these needs, as are the depictions of the human characters eating and sleeping. Safety needs are certainly activated a number of times in the novels as Bella is repeatedly saved in dangerous situations, and as the Cullens are threatened by the Volturi. These needs are fulfilled by resolving the dangerous situation and restoring feelings of well-being and security.

Fulfillment of love and belongingness needs are demonstrated through Bella and Edward's relationship with each other, as well as the relationships between Alice and Jasper, Rosalie and Emmett, and Carlisle and Esme, among others. Carlisle is a well-respected doctor, demonstrating the satisfaction of some of the esteem needs in the hierarchy, his reputation needs in particular. And finally, the fact that the Cullens have attended college multiple times and developed hobbies in order to alleviate boredom is indicative of actualization needs. But more important, Maslow's concepts are relevant to this discussion about the work-family dichotomy because different experiences satisfy different needs. Parenting (and romantic relationships) might fulfill love and belongingness needs but it does not necessarily fulfill esteem needs or actualization needs. On the other hand, succeeding in a career can bring with it fulfillment of reputation needs and can certainly make us feel proud. And continuing to grow in our careers can help us to move toward completion, that is, actualization. As such, it is healthy and useful to have a variety of experiences. Certainly career advancement is not the only way to fulfill esteem and actualization needs. For instance, the Cullens fulfill them through their repetitive enrollment in college studies, as well as Edward's music composition, Esme's house renovations, and Carlisle's additional medical knowledge. But for humans, who do not have the longevity of vampires or the financial resources of the Cullens, careers can certainly be one source of this need satisfaction. Conversely, encouraging women to choose motherhood over careers does not allow for the variety of experiences that permit multiple types of needs to be met. And, according to Maslow, when needs are not met, some type of disturbance, physical or mental, will develop. Thus, adjustment is related to the fulfillment of the majority of Maslow's needs and, therefore, a variety of experiences, including the combination of work and family experiences. Unfortunately, the combination of the two roles for women is not readily depicted in the media.

Rogers' Self-actualization and Conditions of Worth

Finally, the work of Carl Rogers is also especially relevant to the discussion of whether women should combine work and family or whether they should ignore careers in favor of motherhood. Rogers, once nominated for the Nobel Peace Prize, is considered one of the founders of the humanism school of psychological thought and developed a type of therapy consistent with that view, person-centered therapy. For Rogers (1961), a healthy, well-adjusted person is a fully functioning person. Some of the characteristics of the fully functioning person that are relevant to this discussion include creativity, a sense of freedom of choice, and the need to live a rich and full life. Rogers thought that healthy people are able to live their lives creatively, without the need to conform to societal expectations. He thought that they feel free to make choices in determining their own behavior, that they feel responsible for their own experiences. They do not feel restricted by societal demands, nor do they succumb to the pressure from people close to them to behave in certain ways.

According to Rogers, we are all able to become fully functioning people but certain conditions are necessary for us to do so. One condition that is necessary is for us to be accepted and loved for who we are. Rogers (1961, 1980) called this *unconditional acceptance* or *unconditional positive regard.* This term is sometimes misunderstood. Some mistake this term for meaning that we should approve of everything that another does. That is an incorrect interpretation. Instead, it means that we will not judge others even when they engage in behaviors of which we might not approve. It means that we still will care about them regardless of their behavior. Both Jacob and Edward are nonjudgmental toward Bella on occasion. For example, Jacob continues to love her even when she repeatedly engages in (or plans to engage in) behavior of which he disapproves. This is illustrated in *Breaking Dawn* when Bella thinks about her relationship with Jacob after she is turned into a vampire and after she physically attacked him. She thinks, "he was still my friend. Someone who knew the real me and accepted her. Even as a monster" (p. 459). Such sentiments typify what Rogers meant by unconditional positive regard. Jake loves Bella "even as a monster." Edward also demonstrates this unconditional acceptance when, for example, he ultimately supports Bella's decision to continue her life-threatening pregnancy even though he is not in agreement with her decision.

Unfortunately, not all of us experience unconditional positive regard. Instead, we are presented with conditions of worth (Rogers, 1959). Because we have such an intense need for positive regard, because we have such an intense need for others to like us and love us, we sometimes are willing to engage in behaviors just to please someone else. And sometimes we are uncomfortable with those behaviors. In some cases we set aside our own needs to satisfy the needs of others just to gain their approval. In those instances we feel as though if we do not behave in ways that others want us to, they will withdraw their affection or regard. We are concerned that others will not see us as worthy unless we engage in behavior of which they approve. These are *conditions of worth*. Although Edward unconditionally accepts Bella's behavior on occasion, Bella is also often faced with conditions of worth when she acts against the wishes of Edward. While he continues to claim to love her, he shows a tremendous amount of reproach when she behaves in ways he does not approve. Consider, for example, Bella's description of Edward, who is waiting to confront Bella after she visits Jake (which he did not want her to do): "His face was hard and his posture tense. He glared at me wordlessly" (*Eclipse*, p. 140). Bella cringes in response to Edward's disapproval. Such reactions are depicted numerous times and can be found throughout the *Twilight* novels. Likewise, Jacob sometimes expresses conditions of worth toward Bella, especially when she discusses her plans to become a vampire with him at the end of *New Moon* and the beginning of *Eclipse*. Jacob struggles with his anger and control as he almost changes into his werewolf form in response to Bella's decision to become a vampire. Likewise, at the beginning of *Eclipse*, as this disagreement between Jacob and Bella continue, and as Jacob refuses to talk to Bella, he writes her a note that, in part, says, "'You made the choice here, okay? ... What part of 'mortal enemies' is too complicated for you to ... [understand?]'"(p. 3), although both of these sentiments are crossed out and replaced with thoughts that tell Bella that Jake misses her. And in *Breaking Dawn*, when Bella discusses her upcoming honeymoon with Jacob, he expresses his disapproval by grabbing her and shaking her.

If these concepts are applied to the discussion of the work-family dichotomy, one can see that one of the reasons that many of us do not become fully functioning people, and why women are reluctant to combine work and family life, is because we experience conditions of worth. We are all influenced by societal standards, by other people's expectations of us. Consider the countless couples who, when they get married, are asked by well-meaning relatives how many children they want, not *if* they want children. If we do not live up to their (societal) expectations, then we are often met with disapproval or conditions of worth. And society expects women to have children, to want to have children, and to put aside careers in favor of child rearing. Society, like the *Twilight* novels, pressures women into motherhood roles—which might or might not be what they want—by indicating that that is the appropriate behavior for them and by glorifying images of these roles, as was discussed in the chapter on the motherhood mystique. Women are presented with conditions of worth and they, therefore, engage in socially desirable, traditionally feminine behaviors, such as motherhood roles, in order to earn approval. This does not mean that women are unwilling to take on motherhood roles. In fact, the majority of women do want to be mothers (Etaugh, 1993). But it does mean that many women do not consider these roles before taking them on. Many women automatically assume that they want (or should want) to be mothers without considering the possibility that perhaps they do not. They absorb societal and familial expectations and act as though they are their own.

The fact is that a large segment of our society still approves of stay-at-home mothers and provides conditions of worth in the form of disapproval toward mothers who work outside the home. Evidence for this can be found in the data from the Pew Research Center (2007), which found that 44% of stay-at-home mothers thought that the increase in the number of mothers working outside the home was bad for society. This segment of society still assumes that women should be the ones to sacrifice careers in favor of family responsibilities and frowns upon women who combine work and family life, suggesting that such mothers are selfish, that their children are neglected and raised by people other than the parents, that is, daycare staff. With this type of disapproval, with these types of conditions of worth, is it any wonder that this work-family dichotomy survives and that the

Twilight novels that depict socially desirable, traditional roles for women are so popular?

Summary and Implications

The majority of women and men in our society do not consider the double standard involved in women choosing between careers and motherhood and men not needing to make this choice. Nor do they consider that women's tendency to take the "mommy track" in order to combine work and family robs women of financial independence and places unnecessary pressure on men to provide financial support for them. Part of the reason they do not question such assumptions is because the media provides an extensive amount of images supportive of the work-family dichotomy. Movies, television programs, and books such as the *Twilight* novels still routinely depict traditional roles whereby the female characters are stay-at-home moms and the male characters are the primary breadwinners (Barner, 1999; Brown, 1998; Jennings, et al., 1980; Lauzen, et al., 2008). Such media sources (like the *Twilight* novel *Breaking Dawn*) send subtle messages that suggest the noble thing for women to do is be self-sacrificing, to have children and dedicate their lives to the raising of those children, that careers are irrelevant for women, especially in comparison to relationships and family life. Such implications support the work-family dichotomy and the assumption that women should have to choose between careers and family life. But psychologists have long noted the benefits of combining career and family. Such a combination allows for a variety of enriching experiences that contribute to psychological growth and adjustment, and there is research evidence to suggest that those who combine work and motherhood (or fatherhood) are healthier and happier financially, psychologically, and physically (Barnett & Hyde, 2001). Unfortunately, many women do not adopt both types of roles because of societal pressure and sex-typed assumptions. What is especially problematic is that such novels as *Breaking Dawn* are marketed toward female tweens and teens; therefore, such messages can be absorbed by them, influencing their career aspirations.

The subtle messages in books such as *Breaking Dawn* and other media sources not only assist in the endurance of these biased and sex-typed assumptions supporting the work-family dichotomy but they also hinder social change that assists women who do combine breadwinner roles with motherhood, many of whom do so not out of "choice" but out of financial necessity. Many question the necessity of social change regarding family policies, but the United States lags behind other countries in policies providing childbearing leave, support for breastfeeding, paid annual leave, maximum length of the work week, and leave for illness and family care, as well as other social conditions (Heymann, Earle, & Hayes, 2007). However, such policies can potentially improve conditions for working families, facilitating work-life balance. Providing policies that reduce conflict between work life and family is beneficial to mothers and fathers alike, as well as children, and assists women as they continue to strive for equality. Additionally, supportive family policies are good business. As the American Psychological Association (2011) notes, these types of policies are beneficial to employers because of improved employee morale, job satisfaction, and loyalty. Consequently, employers benefit from increased productivity, reduced absenteeism, and decreased turnover. In fact, according to the Institute for Health and Social Policy, "Globally, the most economically competitive countries provide, on average, longer parental leave, as well as more leave to care for children" (Heymann, Earle, & Hayes, 2007, p. 9). If we truly want to encourage economic gender equity, family-friendly policies are necessary.

CHAPTER FIVE

The Damsel in Distress

Rescuers and Rescuees

In the last few chapters the traditional sex-typed behaviors of the female characters in the *Twilight* series have been examined. Further expanding that discussion, this chapter examines the fact that Bella is the prototypical "damsel in distress," as the sheer number of times Bella needs to be rescued or aided in some way is extensive. In just the first book of the series, *Twilight*, Edward saves Bella from being crushed in a car accident when another student's vehicle careens out of control after skidding on ice in the school parking lot. He then protects her from his family, Rosalie in particular, who thinks Bella should be eliminated in order to protect their vampire identity, which could be exposed because of this incident. (For further revelation of Rosalie's attitude toward Bella see Meyer's partial draft of *Midnight Sun* located on her Web site, pp. 80–88.) Edward rescues Bella in Port Angeles from would-be rapists. He, likewise, protects her from the visiting vampires James, Victoria, and Laurent, who happen across the baseball game in which the Cullens and Bella are participating. And Bella is also rescued by the Cullens from the vampire James again, who wants to kill her and who tracks her, as if in a game.

Similarly, in the second novel of the series, *New Moon*, Edward rescues Bella from Jasper who loses control and attacks her during her birthday party at the Cullens. Then Jake takes over Edward's role as Bella's protector after Edward leaves her. Jake and his pack of werewolves save Bella from the vampire Laurent, who is in need of nourishment, when he finds her in a meadow alone. The werewolves also protect Bella from the vampire Victoria, who wants to take Bella's life in revenge for Edward killing her mate, James, in the previous novel. And Jake, in particular, saves Bella from drowning when she jumps off a cliff in order to fulfill a need to hear Edward's voice, which materializes when she places herself in danger.

Bella's need to be rescued also continues in the third and fourth novels of the series. In *Eclipse*, Bella is again saved from the vampire Victoria and her army of newborn vampires. In *Breaking Dawn*, Bella's life is in danger again, this time from the half-vampire/half-human child she and Edward conceived while on their honeymoon. Edward saves Bella by changing her into a vampire when the birth of their child almost kills her. Jake likewise protects Bella in *Breaking Dawn* when his werewolf pack wants to kill Bella and her unborn child, whom they view as an abomination.

Author Stephenie Meyer vigorously disagrees with the assessment of Bella being a damsel in distress. She states,

> I am all about girl power—look at Alice and Jane if you doubt that. I am no anti-female, I am anti-human. I wrote this story from the perspective of a female human because that came most naturally as you might imagine. But if the narrator had been a male human, it would not have changed events. When a human being is totally surrounded by creatures with supernatural strength, speed, senses, and various other uncanny powers, he or she is not going to be able to hold his or her own. Sorry. That's just the way it is. We can't all be slayers. Bella does pretty well I think, all things considered. She saves Edward after all. (Meyer, n.d.c, para. 21)

Although Meyer's explanation certainly seems logical, several contradictory points need to be made. For example, while it is certainly true that humans would have difficulty holding their own in a fight with supernatural creatures, this reasoning does not apply to the number of times Bella needs to be rescued in purely human situations (e.g., the car incident in the school parking lot, the would-be rapists in Port Angeles, the near-drowning incident after cliff diving). She is not in need of rescue *from* these supernatural creatures; she is rescued *by* these supernatural creatures, who also happen to be male. Furthermore, although there are female supernatural creatures in the novels, they are not as readily portrayed in the role of Bella's rescuer as the male supernatural creatures. Additionally, although Meyer uses a female (Bella) in the role of the narrator in most of the series because that is what felt comfortable for her as a writer, she suggests that the story would be essentially the same if the narrator were a male

(Meyer, n.d.c), that is, a male narrator would be in need of rescue to the same extent that Bella is. Unfortunately, such scenarios are rarely depicted in the media, and although it is possible, a male protagonist would not be as likely to be in need of rescue from potential rapists. As such, Meyer's explanation of Bella's repetitive need to be rescued does not completely eliminate this common feminist criticism of the series.

It should also be noted that Bella's need to be cared for also goes beyond the need for physical rescue. Throughout the series she also is in need of repeated psychological and emotional support. Although there are other examples, the most notable, and the example to which most critics of the series object, can be found in *New Moon* when Bella gets lost in the woods and collapses to the ground after Edward leaves her. She is then found and carried home by Sam Uley. She is barely able to function for months after the breakup. In fact, later in the book Jake finds Bella curled up in a ball on the beach, unable to move, because the pain of losing Edward is too much for her. As argued in a later chapter, many of these emotional reactions indicate poor adjustment and coping styles, but Meyer is also comfortable with Bella's need for psychological support in response to these scenarios. She states,

WHAT IF . . . What if true love left you? Not some ordinary high school romance, not some random jock boyfriend, not anyone at all replaceable. True love. The real deal. Your other half, your true soul's match. What happens if he leaves? The answer is different for everyone. Juliet had her version, Marianne Dashwood had hers, Isolde and Catherine Earnshaw and Scarlett O'Hara and Anne Shirley all had their ways of coping. I had to answer the question for Bella. What does Bella Swan do when true love leaves her? Not just true love, but Edward Cullen! None of those other heroines lost an Edward Cullen (Romeo was a hothead, Willoughby was a scoundrel. Tristan had loyalty issues, Heathcliff was pure evil, Rhett had a mean streak and cheated with hookers, and sweet Gilbert was much more of a Jacob than an Edward). So what happens when True Love in the form of Edward Cullen leaves Bella? I let Bella answer the question for herself, writing to see what she would do. It was hard to write her pain, because I had to live it to write it, and I was often writing through my tears. At the same time, it was always *interesting*. Bella surprised me with her grit and doffed determination. She pushed through the agony, living for others—Charlie in this case—as has always been her style. (Side note: there are those who think Bella is a wuss.

There are those who think my stories are misogynistic—the damsel in distress must be rescued by strong hero. To the first accusation, I can only say that we all handle grief in our own way. Bella's way is no less valid than any other to my mind. Detractors of her reaction don't always take into account that I'm talking about true love here, rather than high school infatuation. ...) (Meyer, n.d.c, para. 15)

But there are a number of flaws in the assumptions underlying this defense of Bella's response to Edward ending their relationship, and her subsequent need for emotional and psychological support. First, there are certainly different types of love relationships, with some being genuine and others being approximations of, or substitutes for, genuine love relationships—just as Stephenie Meyer notes that some relationships are "true love" and others are more replaceable infatuations—but Meyer assumes that there is such a thing as a "true love," a perfect love, and that everyone has the same definition for this concept. There is, however, no universal definition of "true love" and Meyer's emphasis on this concept, complete with capital letters for accent, indicates an overvaluing of love, as will be discussed in detail in a later chapter. In fact, psychologists suggest that there are a variety of types of love, that different people prefer different love styles, in general, and that individuals reserve different love styles for different people (Lee, 1973, 1988; Sternberg, 1986). Such research indicates different standards for satisfactory love relationships. A second problem with the assumptions in this explanation for Bella's reaction to the loss of her relationship with Edward is that Meyer implies that Edward Cullen is the epitome of "true love." She implies that Edward Cullen is somehow a better true love than all the other examples on her list. She implies his perfection without noting his faults although she notes the faults of the other fictional characters. Meyer suggests that because Bella has lost Edward Cullen, in particular, her loss of true love is even greater than others who have lost true loves. However, although many fans are attracted to the Edward Cullen character, other fans (and nonfans) are not, and so do not necessarily agree that Bella's mourning and subsequent need for emotional and psychological support is warranted. What is most applicable to this discussion, though, is that Meyer implies that Bella's reaction to the loss of Edward is just as acceptable as anyone else's reaction, that crumbling to the ground and being barely functional for months afterward is just as reasonable as other responses. Certainly Meyer is correct in saying that different people will have different coping styles in similar situations, but from a psychological perspective, some reactions are indicative of maladjustment. As mentioned, and as will be discussed in more detail in a later chapter, Bella's coping mechanisms are not healthy, and implying that such dysfunctional responses are just as acceptable as other (normal) coping mechanisms is specious. Consequently, although Meyer suggests that Bella's reaction to the loss of her relationship with Edward, as well as her need for emotional and psychological support, is warranted and reasonable due to the loss of something rare and wonderful, others, many psychologists in particular, would not agree due to the extremity of her response, as well as due to individual differences in love needs and definitions.

Many fans agree with Meyer and do not perceive Bella as a damsel in distress, minimizing the importance of the noted scenarios. They see Bella as a strong female character who does some rescuing of her own. For example, it could be argued that Bella also rescues Edward from his lonely existence, as he has not been able to find a "soul mate" in close to 100 years. It should also be noted that Bella saves Edward's life in *New Moon* when he is about to commit "suicide" by exposing his true nature to humans in order to provoke the Volturi into eliminating him. And certainly readers see Bella as instrumental in the protection of the Cullens from the Volturi at the end of *Breaking Dawn*. But the sheer number of times Bella *rescues* versus the number of times she *is rescued* is extraordinarily lopsided. Furthermore, the nature of Bella's rescuing behavior is not just quantitatively different but qualitatively different from those displayed by the male characters in the series. Her mere existence saves Edward from a lonely life. She simply shows up and reveals herself to Edward to save him from stepping into the sunlight and exposing his glistening skin to humans, thus preventing a chain of events that could culminate in the Volturi killing Edward. Again it is just her presence that results in Edward's salvation. Even the nature of Bella's rescue of the Cullens from the Volturi at the end of *Breaking Dawn* is substantially different than that of Edward's rescues of Bella on other occasions. Hers is a type of cocooning of her friends and family in a protective bubble, whereas his is a much more physically active and aggressive pattern of behavior. Bella's shield results in the Volturi's willingness to negotiate with the Cullens and the "army" they developed, rather than the physical war for which the rest of the Cullens prepared. Meyer explains this ending. She states,

> I'm not the kind of person who writes a Hamlet ending. If the fight had happened, it would have ended with 90% of the combatants, Cullen and Volturi alike, destroyed. There was simply no other outcome once the fight got started, given the abilities and numbers of the opposing sides. Because I would never finish Bella's story on such a downer—*Everybody dies!*—I knew that the real battle would be mental. It was a game of maneuvering, with the champion winning not by destroying the other side, but by being able to walk away. This was another reason I liked the chess metaphor on the cover—it really fit the feel of that final game. I put a clue into the manuscript as well. Alice tore a page from *The Merchant of Venice* because the end of *Breaking Dawn* was going to be somewhat similar: bloodshed appears the inevitable, doom approaches, and then the power is reversed and the game is won by some clever verbal strategies; no blood is shed, and the romantic pairings all have a happily ever after. (Meyer, n.d.a, para. 4)

Meyer's concern for a happily-ever-after ending should be noted, but more important, it should be noted that Bella's rescues are less dramatic than those of the male characters and, therefore, imply different types of protective abilities for males and females.

It should likewise be noted that the number of people who are interested in potentially harming Bella is significantly larger than those interested in harming Edward or the other Cullens. The primary adversaries of the Cullens, including Edward, are the Volturi, who are hostile toward them because of what they perceive as a power struggle. But Bella is repeatedly rescued from strangers who mean to do her harm: would-be rapists and James the vampire in *Twilight*; vampires Victoria and Laurent in *New Moon*; Victoria again, and her army of newborn vampires, in *Eclipse*. Bella also is in need of assistance because of accidental occurrences: the vehicle in the school parking lot in *Twilight*; her life-threatening pregnancy in *Breaking Dawn*. These dangerous situations are all out of Bella's control whereas Edward's (and the Cullens') threatening situations can be seen as of their own making through their interactions with the Volturi. As such, the implication is that women can be in need of assistance at any time because the world is a dangerous place where women can randomly experience danger, but men will not. Additionally, Bella places herself in danger due to her own carelessness. Certainly she is portrayed as clumsy, as is referenced throughout the texts, but Bella is also reckless in the sense that she begins to participate in extreme sports without protective gear and without proper lessons (cliff diving without instruction, motorcycle riding without a license). As argued in a later chapter, these behaviors are indicative of suicidal tendencies, but what is important to this discussion is that these storylines depict Bella as careless and, therefore, in need of protection, whereas the male characters in the novels are portrayed—for the most part—as cautious, strategic, and meticulous in their behavior and planning. In sum, the stories suggest that men do not experience danger unless they provoke some type of threat. For women, the threat is ever present and they, therefore, are in need of (men's) ever-present protection.

As noted, Meyer defends Bella's need to be repeatedly rescued and protected, claiming that it is due to her human nature, but she further clarifies Edward's protectiveness of Bella in particular, noting that his protective need is also about shielding her from the monster side of himself. She specifically defends his leaving Bella in *New Moon* as a selfless and protective act (rather than an thoughtless and selfish one) stating,

> Someday, when *Midnight Sun* (Edward's version of *Twilight*) is available, I think you'll understand better what was going on in the boy's head. See, just as Bella doesn't think she's good enough for Edward, Edward sees himself as a soulless monster destroying Bella's life and endangering her afterlife. The incident with Jasper acts as a catalyst, forcing him to act. He is determined to save Bella. He thinks the best way to do this is to take the vampires out of her life. Is he being silly? In some ways, yes. But he can't see any other way to protect Bella. Edward's dealing with the idea that if he hadn't been quick enough, if he hadn't read Jasper's thoughts just in the nick of time, then would that—death—have been better for Bella than a life with Edward? If she died at eighteen and went to heaven, would that be better than an immortal but soulless and damned existence? Edward thinks so. However, he knew he'd never be able to watch her die. Consequently, he'd better get away from her before something happens that makes biting her a necessity. (Meyer, n.d.c, para. 12)

But even given this justification of Edward's protectiveness, such reasoning does not explain why Jacob also repetitively needs to rescue Bella and, therefore, does not fully justify or excuse the sex-typed portrayals of Bella as the damsel in distress, who is rescued by her male Prince Charmings.

These repetitive depictions of the damsel in distress being rescued and comforted by the brave knight are problematic because they imply a feminine fragility and a masculine strength, a feminine powerlessness and a masculine resourcefulness, a feminine passivity and a masculine industry. Books with these types of storylines, such as the *Twilight* series, indicate that women are in continuous *need* of protection, in need of rescue, especially by men, because the world is a dangerous place for women. Such storylines imply that women are not, and cannot be, self-sufficient, but that men are. This double standard is harmful to both men and women: Portraying women in such a dependent manner can be detrimental especially to the developing self-concepts of adolescents, for whom the *Twilight* series is marketed. Adolescent readers can come away with the idea that femininity is equated with powerlessness, fragility, and dependence, and such assumptions can have a negative effect on a female teen's self-confidence and on her developing sense of independence. In fact, as discussed elsewhere, Bella enjoys being self-sufficient and strong after she is changed into a vampire, and some might argue that this change, along with her dissatisfaction with her need to be repeatedly rescued, indicates that Bella is a role model for feminine strength and independence. While this is conceivable, it should be noted that during more than 75% of the series (during more than the first three books of the four book series) Bella plays the role of the victim instead of the rescuer. As such, these repetitive storylines depict the world as a dangerous place for women, and they needlessly create fear, anxiety, and trepidation. For men, such images and their potential, subsequent assumptions about masculinity create unrealistic and unattainable standards that require them to aid women even in situations in which they might not have expertise. In fact, there is some indication that *Twilight* has had an influence on expectations for romantic partners and relationships (Behm-Morawitz, et al., 2010).

It could be argued that since the *Twilight* saga is really just a series of stories, not real life, such concerns are unfounded, that just because we read stories like this does not mean that we assume that women always need to be helped or rescued and that men are the ones who always do the helping. But as discussed in previous chapters, research suggests that repeated exposure to these sex-typed images do influence our perceptions of men and women (Bussey & Bandura, 1999). Consequently, while novels, movies, and television programs need the thrill of a character in trouble and the suspense of an attempted rescue, in order to attract and maintain audiences, it must also be noted that the gender role assumptions of readers of such novels and viewers of such movies and television programming can be influenced by this type of storyline. Even though most people can tell the difference between these stories and real life, repeated exposure to this scenario can subtly affect our behavior and our attitudes because when we are continuously exposed to the same ideas over and over again, it is difficult to conceptualize other ideas and other scenarios. These storylines are problematic specifically because there are relatively few examples of women rescuing men but numerous examples of men rescuing women (Barner, 1999; Brown, 1998; Jennings, et al., 1980; Lauzen, et al., 2008), and in the case of the *Twilight* series, Bella is rescued much more frequently than she plays the role of rescuer. This inequity makes readers and viewers form attitudes that are sex-typed through social learning because the stories that they are reading or seeing are sex-typed. Furthermore, teens and tweens, who are forming their ideas about gender roles and romantic relationships, can come away from romance novels, like those in the *Twilight* saga, with inaccurate perceptions of what behaviors are appropriate for males and females and what romantic relationships should be like (Behm-Morawitz, et al., 2010). In fact, there is considerable evidence that young women determine how to interact with young men through their examination of such portrayals in movies, television, and magazine stories, as well as other media (Brown, et al., 2006; Galician, 2004; L'Engle, Brown, & Kenneavy, 2006). Consequently, they can come away believing that traditional gender roles are appropriate and indicative of ideal love relationships. To be more specific, they can come away with the idea that in (heterosexual) romantic relationships, it is the role of the man to protect the woman and that the woman is in need of his protection. Additionally, what is troublesome is that once these ideas are formed, they are difficult to change because these ideas that have been developed are schemas, as is discussed next.

Schemas

The different perceptions of Bella as a heroine or damsel in distress can be explained through the use of schemas. Schemas are hypothetical cognitive structures (Bartlett, 1932; Alba & Hasher, 1983). They do not physically exist but are useful in the understanding of our thought processes and subsequent behaviors. You can think of schemas as lenses through which we see the world. You have probably heard the phrase "seeing the world through rose-colored glasses," which suggests that the person who does so sees the world as more beautiful than it actually is because the world looks rose-colored. The implication is that the rose-colored lenses have an influence on how the world is viewed and, ultimately, on how we behave in the world. The same is true for schemas. A schema is an idea or vision of what something is like—what an event will be like or what a type of person acts like. For example, we know what to expect when we go to a doctor's office because we have a schema of what that type of visit is like, a script, if you will, of what will take place during that visit.

Schemas develop through experience (Bartlett, 1932). Thus, we form these cognitive structures through our interactions with others, through the process of experiencing an event, and so forth. And we draw conclusions about these people or social groups or events after having had multiple similar encounters with them. These conclusions form our schemas. For example, a child might develop a schema about dentist visits through repeated appointments with the dentist. S/he initially would not have any idea about what a visit to the dentist is like because s/he would not have had any experience with one. After a parent explains what will happen during the visit, and after the initial visit, the child will begin to develop ideas (draw conclusions) about what it is like to go to the dentist. Later, with additional dental appointments, those ideas will become solidified until a schema is formed. Consequently, if early experiences with a dentist are unpleasant (perhaps multiple cavities filled), a child might form a schema about dentists that involves pain and anxiety. If early experiences are neutral or even pleasant (perhaps the child likes the taste and feel of the tooth polish), then their schema for a dentist visit will include more agreeable characteristics. Note, however, that in both cases the children's schemas will probably overlap somewhat in that they will both include understanding that such an appointment will involve sitting in a dental chair with a bib around one's neck and instruments being used to examine one's teeth. But also note that even though two people might develop the same schema, and the characteristics of that schema might overlap somewhat, it can also consist of different ideas, in this case whether a visit to the dentist is pleasant or unpleasant, because the initial development of those schemas involved different (although similar) experiences. In other words, the same schema in two people can be very different and this can explain why people who have similar experiences can interpret them in very different ways.

Once schemas form, they influence how we interpret experiences, what information from an experience we will place into our memories, and what, ultimately, we will remember (Conway & Ross, 1984; Fiske, 1993; Wyer & Srull, 1994). Thus, we tend to interpret experiences in a way that is consistent with our schemas, encode information that is consistent with our schemas into our memories, and remember events in ways that are consistent with our schemas. This is true even if it means interpreting, encoding, and remembering experiences in inaccurate ways (Hastorf & Cantril, 1954). As such, when we are presented with repetitive sex-typed images in which women, who find themselves in peril, are rescued by competent and capable men trained in defense, first aid, and other emergency skills, we can develop schemas that indicate that those are appropriate roles for women and men. And then we interpret the world utilizing that schema. Consequently, if we are presented with a contradictory scenario of, say, a woman rescuing a man, we can misinterpret the experience and remember it as a man rescuing a woman because we rely on that traditional gender role schema. This gender schema can cause us to misinterpret the event, make us place this misperceived event into our memories (incorrectly), and then remember it inaccurately later. Therefore, these cognitive errors make it difficult to change our schemas because every time we are presented with an idea or event that is inconsistent with our schema, we reinterpret it to make it consistent (Jones, Rock, Shaver, Goethals, & Ward, 1968). Therefore, it is difficult for readers of the *Twilight* series to accept opposing views of Bella in the novels because, when reading the stories, our schemas allow us to focus only on information that is consistent with our interpretation of the character and the saga. If we do come across scenes that are inconsistent with our perceptions of the series (with our schema for the series or for heterosexual relationships or gender appropriate behaviors), we often do not notice it, or we reinterpret the scene so as to match our already existing schema. To be more specific, those who perceive Bella as a damsel in distress find it difficult to accept that others perceive her as a heroine because their schema for the series (and Bella) only allows them to notice scenes that confirm their schema, and vice versa. Those who perceive Bella as a heroine cannot accept that others perceive her as someone who is always in need of rescue because their schema for the series (and Bella or women in general) only allows them to notice scenes that confirm their schema. In sum, the discrepant views of Bella are due to differential cognitive structures utilized to interpret the series.

Benevolent Sexism

Some of the disparity in readers' perceptions of Bella, as well as of Edward, can also be explained through the understanding of *benevolent sexism*. Benevolent sexism (Glick & Fiske, 1996, 1997, 2001) is a subtle form of sexism, one that can only be noticed through the deeper examination of behavior, that is, deconstruction, and can be distinguished from *hostile sexism*. Whereas benevolent sexism consists of prejudicial attitudes and discriminatory behaviors that seem favorable to women but in actuality are not, hostile sexism only conveys antipathy toward women. Those who exhibit benevolent sexism can seem to value women, but do so only if they cooperate and display behavior that is deemed appropriate for women. Those who exhibit hostile sexism show no appreciation of women and instead resent them (Cuddy, Fiske, & Glick, 2004). While most people, both men and women, object to more blatant, hostile forms of sexism, they fail to notice this more covert form. For example, most people would object to women being paid less money than men for equal work, but many are not offended by Edward's (benevolently) sexist behaviors in the *Twilight* novels. They might not even notice that they are sexist. In fact, many readers of the series not only do not label Edward's behavior as sexist they also seem to actually enjoy that quality of his character. As an illustration, consider that in the survey on readers' perceptions of the *Twilight* series conducted for *Deconstructing* Twilight, many respondents who like the Edward Cullen character said they did so because he was protective of Bella. One reader noted that Edward's best qualities included the fact that he "is sincere, caring, and protective. Every girl's dream!" Another reader noted that Edward's best qualities are "his looks, how he takes care of Bella, and protects Bella." This paternalism appeals to many fans of the series, most likely because the behavior can make people feel cared for, but, as will be discussed, many of Edward's "protective" behaviors do not just demonstrate his concern for Bella but also are very controlling and are illustrative of benevolent sexism. Behaviors characteristic of benevolent sexism—behaviors that can seem quaintly old-fashioned and chivalrous, like men opening doors for women— can seem harmless but in many cases are not. In fact, people who score higher in benevolent sexism are more likely to excuse sexist behaviors and tolerate gender discriminatory behaviors (Moya, Exposito, & Casado, cited in Glick & Fiske, 2001).

Benevolent sexism consists of three factors: protective paternalism, complementary gender differentiation, and heterosexual intimacy (Glick & Fiske, 1996). Protective paternalism refers to men's need or desire to protect women. Complementary gender differentiation is a matter of perceiving women as being different from men in a positive way, one in which men and women complement or complete each other. Heterosexual intimacy refers to viewing women romantically and valuing their sexual purity. Often it is a matter of figuratively placing women on a pedestal, commending their virginity, their ability to have children, and the institution of motherhood. It is important to understand each of these concepts because they are often not perceived as sexist and, in fact, are often perceived in a positive light, as desirable behaviors. As noted, they are perceived as chivalrous, romantic, and noble. Nonetheless, even though some people find these behaviors appealing, when they are examined carefully, one can see the inherent sexist attitudes that encourage them.

Protective Paternalism

Protective paternalism is an attitude that suggests that women are in need of men's protection. Paternalistic behavior is typical of parents who try to shield their children from harm, sometimes by restricting their behavior, but in this case the paternalistic behavior is directed toward adult women. Protective paternalism subtly implies that women are weak, either physically or psychologically, and that they are in *need* of men's protection. In fact, Meyer repeatedly portrays Bella as fragile. Both Edward, and to a lesser extent Jacob, describe Bella in this way, as does Bella herself, on numerous occasions: In *Midnight Sun*, Edward compares Bella to a soap bubble, indicating how vulnerable and delicate she is. In *New Moon*, Jacob describes Bella as a "porcelain doll" (p. 179), also implying that Bella is fragile. Some might argue that Edward and Jacob both perceive Bella in this way, and are, therefore, protective of her, because both male characters are supernatural beings complete with superhuman strength, and they, therefore, could potentially hurt or kill her, as could others of their kind. Fans could further suggest, as does Stephenie Meyer (n.d.c), that Edward is especially aware of this possibility and, therefore, acutely vigilant to prevent it, as referenced throughout the series. But there are many references throughout the series that also refer to Edward's need to protect Bella from human experiences. In Meyer's draft of *Midnight Sun*, for example, although Edward references the fact that Bella needs protection from his vampiric nature, he also wants to protect her from Jessica's snide thoughts. And Edward and Jacob protect Bella, not just from themselves, but from car accidents, rapists, and drowning. Furthermore, there are a variety of references in the *Twilight* novels to human men feeling protective toward women also: Jasper refers to his tendency toward protecting women even before he was changed into a vampire. In *Eclipse*, he notes, "'I had not been taught to fear women, but to protect them'" (p. 294) as he describes the events that led up to his becoming a vampire. Edward notices the protectiveness in Mike's thoughts toward Bella in another scene in Meyer's draft of *Midnight Sun* that takes place in the cafeteria during which Bella feels unwell and does not eat because of Edward's initial hostility toward her. Mike feels anxious for (and possessive of) Bella when she says she feels unwell. Likewise, Edward reads Ben's protective thoughts toward Angela in a scene in *Midnight Sun* in which Ben is manipulated into asking Angela out. In this scene Edward asks for Emmett's assistance. Edward has Emmett ask him, within hearing distance of Ben, whether Edward has asked Angela out, even though this was never a possibility. Edward hopes to make Ben jealous enough to ask Angela out in order for Edward to reward Angela for being kind to Bella. Ben does ask Angela out but not before Edward reads Ben's thoughts suggesting that Edward would not be safe for Angela to date. Consequently, although there might be some truth to the necessity of Edward (and Jacob) protecting Bella from their own supernatural nature, and other beings similar to themselves, there are numerous references to other situations that imply that women need to be protected generally by (human) men.

There is substantial evidence that Edward's protective tendencies toward Bella reach beyond simple concern, instead demonstrating paternalistic tendencies representative of benevolent sexism. In addition to repeatedly saving Bella from imminent harm, Edward tries to prevent the *possibility* of harm, just as parents do toward children. Note Edward's thoughts when he realized he loved Bella. He tells Jacob in *Eclipse* that there were only four possibilities for their relationship: (1) that Bella didn't love him as much as Edward loved her, would, therefore, end the relationship, and move on to a different relationship as a human; (2) that Edward would stay with Bella throughout her human life but this was a dangerous alternative because of the possibility of her being harmed by him or other vampires; (3) that Edward would leave Bella (as a human) and never see her again, which he did, and which resulted in Bella's emotional devastation; or (4) that Edward would turn her into a vampire. As he discusses each of these alternatives with Jacob, it is evident that Edward is concerned for Bella's safety and happiness, but it is also evident that Edward is making choices *for* Bella, based upon what *he* thinks is best for her. As he discusses the second option, he describes it as "'the one *I'd* [italics added] originally chosen'" (*Eclipse*, p. 500) and that it did not work out as well as he had hoped. He then indicates, "'So *I* [italics added] chose option three. Which turned out to be the worst mistake of my very long life...'" (p. 501). Edward's thought processes seem to indicate that his protectiveness is reasonable, but in protecting Bella, Edward attempts to restrict Bella's behavior and make decisions for her because *he* thinks it is in her best interest. He behaves as a parent, as though he is an authority, as though Bella is in a position subordinate to him. Just as parents "know better" and, therefore, place rules and restrictions on their children, so too does Edward try to place restrictions on Bella's behavior. Paternalism is detrimental in adult relationships precisely because of this: It robs another person of their right to make decisions for themselves. Meyer defends Edward's paternalistic behavior, his thinking that he knows what Bella needs better than Bella herself, although, as just noted, he was obviously mistaken in determining a number of courses of action for Bella. Meyer explains,

> Edward finally realized the intensity of Bella's feelings for him, something he has always underestimated. Here's the thing about Edward: he knows human nature pretty well. He's seen a hundred thousand human relationships from the inside, and none of them have come close to touching the depth and everlasting devotion of Carlisle's and Esme's love, or Alice's and Jasper's or even Rosalie's and Emmett's. Can you blame him for thinking himself—after one hundred years of immortal experience—capable of a more profound love than his eighteen-year-old human girlfriend? Edward is, understandably, a bit of a know-it-all. He learns a lot through this experience, the most important being that Bella's feelings for him are an exception to the human rule. Something else he learns (not quite as important, but still good to know) is that, despite all his knowledge, he is fully able to make hideous mistakes in judgment. (Meyer, n.d.c, para. 26)

Clearly Meyer indicates that readers should be accepting and understanding of Edward's paternalism but understanding behavior does not make it acceptable. Readers can understand *why* Edward is paternalistic but this understanding doesn't make it any less problematic. As explained in the next chapter, controlling behavior is often indicative of early stages of abusive relationships (National Domestic Violence Hotline, n.d.). Unfortunately there are numerous examples of Edward attempting to restrict Bella's behavior physically and otherwise, some of which are representative of early abusive relationships. One example can be found in the last chapter of *New Moon* where Jacob confronts Edward and Bella after they return from Volterra. During the depicted argument, both Jake and Bella are distressed because Jake feels as though he cannot continue his friendship with Bella if she continues to see Edward, and because she intends to be changed into a vampire in the near future. Bella wants to go to Jacob to comfort him and convince him that nothing has changed between them, but in order to protect her from the possibility of a werewolf attack, Edward physically restrains Bella and does not *allow* her to go to Jake as he struggles to prevent himself from changing into wolf form. Edward is concerned about Jake's lack of control, but Bella does not think she is in any danger. Edward, however, assumes that his assessment of the potential danger is correct and that Bella's is incorrect. Consequently, Bella is unable to fulfill her needs and desires; she can only submit to Edward's will. In fact, early in the next novel, *Eclipse*, Bella wants to make up with Jake, to go to see him, but Edward says, "'You know it's out of the question for you to be around a werewolf unprotected'" (p. 28). Later in *Eclipse*, when Bella tries to go to La Push to see Jake again, Edward actually dismantles part of her truck's engine to prevent her from doing so. Still later in *Eclipse*, when Bella tells Edward, "'I have to see Jacob,'" Edward replies, "'Then I'll have to stop you'" (p. 34). Likewise in *Eclipse*, Bella knows that Edward will not "allow" (p. 51) her to go to a party that would include numerous werewolf guests because he thought it was too dangerous, even though her own father would also be there. Such behavior can undoubtedly be described as controlling and is characteristic of paternalism and benevolent sexism, as Edward places limits on Bella for her protection.

At times Edward acknowledges his own overprotectiveness, as does his family and Bella's friends, and there is some indication that he attempts to change his behavior. For example, he tells Bella in *Eclipse* that she should go to a different gathering in La Push—that she doesn't need to ask his permission to go. He tells Bella, "'You don't have to ask my permission Bella. I'm not your father...'" (*Eclipse*, p. 230). He also tells her that he is going to trust her judgment, but the reader is left with double messages. Even though this indicates some development on Edward's part, that Edward now trusts Bella's ability to make decisions for herself, he then suggests that she ask her father for permission. In fact, one wonders whether Edward is being so reasonable because if Bella is on the La Push reservation she will be safe from the newborn vampires who are apparently tracking Bella, which Edward had just discovered. Other evidence suggests that Edward is willing to allow Bella to see Jacob in this scene because he is manipulating her: Later in *Eclipse*, Edward admits to Jacob that he decided to play the role of a nice, patient guy while waiting for Bella to choose between the two of them (Jacob and Edward). Edward indicates that forcing her to choose between the two of them was hurting her, and this is why he no longer is restricting Bella's contact with Jacob. It is implied that Edward is playing this nice guy role in order to manipulate Bella's choice, to make her choose Edward himself. As such, Edward's change of heart, his decision to minimize his controlling and paternalistic tendencies, is really just another manipulative tactic to control Bella rather than a change in his paternalistic tendencies.

Despite the fact that Bella is so extraordinarily in love with Edward, she feels some dissatisfaction with this paternalistic aspect of his behavior. In *Twilight*, she calls Edward "pushy" (p. 104) after Edward forces Bella into his car in order to drive her home after her fainting spell from blood typing in biology class. In *Eclipse*, when Jacob confronts Edward about his family crossing over into Quileute territory and breaking the treaty between the Quileute and the "cold ones," as vampires are referred to, Bella again wants to go to Jacob and hold him, and again Edward physically restrains her. At one point she thinks, "Edward's shielding arms had become restraints" (p. 84). While one can understand the need to try to prevent injury, in many cases Edward is overprotective and smothering. In fact, in the third novel, *Eclipse*, Jacob says to Bella,"'Overprotective, isn't he?'" referring to Edward. He goes on to add, "'A little trouble makes life fun. Let me guess, you're not allowed to have fun, are you?'" (p. 82). Edward's behavior repeatedly crosses the line between protective and controlling. And yet Bella repeatedly forgives Edward his controlling behavior because he means well, because he just "didn't *understand*"

(*Eclipse*, p. 32; original italics). Ignoring or excusing such paternalistic behavior is illustrative of benevolent sexism. Men who are paternalistic do not perceive it as sexist. Instead they see it as a way to cherish, protect, and respect women, just as Edward views his protectiveness of Bella as indicative of his love for her. Similarly, women who are recipients of paternalistic behavior often interpret it as a sign of affection and consideration (Housel, 2009; McClimans & Wisnewski, 2009).

Although Bella objects to being treated like a child, she engages in a variety of behaviors that are childlike, and such behaviors, although problematic in their own right, can further encourage already existing paternalistic tendencies. To illustrate, observe that at one point during her pregnancy in *Breaking Dawn*, Bella sticks her tongue out at Jake, just as a child would, in response to teasing from him about what type of blood she would have for breakfast. Note also the numerous times she climbs into other adults' laps, as a child would climb into a caretaker's lap: In *New Moon* Bella climbs into Edward's lap and asks permission to open her birthday presents. Alice pulls Bella onto her lap in *New Moon* when they are reunited after the Cullens abandoned Bella (and Forks) for an extensive period of time. And in *Eclipse*, Bella goes to sit on Edward's lap as they discuss Bella's relationship with Jacob. Such physical examples of childlike behavior and paternalism can likewise be found in the number of times others carry Bella, even though she can be considered a grown woman. In *Eclipse*, Jake carries Bella to his car after she falls asleep during a visit to the Quileute reservation. Likewise, when Edward picks Bella up at the boundary line, he asks whether she is tired enough for *him* to carry her. Edward then lifts her into his vehicle and even buckles her seat belt for her. In fact, before her visit to La Push, Bella notes the absurdity of Edward driving her to the La Push boundary line and Jacob picking her up there. She tells Edward that it reminds her of when her divorced parents would exchange custodial guardianship for the summer. She felt "like a seven-year-old" (*Eclipse*, p. 236). She complains again about this arrangement later in the book noting, "...dignity was lost when Edward insisted again on delivering me to the border line like a child being exchanged by custodial guardians" (p. 318). Even though Bella is uncomfortable with this treatment, she acquiesces to it and even contributes to it by acting childlike.

Moreover, there are numerous other references to Bella that describe her with childlike terminology. Bella, herself, describes feeling like "a child hugging a grown-up" (*New Moon*, p. 178) when she hugs Jake, who is so much bigger than her. In *Eclipse*, Jake calls her, "a baby" (p. 405) when she is resistant to an idea he has that involves carrying Bella to disguise her scent. Furthermore, Bella describes herself as "cradled" (p. 436) in Edward's arms in a scene in *Eclipse*. And there are numerous references to Bella being "babysat": Bella mentions hating "'being babysat'" (*Eclipse*, p. 316) when she realizes that she must spend time with some of the Cullens after school lets out so that they can protect her from the vampire Victoria and her army of newborns. And Edward, himself, uses the term "babysit" (p. 421) when he calls Alice to essentially act as Bella's bodyguard. Edward also repeatedly refers to Bella as "the girl" in Meyer's partial draft of *Midnight Sun*, even though as a vampire he is frozen at the same age as Bella at that time in the series. He uses this terminology in order to distance himself from her so as not to encourage feelings toward her, but other terms (e.g., the human) could be used to provide such emotional distance. Bella is technically still underage and, therefore, could be referred to as a girl, but Edward's use of the term also conveys a sense of superiority despite the similarity in their human ages.

While some would suggest that criticizing the use of this terminology is unnecessary, that too much is being read into it, such wording is problematic because language influences thought processes and vice versa (Kuehn, 1998). Using wording that depicts women with childlike imagery encourages readers to perceive women as childlike. Consider describing a car accident in the following two ways: The truck *smashed* into the car. The truck *bumped* into the car. Certainly different images are called to mind, with the first denoting extensive damage to the vehicles and the second indicating minor damage. Likewise consider describing an adult in the following two ways. The *woman* typed quickly on her laptop. The *girl* typed quickly on her laptop. Again two different images emerge. In the first the woman might be working at a job, might be a typist or a writer. In the second, the girl might be completing a homework assignment. In the first the woman is most likely an adult. In the second she might be an adult or a child because we often use the term *girls* to refer to adult women even though the term technically refers to a female child. As such, use of *infantilization*, that is, referring to adult women with infantile terms not only reflects our thought processes but also influences our thought processes, in this case about women (Hyde, 2007). And although Bella was underage in *Twilight*, she turns 18 at the beginning of *New Moon* and the majority of examples of infantilization, that is, Bella acting like and being described as a child, took place after she reached adult age.

Infantilization typifies protective paternalism because it places women in a subordinate position relative to men. It places men in parental roles and women in the role of children who need to be protected from any potential harm. But Edward and Bella's relationship is not a parent-child relationship and Edward does not necessarily know better than Bella what is good or not good for her. They are both (almost) adults. One might argue that Edward is "older" in the sense that he has "lived" long as a vampire and, therefore, knows more than Bella who is a teenager. However, Edward, as a vampire, is essentially frozen in time physically, psychologically, and emotionally, according to *Midnight Sun*. As such, he is frozen at the age of 17, the age at which he was changed into a vampire. Relatedly, Bella is often described as mature for her age. For example, when Edward asks Bella how old she is in both *Twilight* and in *Midnight Sun*, she replies that she is 17 but explains that her mother thinks "'I was born thirty-five years old and that I get more middle-aged every year'" (*Twilight*, p. 106). Edward states that she does not seem 17, implying that Bella seems older than she actually is. In any case, a healthy, equal relationship cannot exist between two people when one thinks he or she has superior knowledge in comparison to the other, and when the other party plays a submissive role in response to that perceived superior knowledge or wisdom (McClimans & Wisnewski, 2009). Certainly, in any relationship both parties do not have equal knowledge in all situations. For example, one person in a couple might know more about financial matters; the other person might know more about how to update plumbing. But in the *Twilight* series,

Edward consistently is portrayed as the one who is better informed. He is depicted as all-knowing. In fact, he is repeatedly described by Bella as godlike, and, Stephenie Meyer, as noted, similarly describes him as a "know-it-all" (Meyer, n.d.c, para. 26).

Other examples of paternalism in the series are found in behaviors that are often romanticized and admired by readers, but if they are examined on a deeper level, or deconstructed, it is evident that such behaviors (that exemplify benevolent sexism) can have harmful effects. As an illustration, consider again that in *New Moon* Edward leaves Bella because he wants her to be able to experience a normal human life. In fact, in *Midnight Sun*, it is evident that Edward has been planning Bella's future for her ever since he first watched her sleep. He had planned to leave her since the beginning of the series. He admits that he wasn't strong enough to leave her but that he would continue to try to become strong enough to do so, in order to protect her human life. And in response to the accidental attack on Bella by Jasper, Edward's adoptive vampire brother, he does so. He leaves Bella in order to be protective, to ensure that she is safe from him and other vampire attacks. While on the surface this seems admirable and self-sacrificing, when one looks deeper, one can see an inherent sexism. Edward thinks he knows what Bella needs better than she knows herself. He ignores her wishes of continuing their relationship because he sees himself as a soulless monster and does not want that "life" for Bella, and because he thinks she does not love him as much as he loves her. He hurts her emotionally in order to "protect" her physically. Ultimately, his plan is unsound and unforgivably wounding to Bella, which he later realizes and for which he apologizes profusely. But note that this paternalism results in Bella's emotional breakdown. She crumbles to the ground when Edward leaves her in the woods. She does not try to get up. She is unresponsive, almost catatonic, immediately after his departure. For months afterward Bella shows signs of clinical depression, complete with suicidal tendencies, symptoms of posttraumatic stress disorder (PTSD), and recurring nightmares. Similarly, Edward initially treats Bella very poorly in the beginning of the series. He ignores her; he is rude to her. He is often cold and indifferent. At one point he says, "'I'm sorry. I'm being very rude, I know. But it's better this way, really'" (*Twilight*, p.

74). Edward treats Bella poorly so that she doesn't become interested in him romantically because he wants to avoid starting a relationship; he is concerned that if he started a relationship with Bella he would put her in danger, from vampires in general, but from himself especially. Edward thinks his rude behavior is justified because its motivation is to protect Bella, but it leaves Bella confused about the status of their relationship because the reason for it is unknown to her. In both examples, Edward's behavior is emotionally harmful to Bella even though he perceives it as "for her own good."

Paternalistic behavior can be damaging in more general ways as well. If used repeatedly, paternalistic behavior can make the person who is being protected feel incompetent and unsure of themselves and their abilities, including their ability to make capable decisions for themselves. Consider, for example, when Bella is about to go to La Push for the first time in *Twilight*. Edward does not accompany her because he would break the treaty with the Quileute if he ventured onto their land. Edward tells Bella to "'try not to fall in the ocean or get run over or anything'" (p. 109). This might seem like something that someone would say as a joke, but Edward is sincere—even though he has a smile on his face—because he views Bella as "'one of those people who just attract accidents like a magnet'" (p. 109). This is especially evident in the partial draft of *Midnight Sun* on Meyer's Web site: Edward acknowledges to himself, and to readers, that he is concerned for Bella's safety, both in general and from himself in particular. Bella, however, has no knowledge of Edward's good intentions and instead is offended by his comment. Clearly, such comments can be offensive even if they are meant well. But also consider how people, children or adults, could also react if they are repeatedly admonished in the same way. They would eventually start to doubt their abilities, lose their self-confidence, and begin to see the world as an unsafe place.

Paternalism must be examined from both sides of the relationship. On the one hand, one person feels as though s/he understands what is best for the other person by taking a superior, dominant role in the relationship. This person also seems to have an excessive need to control the partner's behavior. In some cases, this need to control comes from concern. The paternalistic partner controls in order to protect the other partner, but even this type of overprotective behavior can be about protecting not the person who is being controlled, but rather the person doing the controlling. The paternalistic partner controls the other's behavior in order to prevent him/herself from feeling the pain of seeing someone s/he loves suffer or even die. In fact, again and again in the series, Edward talks about how he cannot live without Bella. In *Eclipse*, Edward states, "'...I've come too close to losing you in the past. I know what it feels like to think I have. I am *not* going to tolerate anything dangerous'" (p. 33). On the other hand, the person being protected is taking a submissive role. S/he passively agrees to the suggestion or command of the paternalistic partner, perhaps out of a lack of confidence and self-esteem. This partner is acting in a childlike manner because s/he really does believe that the other partner knows better. The overly protective behavior of the partner has damaged the confidence and self-esteem of the party being protected. It has made it seem as though the world is always a potentially dark and dangerous place. The submissive partner might even *want* the other to make decisions for her/him. It frees her/him from the responsibility of making perhaps an incorrect decision. In fact, Bella is frequently portrayed as acting in a childlike manner in response to Edward's more paternal conduct. She repeatedly consents to his treatment of her, even though she also sometimes resents it. In both cases, whether a partner is in a dominant or submissive role, the partners are freely choosing to engage in these controlling or childlike behaviors, even though they have the free will to resist. They often do not realize that they are able to act in different ways. They likewise might feel as though they *should* behave in these ways, perhaps because they see it as gender appropriate. This is problematic because paternalism is not a characteristic of a healthy relationship, as will be discuss in greater detail in a later chapter. An equitable relationship cannot persist if one partner thinks that s/he is more knowledgeable than the other and if one partner wants to control the behavior of the other. That means that the paternalistic partner needs to give up his/her feelings of superiority and control. It also means that the submissive partner needs to resist the other partner's attempts at control instead of passively acquiescing to demands. Submissive partners need to take responsibility for their own safety, their own decisions, instead of giving that responsibility to their more dominant partner. And as noted, Edward does begin to relinquish control over Bella's behavior toward the end of the series after he realizes that his attempts to plan out her life have resulted in repeated emotional and physical turmoil for her. Likewise, Bella begins to act more confidently and independently at the end of the series after being changed into a vampire.

Complementary Gender Differentiation

Complementary gender differentiation is the second factor in benevolent sexism. It is a matter of perceiving men and women as being different from each other and that those gender differences are beneficial. It suggests that men and women complement each other because each sex has different characteristics from the other. Thus, a relationship with a member of the other sex can have the potential to "complete" each partner. Consequently, when complementary gender differentiation exists, women are praised for their traditionally feminine characteristics (and men are praised for their traditionally masculine characteristics) and both sexes are encouraged to behave in ways consistent with those characteristics (which are different from each other). The implication is that women can successfully perform traditionally feminine roles because they come naturally to them and that men successfully perform traditionally masculine roles because they come naturally to them. The implication is also that women will not be able to perform masculine roles as successfully as men because they do not come as naturally (and vice versa). For example, consider a heterosexual couple determining who should give up a job to stay home and take care of their newborn. It is often assumed that it should be the mother because she is so naturally nurturing. At face value, this statement seems positive—the mother is complimented on her natural nurturing abilities—but if it is examined on a deeper level one will notice that the assumption that mothers are naturally more nurturing than fathers minimizes such abilities in men. It likewise implies that mothering abilities are biologically based and, therefore, unchangeable in women. This assumption also suggests that the mother retain her traditional caretaker role. And while there is nothing wrong with this role, it is of concern that the father never considers the possibility that he should improve his child-rearing skills so that there can be a choice about who should care for the children, most likely because he thinks he is biologically incapable of doing so.

There are fewer cases of complementary gender differentiation in the *Twilight* series than other components of benevolent sexism, but one can still find examples of them. One such example can be found when Bella decides to take over the cooking and food shopping chores shortly after moving in with her father, Charlie. She notes early on that "Charlie couldn't cook much besides fried eggs and bacon" and "that he had no food in the house" (*Twilight*, p. 31). Later in the series, in the beginning of *Eclipse*, Bella notices that Charlie is cooking. He is making a simple dinner of spaghetti with sauce and yet he seems incapable of doing so. The pasta is clumped up in a mass and he put the jar of sauce in the microwave with the lid on, potentially damaging the microwave with his ineptitude. Bella intervenes. Both Charlie's and Bella's behaviors are consistent with complementary gender differentiation because Bella is portrayed as talented in, and subsequently placed in charge of, cooking, a traditionally female task, and Charlie is portrayed as inept at this skill. In this particular example it is Bella herself who believes her cooking and food shopping skills are superior to her father's and, therefore, they should be her chores. Thus, it isn't just men who use this type of thinking to maintain traditional gender roles, in this case to maintain the traditional feminine role for females. Similarly, women relegate men to traditionally masculine roles by thinking that their husbands, boyfriends, or men in general are better than them at certain tasks, say fixing the car, and, therefore, should perform that duty. As noted, the implication is that because someone is better at a task than another person (or at least that they are perceived to be so), they should be the one to complete the task. The problem with this thinking is that it is limiting. It does not allow us to expand our repertoire of behavior. We just keep doing the same thing again and again because we are good at it instead of trying something new and, through practice, becoming good at that new task. Consider where women would be if they had listened to people in the 1960s and 1970s telling them that men naturally made better doctors, lawyers, chefs, and so forth because they had the necessary qualities for these occupations and that women did not! Accepting such similar thinking would certainly have hampered the progress of the women's movement!

Heterosexual Intimacy

Heterosexual intimacy is the third factor in benevolent sexism. It is a romantic attraction toward women by men, but one that is based on inaccurate and glorified images of them, particularly of their sexual purity and ability to become pregnant and bear children. It is a matter of placing women on a pedestal, of men almost worshipping women. For example, the Ambivalent Sexism Inventory (Glick & Fiske, 1996), a scale that measures both hostile (overt) and benevolent (covert) sexism, includes the following items, which are indicative of this aspect of benevolent sexism:

> "Women should be cherished and protected by men."
> "A good woman ought to be set on a pedestal by her man."

Chivalry and traditional gentlemanly behavior, such as men opening doors for women and paying for dates, reflects this adulation of women and is illustrative of the heterosexual intimacy factor that is a component of benevolent sexism. Behavior that represents chivalrous attitudes is readily apparent in the *Twilight* series. For example, Edward is preoccupied with such behavior in *Midnight Sun*. To illustrate, note Edward's thoughts after he saves Bella from being crushed in the school parking lot by a vehicle that skids on ice. After the rescue, Bella realizes that there is something different, something superhuman, about Edward, but she does not discuss this with anyone but Edward himself. Edward is concerned about Bella's deduction and thinks it would be best to discredit Bella, implying to the school population that she had sustained a severe head injury (and, therefore, possibly does not remember the event correctly) so as to protect his (and his family's) identities as a vampire. But Edward does not discredit Bella, believing that to do so would be ungentlemanly. Heterosexual intimacy is also exemplified in the *Twilight* series through Edward's need to be gracious and gallant; he is frequently described as holding doors open for Bella, for example. But his behavior goes beyond courtesy and good manners and is excessive in his treatment of Bella, representing adulation and reverence more than realistic affection. Note that in *Twilight*, after Edward rescues Bella from would-be rapists, he takes Bella to a restaurant and pays for her dinner even though he does not eat or drink anything. In fact, Bella comments to herself about Edward's generous nature while on their honeymoon in *Breaking Dawn* because of repetitive scenes such as these. She wonders whether Edward learned this behavior from Carlisle. Similarly, in *Eclipse*, Bella notes that, after returning from the trip to Florida to see her mother, Edward is adamant about carrying her bag into the house even though it was small. These niceties seem simply like considerate behavior and in many instances, both in the novels and in real life, they are. However, Edward insists on them because he places Bella on a pedestal. He idolizes her (and women in general) and this is indicated to readers in Edward's belief that Bella is completely unselfish even though, as will be discussed in a later chapter, she displays many selfish tendencies. It is also indicated in Edward's continued belief in Bella's loyalty despite her continued relationship with Jacob and the fact that she kisses Jacob while she is engaged to Edward. In fact, Edward's excessive admiration of Bella is later extended to Renesmee, whom, as noted in previous chapters, is regarded with reverence, perhaps because she is an extension of Bella. As such, Edward's respect of Bella seems unrealistically optimistic and, therefore, results in chivalrous behavior that typifies the heterosexual intimacy aspect of benevolent sexism. Subsequently, because Edward has such a glorified image of Bella, he expects certain behaviors of her, and this results in his insistence that Bella accept these displays of respect and admiration even though they appear to make her feel uncomfortable in many instances. Consider that in Meyer's draft of *Midnight Sun*, Edward thinks to himself that Bella would have to get used to his chivalrous acts whether she wanted to or not as he notices that she did not wait for him to open a door for her. In fact, it is notable that Edward indicates in *Midnight Sun* that one of the reasons he is so attracted to Bella is because she reacts to his chivalry differently than any other woman he has encountered: She is uncomfortable with it and ungrateful for it, indicating that he is aware of her discomfort with such traditional behavior, and still he insists upon it. *That* is what is problematic about the heterosexual intimacy aspect of benevolent sexism, that when a man insists on such chivalrous acts, the woman can feel pressure to behave in ways consistent with those acts as is seen with Bella. Edward requires certain traditional behaviors of Bella, which conform to his expectations of womanly behavior. And because the woman feels as though the man is paying her a compliment, showing her respect, which is what he intends, the woman feels as though she needs to go along with the scenario he set up. After all, if she does not, she appears ungrateful and she is actually suggesting that she is not worthy of his adoration, that she should not be viewed in as positive a light as he seems to perceive her, and that is a difficult thing for anyone to do. But these are favors for which she did not ask, and with which she, like Bella, might feel uncomfortable. These acts can fulfill his need to feel chivalrous but not her need to feel independent.

Clearly a man opening a door for a woman is a minor issue, one hardly worth concern considering the gender differential in pay, abusive behaviors toward women, and the rape rate. At this point in time, such behavior can be viewed as charming and courteous, but other chivalrous behavior has farther-reaching implications, encouraging women to conform to other, more significant traditional behaviors. For example, in the series Edward repeatedly resists Bella's sexual advances and insists on marrying Bella before having sex, a gentlemanly gesture especially in this day and age of ubiquitous sex. This is noted in *Eclipse* during extensive negotiations between Edward and Bella about whether they should marry and/or become sexually active. Bella says to Edward, "'So that's it. You won't sleep with me until we're *married*'" (*Eclipse*, p. 455; original italics), to which he replies in the affirmative. Bella, however, shows a great deal of reluctance to get married, and yet, because Edward insists on this ritual, Bella reluctantly conforms to his wishes and marries him in an elaborate ceremony, complete with flowers, bridesmaids, and white dress, in exchange for Edward agreeing to try to make love to Bella while she is still human. This conformity does bother Bella who notes in chapter 1 of *Breaking Dawn* the numerous times she has given in to Edward's demands just so that she will be able to make love to him while she is still human. In fact, Bella continues to accept and even incorporate Edward's wishes as her own, insisting on doing things the "right way," that is, getting married before consummating the relationship, as originally planned, even when Edward gives her the opportunity to cancel wedding plans, engage in sexual behaviors while still human, and later become a vampire without meeting his conditions. Although some aspects of this old-fashioned abstinence-until-marriage storyline are appealing, other aspects of it are problematic, in particular the fact that, for much of the series, Edward makes the decision for both he and Bella about whether they should engage in sexual behaviors. It is not until late in the series that Edward shows any inclination to negotiate on this topic. As noted, when he does so, he initially agrees to have sex with Bella as a human, but only if she marries him and waits until after they are married to consummate the relationship. This seems like a legitimate request: Clearly, Edward should have control over his own sexuality, just as a woman should have control over whether she should have premarital sex or not. But the issue here is not about whether the couple should or should not engage in premarital sex. The issue is that, for an extensive portion of the series, Bella does not have this control, cannot make this decision. Only Edward does, until he finally decides to negotiate with Bella. The point is that when two partners in a relationship have desires that are polar opposites, as Bella's and Edward's were with regard to premarital (human) sex, compromise is necessary. But although Edward does negotiate later, he is initially determined to not compromise. What is especially notable about Edward's disinclination to compromise is that his resolve to be abstinent is not about himself but because he thinks it is best for Bella. Certainly some of this concern is due to anxiety about physically harming Bella with his superhuman strength during the sex act and as is indicated later, when Edward and Bella do consummate their marriage, this is a legitimate concern, as Bella is extensively bruised the next morning. But Edward is also reluctant to compromise on this matter because he is old-fashioned and chivalrous. He thinks it is the right thing to do for Bella because he does not want to take advantage of her sexually. He believes that she deserves marriage before having sex, that to have sex before marriage would show her disrespect. He is protecting her virginity—not his own—and this is indicated in *Eclipse*. During Edward and Bella's negotiations about becoming sexually active,

Bella exclaims, "'That's it, isn't it? . . . You're trying to protect your virtue!'" Edward responds, "'No, silly girl . . . I'm trying to protect *yours*'" (p. 453). Concern for Bella's virginity is also found when Edward rescues Bella from potential rapists in *Twilight*. He is, understandably, enraged and outraged by her attackers and certainly rescuing Bella from this situation was a noble and moral thing to do, the right thing to do, but protecting Bella's purity from himself when she clearly wants to be sexually active with Edward is a completely different scenario. Edward has different standards for his own behavior (although he does remain abstinent) than he does for Bella's behavior. He believes that she should remain virginal until marriage. Such chivalrous behavior is further indicative of Edward's idealized image of Bella, thereby requiring certain standards of conduct from her, and does not take her desires into consideration. During their discussion about becoming sexually active, Bella tells Edward, "'So you can ask for any stupid, ridiculous thing *you* want—like getting *married*—but *I'm* not allowed to even discuss what I—'" (p. 443 of *Eclipse*). In response Edward puts his hand over her mouth and replies, "'No,'" referring to his refusal to consider having sex with her. Edward again is pressuring Bella to behave in ways that he requires rather than in ways that support Bella's own needs and values and, therefore, deprives Bella of a voice—literally—in her own decision making, at least initially. One partner withholding sex from the other partner *because s/he thinks it is best for the other partner*, or because the (female) partner is too good or pure to engage in such behavior, is paternalistic and indicative of the heterosexual intimacy aspect of benevolent sexism, especially if it is contradictory to their partner's desires. In other words, refusing to engage in sexual behaviors is perfectly acceptable if the reason is related to one's own moral needs and value system, but refusing to engage in sexual behaviors because one thinks s/he knows what is best for her/his partner is controlling. As such, chivalrous behavior is restrictive and limiting just as paternalistic behavior can be restrictive, and both are components of benevolent sexism.

Consider another example that illustrates the limiting behavior of chivalry where a husband feels as though it is his job to be the family's provider. He does not think that his spouse should "have to work" outside the home, that she deserves to be able to stay home. On the surface this seems as though it is a self-sacrificing expression of love. It implies that he holds her in such high regard that he wants to give her this gift of not having to work outside the home. But isn't this confining? Doesn't this restrict her behavior to the housekeeping/childcare realm? And doesn't she seem ungrateful if she does not take advantage of the possibility? After all, don't many people in our society dream of winning the lottery so that they can quit their jobs and not have to work? But work does not have to be a negative experience. It can be a fulfilling, enriching experience, depending on the job or career. And if this spouse pressures her to not work outside the home so that he can take care of her, doesn't that mean that he has also deprived her of this enriching experience? Hasn't the one partner made that decision for the other?

In addition to pressuring women to act in a certain way that is consistent with attitudes reflective of heterosexual intimacy, the chivalry aspect of benevolent sexism is problematic because the adoration that characterizes it is unwarranted and based on unrealistic perceptions of women. Does this mean that women are not deserving of respect? Of course not, but viewing them as flawless creatures is unrealistic and creates difficult standards to achieve and maintain. When a woman is placed on a pedestal, it is very easy to fall off. There is only one way to go and that is down. In fact, Bella feels as though she has fallen off the pedestal after she kisses Jacob in *Eclipse* and begs Edward to get angry with her and call her names. He resists this temptation, which is certainly admirable, but in so doing chooses to keep Bella on that pedestal. Instead, Edward blames Jacob, whose mind he has read, allowing Edward a glimpse of Bella's disloyal and inconstant behavior. Edward's forgiveness is certainly preferable to anger or abusive behavior, but adherence to these standards places unnecessary pressure on both men and women. In this example Bella is required to act in ways beyond reproach but Edward also requires of himself extraordinary acts of forgiveness, patience, and kindness. And while these are noble sentiments, they require unnecessarily rigid standards of behavior for both men and women, standards that most people will ultimately be unable to meet. Subsequently, the failure to live up to these standards can result in feelings of disappointment and guilt, not to mention maladjusted behavior, as will be discussed in a later chapter.

One final point about chivalry, that is, the heterosexual intimacy aspect of benevolent sexism, must be made. Although chivalrous behavior requires men to be courteous to women under all circumstances (and this is certainly admirable, if unrealistic, behavior) courtesy should not be gendered. What is often overlooked, in defense of such niceties, is that men, too, are deserving of courteous behavior. If a man is carrying a heavy package, should he feel the need to open a door for a woman who approached the door at the same instant? Shouldn't she feel comfortable opening the door for him if he appears to be in need of assistance? And wouldn't she seem self-centered if she waited idly by for him to open the door for her? Similarly, if someone attacks a woman, she should expect her boyfriend or husband to come to her rescue. But likewise if a man was attacked, he should be able to expect that his girlfriend or wife would assist him as well. We are all deserving of courtesy and we all should expect such behavior of our partners regardless of our gender. Preferential treatment and courtesy should not be expected, or determined, by one's sex and, therefore, should not be limited to women. As such, it is not necessary to discourage courteous behavior directed from men toward women (as long as it is indeed courteous and not controlling behavior), but it is necessary to also encourage courteous behavior directed from women toward men.

Summary

There are two problems with the damsel in distress scenarios portrayed in romance novels like the *Twilight* series. The first involves the potential for social learning, a topic discussed throughout this book. The novels portray male characters as protectors, rescuers engaging in behaviors like those typical of first responders (police officers, fire fighters). They demonstrate superhuman (or perhaps, in this case, we should say supernatural) helping behaviors. Characters who model these types of rescue behaviors can be of value because they demonstrate responsible and compassionate human values, values and behaviors that we want our children (and others) to learn and, if they are capable, in some cases, imitate. There are too many cases of the bystander effect in emergency situations (Darley & Latané, 1968), that is, cases where someone is in need of assistance because they are ill or hurt and passersby ignore them! Role models demonstrating helping behavior are, therefore, of value, although it is not necessarily mandatory to place oneself in danger in order to lend assistance to someone who needs it. However, as mentioned, one of the problems with this storyline is that primarily male characters are portrayed as protectors or rescuers. Thus, males have role models that might encourage them to become fire fighters and police officers but females have dramatically fewer. In fact, their role models tend to be women who are victimized or in need of assistance in some other way. Even Bella objects to her damsel in distress roles at one point! In *Twilight* she states, "'I can't always be Lois Lane. . . . I want to be Superman, too'" (p. 474), in an attempt to convince Edward to change her into a vampire so that their relationship will be more equitable. And equity is vital to the health of a relationship, as feminists have argued for decades (McClimans & Wisnewski, 2009). Consequently, because characters in books can be symbolic models, children, as well as adults, can learn attitudes and behaviors from those characters. Furthermore, because the novels in this series are marketed toward tweens and teens, the storylines and characters can have a dramatic influence on readers of this age, especially on their attitudes about gender roles and romantic relationships since this can be the time they develop ideas (schemas) about these experiences.

The message that girls (and women) can get from these damsel in distress scenarios, then, is that the world is a dangerous place and that they are in need of men's protection. But consider how awesome it would be if, instead of learning to be fearful from victimized characters in novels, our daughters (and adult women) were presented with role models who could take care of themselves, who were confident and unafraid of, say, walking alone at night, women in control of their own lives, responsible for their own safety! Bella, for example, is empowered at the very end of the *Twilight* series. She is able to not just take care of herself but also protect her loved ones after she is changed into a vampire and develops her supernatural protective shield. Unfortunately, the number of these episodes is minimal compared to the number of scenarios where she is rescued.

The second problem with damsel-in-distress storylines is that they exemplify benevolent sexism, which promotes gender inequality and reinforces men's power by (seemingly) using it to benefit women. Bella (as a human) is portrayed as fragile and in need of repeated assistance throughout most of the series. She is idolized by the male characters, especially Edward, who behaves in chivalrous, protective behaviors that ultimately control and restrict Bella's behavior. Bella does attempt to resist Edward's chivalrous behavior. As noted earlier, she is not comfortable with it, but Edward continues to pressure her to conform to his expectations until late in the series. Interestingly, despite Edward's benevolent sexism, Bella seems to get everything she ever dreamed of by the end of the series: a loving husband in Edward, a daughter, affluence, but for some women these traditional experiences might not be enough. And while Bella evolves into a more self-sufficient, more independent woman at the end of the series, despite her earlier need to be repeatedly rescued and pro-tected, in real life and in human relationships such growth is unlikely given similar experiences. Bella grows more self-reliant despite her traditional behavior and despite Edward's traditional treatment of her. In real life, sexist treatment of women, even if it is meant benevo-lently, deprives them of growth, encouraging powerlessness in them instead. In fact, women who perceive chivalrous behavior as romantic have lower career aspirations than women who perceive romance in a different light (Rudman & Heppen, cited in Glick & Fiske, 2001). As such, sex-typed portrayals such as these are problematic because they can serve as models for romantic relationships (Behm-Morawitz, et al., 2010), in this case for relationships that are unequal. This is especially troublesome because behavior that exemplifies benevolent sexism is often not labeled as sexist and is, in fact, often thought of in a positive light: Benevolent sexism implies that men's power should be, and will be, used to benefit women. This seems like a noble sentiment, but who has the power in the relationship and in society? Because many do not examine chivalrous behavior closely, the portrayal of such sexist behaviors never gets addressed or noticed. As such, the learning of the gender stereotypic behaviors and attitudes is subtle and also goes unnoticed.

Does this mean that anyone who simply reads the *Twilight* series will become traditional in their gender roles? No. Some children who watch stereotypical television programming can still develop fairly equalitarian attitudes (Jennings, et al., 1980). But others will not be able to ignore or decode the sex-typed messages in gender stereotypic media because, when we are repeatedly exposed to the same storyline, it becomes difficult to imagine a storyline different from that one. And so much of television programming and movies (and romance genre books) are still sex-typed (Barner, 1999; Brown, 1998; Jennings, et al., 1980; Lauzen, et al., 2008). Does this mean that people shouldn't read the *Twilight* series or other romance novels? No. Censorship is never the answer, but moderation, variety, and education are. Awareness of the socializing effects of the media, whether we are talking about books, magazines, television programs, movies, video games or other forms of media, is necessary to minimize their effects and in order for progression toward gender equity to continue.

So what makes the difference? Why do some children develop sex-typed attitudes after viewing sex-typed media and others do not? As noted, moderation, variety, and education are the answers. In order to minimize the effect of sex-typed media it is essential to limit exposure to sex-typed media. This does not mean we should prohibit the reading of sex-typed books, the viewing of such films, or the playing of such video games. In fact, exposure to sex-typed media is also beneficial in some ways: It is not a perfect world. It is not a postgender world. Discussing (in other words, education about) sex-typed images to which we have been exposed is important in the preparation to function in our gender-defined world and in order to be better prepared to work toward a more gender equitable society. And certainly the *Twilight* series has generated a great deal of discussion about gender roles (Wilson, 2011; Reagin, 2010). But providing alternative gender role models is also important in minimizing the effects of sex-typed media. Variety minimizes exposure to sex-typed messages and this, subsequently, will allow for the development of a variety of ideas about gender roles and adult romantic relationships. In other words, exposure to alternative gender roles and alternative models for love relationships can minimize the effects of more gender stereotypic portrayals. In sum, although romance novels like the *Twilight* series portray traditional gender roles and can encourage the development of sex-typed attitudes and behaviors, discussing and deeply examining the behaviors portrayed so as to see past the surface behavior to the implicit messages also present can combat the influence of such media.

The Embodiment of Patriarchy

Edward, the male protagonist in the *Twilight* series and Bella's love interest, is the prototypical hero in romance novels. He is handsome, strong, competent, and protective, but he is also arrogant, forceful, and patronizing. Even some fans who find the Edward Cullen character appealing note that his negative qualities include being overbearing, overprotective, and controlling (Wilson, 2011a; McClimans & Wisnewski, 2009). Unfortunately, these aspects of Edward's personality are often ignored or minimized by many fans; the fact that such characteristics are patriarchal in nature is often dismissed or neglected. But while it is vital in real life to ignore the faults and weaknesses of others in order to maintain healthy and harmonious relationships, in this case ignoring the shortcomings of partners, such as those of Edward (and Jacob), can have catastrophic consequences, resulting in dangerous, even life-threatening, situations. This might sound melodramatic, but this danger does not revolve around the fact that Edward is a vampire who can potentially kill those interested in a romantic relationship with him or the fact that he can potentially make them into the undead. Nor does it revolve around the fact that Jacob can potentially maim and kill love interests with his werewolf instincts. Rather, the concern revolves around the fact that these romantic leads, like many leads in romance novels, share an alarming number of characteristics with domestic abusers.

Characteristics and Behaviors of Abusers

Access any Web site for a shelter or organization that assists people who are in abusive relationships and you will find similar information on the characteristics of abusers, the types of abuse that exist, and the typical abuse cycle. The National Domestic Violence Hotline (n.d.) Web site, for instance, notes that abusers tend to share a variety of characteristics and engage in similar types of abusive behaviors, the purpose of which is to control their victims. As noted in the following table, abusers tend to belittle their partners with name-calling, insults, or other mechanisms meant to embarrass and demean their victims. They also can intimidate them with threatening looks, looks that can invoke fear even though they have not physically harmed their partner yet. And they tend to be very controlling—of finances, by making all the decisions in the relationship, and by determining which family members and friends the victim is allowed to see. Feminists often see abusive behaviors as typifying the patriarchy (Ould, 1998; McClimans & Wisnewski, 2009), a system whereby males have the power and authority in society. In a patriarchal system women are subordinate to men, and men's privilege can take social, political, financial, and physical forms. Thus, men can hold a higher social status than women, hold a greater number of political offices in comparison to women, and control more financial resources in comparison to women. Historically, in patriarchal societies men have also controlled women physically, utilizing abusive behavior in order to prohibit them from engaging in certain behaviors or coerce them into engaging in other behaviors, such as nonconsensual sex. That is, physical force or the threat of physical force was often used to usurp or maintain masculine sociopolitical power. Consider that in the not-so-distant past, it was even legal to beat one's wife (Fleming, et al., 1982). Thus, abusive relationships are seen as evidence of patriarchal behavior. As is discussed throughout this chapter, abusive behaviors can take a variety of forms, all with the purpose of controlling the victim (typically, but not always, a female) and placing the abuser (typically a male) in a superior position (Center for Relationship Abuse Awareness, 2010a), as is illustrative of patriarchy. Consequently, this chapter will demonstrate that both Edward and Jacob attempt to control Bella through the use of patriarchal tactics, many of which can also be interpreted as abusive.

Table 1. Behaviors of Abusers.

Behaviors of Abusers

Does your partner:
    * Embarrass you with put-downs?
    * Look at you or act in ways that scare you?
    * Control what you do, who you see or talk to, or where you go?
    * Stop you from seeing your friends or family members?
    * Take your money, make you ask for money, or refuse to give you money?
    * Make all of the decisions?
    * Tell you that you are a bad parent or threaten to take away or hurt your children?
    * Act like the abuse is no big deal, it's your fault, or even deny doing it?
    * Destroy your property or threaten to kill your pets?
    * Intimidate you with guns, knives, or other weapons?
    * Shove you, slap you, choke you, or hit you?
    * Threaten to commit suicide?
    * Threaten to kill you?

Source: National Domestic Violence Hotline Web site, http://www.thehotline.org/is-this-abuse/am-i-being-abused-2/

Threatening Behavior

Some abusive partners intimidate their victims with weapons, for example, threatening them with guns or knives (National Domestic Violence Hotline, n.d.). Edward, however, does not need weapons to intimidate Bella. His vampire skills can do so, but Edward often intimidates Bella merely by looking at her in a threatening way. In fact, there are numerous instances of Edward looking at Bella in ways that could be only be interpreted as frightening, especially at the beginning of their relationship. Note that when Bella meets Edward for the first time in their biology class she goes to sit next to him because it is the only seat available. He glares at her. She notes, "He stared at me again, meeting my eyes with the strangest expression on his face—it was hostile, furious. ... I [was] bewildered by the antagonistic stare" (*Twilight*, p. 23). As the class wears on, Bella sneaks another glance at Edward

> and regretted it. He was glaring down at me again, his black eyes full of revulsion. As I flinched away from him, shrinking against my chair, the phrase *if looks could kill* suddenly ran through my mind. (p. 24, original italics)

Later, when Bella and Edward meet up again, he turns toward her "with piercing, hate-filled eyes" (p. 27). Such imagery clearly illustrates threatening behavior that typifies many abusive relationships: The looks are certainly hostile, and Bella is obviously frightened and confused by Edward's reaction to her, especially because Bella interprets this behavior as unprovoked.

Although Bella, and readers, are unaware of the source of Edward's hostility, it is explained in Stephenie Meyer's partial draft of *Midnight Sun*. As Edward narrates the story, it becomes clear that his antipathy toward Bella has its origins in his "vegetarian" lifestyle. As a "vegetarian" vampire Edward has worked long and hard to control his desire for human blood, opting instead to feed off other animals instead of humans, but Bella's sweet-smelling blood threatens to interrupt his lifestyle, threatens his self-imposed restraint. As such, he is concerned that he will lose control and that his inhibitions against killing humans and drinking their blood will dissolve. If he kills Bella and drinks her blood, he will binge and not be able to stop until he has had his fill, resulting in a mass murder of the other students in the class in which he is sitting with her, and incurring his father's (Carlisle's) disappointment. Beyond Edward's concern for the life of these students, and Carlisle's potential disappointment with him, Edward is also angry because his behavior not only threatens to expose his true vampiric nature to the human world but also the nature of his entire family. Such exposure will result in them potentially being hunted or, minimally, the necessity to relocate and begin a new charade of being human, which some family members are reluctant to do. But although Edward is angry with himself for his potential loss of control, he also initially blames the potential for these situations on Bella who has no control over the scent of her blood. Note, then, the implication that Bella is responsible for Edward's behavior, for his potential loss of control, a dangerous implication given that similar excuses have been made for sexual assault and domestic violence, that is, it was the victim's fault. Abusers often blame the abused for the violent treatment their victims receive (Center for Relationship Abuse Awareness, 2010b; National Domestic Violence Hotline, n.d.). But this justification of Edward's behavior is also problematic in that it justifies his hostility, potentially leading readers to believe in its acceptability. In fact, reader acceptability of such treatment is exemplified in that the romance genre is one of the best-selling genres (Romance Writers of America, 2012) and such initial hostile treatment of the female protagonist in romance novels is typical (Bustillos, 2012; Sterk, 1986). But while Edward's behavior can be explained as being due to his vampiric nature, clearly the same explanation is not applicable to other stories in the romance genre whose male protagonist is human. Certainly, the *Twilight* series is not responsible for explaining similar behavior in other novels. The point is that many readers find this type of male protagonist attractive despite his initial malice because such storylines indicate that as long as they continue a relationship long enough, the hostility will turn into "true love" as happens between Bella and Edward. Observe, for example, that despite all this nonverbal antipathy, Bella still views Edward as attractive, even in the initial stages of their acquaintance when Edward demonstrates his aversion to her. In fact, Bella describes Edward as "absurdly handsome" (p. 27) just after this initial hostile meeting. Additionally, after Edward and Bella interact later, Bella is eager to get to school to see Edward even though she "was still frightened of the hostility [she] sometimes felt emanating from him" (*Twilight*, p. 54). Such storylines—that hatred and offensive behavior will turn into true love and considerate behavior—certainly do not reflect real-life possibilities, but social learning theory suggests that readers of these depictions may use them as models for real-life relationships (Bussey & Bandura, 1999; Goodfriend, 2011). Additionally, these portrayals of Bella's romantic interest in Edward pairs characteristic behaviors found in abusive relationships with descriptions of attractive physical characteristics of the male protagonist, Edward, creating a conditioning effect that can create confusion about Edward's real feelings toward Bella and about the characteristics of healthy romantic relationships. Bella notes her confusion as she thinks about Edward's behavior, "I'd just explained my dreary life to this bizarre, beautiful boy who may or may not despise me" (*Twilight*, p. 50). Note the reference to Edward's physical attractiveness along with the reference to Edward's behavior being perceived as hatred. Likewise note that Edward's threatening behaviors alternate with much friendlier, nonthreatening behavior, which additionally normalizes them. That is, in the *Twilight* novels sometimes Edward is charming, and sometimes he is frightening. For example, during these hostile encounters, Bella notes that her "stomach did frightened little flips at the thought of sitting next to him again," referring to Edward in her biology class (Twilight, p. 42), but in that scene Edward is friendly, introducing himself to Bella and being amiable as they complete a lab together. Perhaps this nervousness is due to Bella's attraction to Edward, but it is unclear whether this is the case or whether Bella is truly still frightened of Edward, and this lack of clarity just further blurs the lines between fear and attraction.

Other examples of inconsistent behavior depicting both concern and hostility can be found after Edward rescues Bella from would-be rapists in *Twilight*. After the rescue, Edward and Bella discuss her tendency to attract danger and the number of times she has almost died. Edward tells her, "'Your number was up the first time I met you,'" a statement that can clearly intimidate and frighten anyone. Bella describes her reaction to Edward's declaration,

> I felt a spasm of fear at his words, and the abrupt memory of his violent black glare that first day . . . but the overwhelming sense of safety I felt in his presence stifled it. By the time he looked up to read my eyes, there was no trace of fear in them. (p. 175)

In this scene Edward is nonthreatening as he rescues Bella from attackers but then intimidates her by hinting that he is a dangerous being. Note that Edward brings up his threatening behavior and Bella responds appropriately with fear. She clearly understands that Edward's initial reaction to her, when they met on her first day at her new school in Forks, was hostility, but she somehow overcomes this emotion in order to feel safe with him. Similarly, later in *Twilight*, Edward demonstrates his supernatural abilities, describing himself as the best predator in the world, remarking that Bella would never be able to outrun or fight him off, and frightening Bella in the process. He runs swift laps around the meadow to which they traveled and pulls up trees by their roots, throwing them and smashing them against other trees. Bella's reaction is fear but in response to seeing Edward's expression of sadness about her fear, and his reassurance that he will not hurt her, Bella stifles her anxiety to make *Edward* feel better. Clearly, there is a double message: Edward demonstrates his strength, calls attention to the fact that he can harm Bella, and then reassures her that he won't harm her. The implication of these scenes is that feeling fear in a romantic relationship is customary and tolerable and that it should be suppressed to make the person doing the threatening (the abuser) feel better about their behavior, especially if they are apologetic. But in real life, fear is not a characteristic of a healthy relationship. To illustrate, consider how a parent might feel if they found out that their daughter or son was frightened of someone at school because of hostile looks. And further, consider whether that parent would allow a relationship to develop between their daughter or son and that threatening person. Because these depictions are fictional, some latitude is necessary. Clearly, Edward is a vampire and so readers need not worry about hostility emanating from potential partners for the same reason, but this type of hostile behavior is typical in initial stages of relationships depicted in the romance genre in general (Bustillos, 2012; Sterk, 1986). As such, it is vitally important that readers are aware that such behavior is unacceptable in real life and can actually represent the beginnings of an abusive relationship.

Despite this evidence, some might still argue that the relationship between Bella and Edward is not abusive. Some might suggest that nonverbal behavior, such as the threatening looks described here, is not abusive, despite the fact that experts in the field (e.g., National Domestic Violence Hotline, n.d.) do view it as such. And yet consider the importance we place on nonverbal behavior. Consider how we detect whether someone is lying to us. It is not their words to which we pay the most attention. Rather it is their nonverbal behavior that gives us cues to their true feelings (Ekman & Friesen, 1974). Others might argue that Edward might have felt hostile toward Bella at the beginning of their relationship but that later this hostility dissipated and so their relationship cannot be described as abusive. However, what is overlooked is the fact that even later in their relationship Bella notes similar types of threatening behaviors. In a scene in the last novel of the series, *Breaking Dawn*, after Bella and Edward are married, Bella discovers that she is pregnant and breaks the news to Edward. Edward is angry and frantic because he is concerned about Bella surviving the pregnancy. Bella, however, does not understand Edward's concern. She does not want to deal with his anger and his moodiness and leaves the room thinking, "I couldn't talk to this icy, focused Edward who honestly frightened me a little" (p. 131). In sum, there are multiple episodes of threatening scenes throughout the *Twilight* series and these scenes exemplify just one of the types of behaviors that domestic abusers use to control their partners.

Belittling Behavior

In addition to the threatening behaviors just noted, there is also ample evidence of belittling behavior in the *Twilight* novels, a behavior that is also typical in a patriarchal society (McClimans & Wisnewski, 2009) and of the early stages of an abusive relationship (Center for Relationship Abuse Awareness, 2010b). Despite extensive professions of love between Bella and Edward, Edward frequently trivializes Bella. To illustrate, consider a scene in *Eclipse* where Bella and Edward are arguing about whether Bella should visit Jake. Edward says, "'Bella. You aren't exactly the best judge of what is or isn't dangerous'" (p. 141). Bella does frequently find herself in dangerous situations, some of which are of her own making, so there is some truth to this statement, but note Edward's condescension. He implies that he understands danger but that Bella is ignorant in this regard. In another scene in *Eclipse*, Edward calls Bella "absurd" when she is jealous of other vampires being attracted to him (p. 194). In still another scene, Edward calls Bella "silly" when she doesn't think she looks sexy in a helmet and leather jacket Edward bought her for when she rides a motorcycle (p. 235). Another time Edward calls Bella "obtuse" when she tells him that she is afraid he will not continue to like/love her when she becomes a vampire (p. 274). In many of these scenes, Edward pairs these comments with a compliment. He thinks her jealousy is "adorable" (p. 194). He thinks her silliness is part of her "charm" (p. 235). He calls her "intuitive" (p. 274) at the same time as obtuse. This can lead some to interpret the comments as affectionate teasing, but when combined with the insults, they send confusing double messages about Edward's perceptions of Bella, and this is one of the troubling aspects of the *Twilight* novels: The novels depict behavior that can be interpreted as abusive (in this case insults) in ways that make them seem acceptable expressions of love. Some might dismiss this behavior as being "just a story" but doing so ignores the possibility that such stories can and do affect us, even if we are not aware that they do. As noted throughout this book, teenagers who are just forming ideas about what romantic relationships are like can come away with dangerous ideas about the acceptability of these and other types of abusive behaviors (Goodfriend, 2011). Obviously, novels do not require that storylines or the behaviors of characters follow typical patterns found in real life. If so, novels about werewolves and vampires living among us would not have found their way into the mainstream! Unfortunately though, in real life not only do such comments create confusion, they can, with time, undermine a victim's self-esteem and self-confidence.

In addition to using insults, Edward also embarrasses Bella by frequently laughing at her. For example, after Edward saves Bella from a vehicle that slips on ice and careens out of control in the school parking lot, he laughs, demonstrating his relief about her lack of injury when she says, "'Ow,'" in response to pain she feels (*Twilight*, p. 57). In the hospital where she is examined for injuries, Edward is described as smirking and as chuckling in response to Bella's downplaying of her injuries and the fact that Bella is resentful of the double-standard between her being examined and unable to go back to school when the same was not true for Edward. In fact, Edward is described as "smug" (p. 62). Also in *Twilight*, Edward is amused by Bella almost passing out in biology class in response to a lesson on blood-typing because the thought of a vampire falling in love with someone who cannot stand the sight or smell of blood is amusing to him (and, the author hopes, to the readers!). Certainly some of these scenes are just examples of playful teasing, and we all laugh at others (hopefully when appropriate and they are receptive), but these behaviors, examined in context with other behaviors that Edward displays, also demonstrate a sense of superiority. In fact, during the blood-typing scene Bella tells Edward, "'You were right,'" referring to the fact that he suggested that she should skip biology class, and he replies, "'I usually am'" (p. 98), although he struggles to determine to what she is actually referring. Additionally, with repetition, such behaviors that belittle and embarrass can create long-lasting feelings of self-consciousness and insecurity in the recipient. Although Bella does not seem negatively affected by this type of treatment at Edward's hand, people in similar, real-life situations most likely would be. And although these behaviors seem trivial, it is well known that they can also mark the beginning of an abusive relationship because such relationships often start out with minor incidents but then tend to escalate (Center for Relationship Abuse Awareness, 2010a).

Controlling Behavior

Threatening and belittling behaviors are used to control victims and clearly there are numerous scenes that exemplify these behaviors, but there are also a variety of other scenes in the *Twilight* novels that further demonstrate controlling behavior. Edward, especially, attempts to limit Bella's behavior (McClimans & Wisnewski, 2009). One aspect of Bella's behavior that Edward controls is her sexuality. As discussed in the previous chapter, for most of the series, Edward is the person in the relationship who determines what sexual behaviors will be engaged in and when. Bella notes in *New Moon*, "Edward had drawn many careful lines for our physical relationship" (p. 16). Later in *New Moon* Bella again refers to Edward's reluctance to move their relationship into a more sexual realm. She thinks, "Edward and his rules ..." (p. 50), and when Bella asks for another kiss from Edward because it's her birthday, Edward says, "'You're greedy tonight'" (p. 51). In still another example, this time in *Eclipse*, Bella tries to kiss Edward but he declines. She reaches "for his face, trying to pull [her]self up to kiss him. His arms held [her] tighter, restraining." Edward responds by telling her, "'Must I always be the responsible one?'" (p. 192). Note several things in this particular scene. First, Edward decides whether they will kiss or not, thereby placing him in the role of decision maker. Bella does not have input into whether she and Edward will be sexually active. Second, Edward physically restrains Bella, thereby controlling her physically. Finally, Edward suggests that he is the responsible person, not Bella, belittling her again, implying his superiority and typifying the patriarchy.

As also discussed in the last chapter, many readers find the sexual abstinence aspect of the novels appealing. They interpret Edward's behavior as being gentlemanly, despite his use of physical restraint, because he refuses to take advantage of Bella sexually (and because he does not want to hurt her physically), both of which are certainly admirable sentiments. But, as also indicated in the previous chapter, Edward's behavior exemplifies paternalistic and patriarchal behaviors and represents benevolent sexism: *Edward* decides that Bella should remain virginal until marriage (because of his chivalrous attitudes), rather than Bella herself. *Edward* decides whether they should consummate their relationship or not, rather than the two of them making this decision together. Bella is not allowed to assess the risk of being physically harmed by consummating her relationship with Edward, and ultimately she feels rejected because of Edward's repeated rebuffs of her sexual advances. Edward does finally realize at the at the end of *Eclipse* that his decision-making for Bella was an extensive unfortunate mistake, indicating the exact point being made here, that controlling other people, making decisions for them, is not in their best interests, even if that is the intention. Edward finally realizes that he does not necessarily know what Bella needs better than Bella herself. He finally realizes that Bella does have the ability to adequately understand her own needs and desires. This indicates some psychological growth on Edward's part, but in real life such spontaneous growth is unlikely and motivations for controlling behaviors are likely to benefit abusers rather than abuse victims.

Jacob also tries to control Bella sexually but he does so in a way opposite to that of Edward. While Edward treats Bella in a chaste manner, Jacob tries to physically force and emotionally manipulate Bella into a sexual act: kissing. And while Edward expresses remorse about his behavior, Jacob does so to a lesser degree, clearly enjoying kissing Bella despite being aware of the inappropriateness of his behavior. In one scene in *Eclipse* he kisses Bella even though she resists. The kiss is described as angry. Bella describes the experience: "His lips crushed mine, stopping my protest. He kissed me angrily, roughly, his other hand gripping tight around the back of my neck, making escape impossible. I shoved against his chest with all my strength, but he didn't even seem to notice" (p. 330). Bella smacks him in response, but Jacob's response to the experience is one of pleasure despite the fact that Bella's was not. Later in *Eclipse*, Jacob emotionally manipulates Bella into kissing him, telling her that he will try to get himself killed by the newborn vampires he is about to fight if she does not demonstrate her affection for him. Although Bella initiates the kiss at Jacob's request, Jacob's kissing is portrayed as aggressive. Bella describes it: "…his lips found mine with an eagerness that was not far from violence" (p. 526). Eventually, Bella willingly kisses him back and realizes that she is in love with him also. Subsequently, after Jacob kisses Bella again, this time gently, before departing to fight the newborns, Jacob tells Bella that their first kiss should have been as gentle, indicating some regret for his initial actions. Taken together, these scenes indicate Jacob enjoys kissing Bella despite his use of physical force and despite being aware of the inappropriateness of his behavior. As such, both Jacob and Edward attempt to control Bella's sexuality but do so in completely different ways.

In addition to Edward deciding how far they will go in their sexual relationship, he also makes numerous other decisions for both he and Bella. For example, Edward pressures Bella to apply to colleges she has no interest in attending, going so far as to sending out an application to Dartmouth for her and bribing the school to admit her. In another example, Edward decides what type of car Bella should drive. In fact, in *Breaking Dawn* Bella suspects Edward of disabling her truck so that he could buy her a different vehicle, one that he thought to be more appropriate (and safer) for her. She thinks to herself,

> "I miss my truck" . . . Very, very convenient—too convenient—that my truck would wheeze its last wheeze just weeks after Edward and I had agreed to our lopsided compromise, one detail of which was that he be allowed to replace my truck when it passed on. (p. 7)

Edward also controls what type of information he gives Bella: In *Eclipse*, Edward initiates a trip to visit Renée, Bella's mother. What Bella doesn't know is the reason for the trip. She finds out later, after they have returned home to Forks, that the reason Edward wanted

Bella to visit her mother is because Victoria, another vampire, is searching for Bella in order to get revenge for her mate being killed in the first volume of the *Twilight* series. In fact, the only reason Bella does find out that she is being hunted by Victoria is because of Jake, who meets Edward and Bella on school grounds after their return. Jake is relaying a message to Edward and the two argue. In the course of the argument Bella realizes that they both know something she does not. Bella notices that

> Jacob was staring at us with incredulous eyes. "You didn't tell her anything at all, did you? Is that why you took her away? So she wouldn't know that—?" . . . "Why haven't you told her?" . . . "You don't think Bella has a right to know?" (pp. 79-80)

addressing Edward and the fact that Edward did not tell Bella about the potential danger she was in. Edward explains to Jacob that he was just protecting her. "'Why should she be frightened when she was never in danger?'" (p. 80). Jacob replies "'Better frightened than lied to . . . She's tougher than you think'" (p. 81). Note that this interaction implies that Edward believes he knows what Bella needs better than Bella herself and although, in this scene at least, Jacob understands that Bella should be able to process information and make decisions for herself, in other scenes Jacob also seems to indicate that he knows what Bella needs better than Bella herself. To illustrate, note that Jake tells Edward in *Eclipse* that Bella loves him (Jacob)—she just doesn't know it yet. In fact, in *Eclipse* Jake explains to Bella all the reasons why he would be better for her than Edward. As such, both Jacob and Edward demonstrate paternalistic and patriarchal attitudes. Such attitudes prevent women such as Bella from standing on their own two feet, from trusting in their own abilities to handle situations. They undermine women's confidence and independence. Indeed, Bella indicates that she wants access to the information Edward has and asks Edward for clarification: "'What happened? Tell me *everything*. And screw the protecting me crap, please'" (p. 86). Subsequently, Bella makes Edward promise to not keep information from her again.

Edward is likewise controlling in the sense that he, like many abusers, stops Bella from seeing her friends, Jake especially, although he is less controlling when she wants to spend time with human friends. On page 34 of *Eclipse*, Bella tells Edward, "'I have to see Jacob.'" Edward replies, "'Then I'll have to stop you.'" In another example, this time in *New Moon*, Bella wants to go to Jake to hug him and make him feel better because he doesn't think he'll be able to continue being Bella's friend since she has a vampire boyfriend and he is a werewolf, the enemy of vampires, and because Bella intends to become a vampire herself. But Edward physically prevents Bella from doing so because Edward is concerned that Jacob will lose control, turn into a werewolf, and accidentally harm Bella. Stephenie Meyer, however, notes on her Web site, which includes background information on Jacob's character, that he has exceptional control, especially for a young werewolf (Meyer, n.d.d). Bella describes the incident,

> "Jake" . . . I took a step toward him. I wanted to wrap my arms around his waist and erase the expression of misery on his face. Edward pulled me back again, his arms restraining instead of defending. (*New Moon*, p. 561).

In yet another example, Bella and her father have been invited to a party on the La Push reservation but Bella is noncommittal about attending when Charlie mentions it to her because she knew she "wouldn't be allowed to hit a werewolf party, even with parental supervision," referring to Edward forbidding her to see Jake (*Eclipse*, p. 51). In this last example Edward does surprise Bella by telling her that she does not need to ask his permission to go to a party, that he is not her father, but note Bella's surprise at her expectation being disproven. There were so many other situations where Bella anticipated similar requirements. Thus, Edward, as in a patriarchal relationship, controls Bella's behavior in a paternalistic way. His intentions might be protective but he still clearly limits Bella's behavior physically and otherwise. There is also an especially disturbing scene in *Eclipse* where Bella tries to sneak off to see Jake when Edward is not around. She thinks to herself, "'Like any fugitive, I couldn't help looking over my shoulder a few times while I jogged to my truck'" (*Eclipse*, p. 62), but when she turns the key she finds that her truck won't start, and then she notices Edward in the cab of the truck. Alice, Edward's sister who can see glimpses of the future, warned Edward that Bella might visit Jacob. In response Edward disabled Bella's truck so that she could not, presumably in an effort to protect her from an inadvertent werewolf attack. Whether this is the case or whether his behavior is at least partially due to jealousy is uncertain, but if Edward's behavior is due to jealousy, it just further supports criticism of the series indicating that the novels normalize abusive behaviors (Goodfriend, 2011; Housel, 2009; McClimans & Wisnewski, 2009). In fact, the Center for Relationship Abuse Awareness (2010b) specifically asks, "Does your partner's jealousy stop you from seeing friends or family?" as it lists warning signs of abuse for readers of its Web site. The escalation of control in this particular example should especially be noted. It is no longer just verbal; it is no longer just physical restraint. Now Edward actually sabotages Bella's truck to prevent her from seeing her friend, and this escalation likewise is typical of abusive relationships (Center for Relationship Abuse Awareness, 2010a). Indeed, it should be noted that according to the 2012 World Conference of Women's Shelters, women fleeing their abusers often have been unable to start their cars (Dvorak, 2012). Additionally, it is disturbing that Bella is initially angry with Edward about this incident but then quickly forgives him. Again these types of scenarios can create confusing images of what healthy love relationships are like. They imply that controlling behavior is actually an expression of love and protection because Edward does not want Bella to be harmed by werewolves, but, in actuality, controlling behaviors are restrictive, prohibitive, and demeaning, and they often represent jealousy rather than protection.

Bella is more successful another time she tries to sneak off to see Jacob—when Edward is off hunting—but she knows Edward will be angry. Consider the following conversation that Bella has with Jake during this surprise visit. Jake asks Bella, "'Will he be mad at you?'" referring to Edward. She replies, "'Yes. . . . He really hates it when I do things he considers . . . risky.'" Jake suggests, "'So don't go back.'" Bella responds sarcastically, "'That's a great idea. . . . Because then he would come looking for me'" (*Eclipse*, p. 115). In fact, when Bella does begin to drive home, she finds Edward's car immediately behind her as she leaves the reservation. "'Aw crap,' [she] whimpered" (p. 132). This depiction is also disturbingly similar to real-life experiences of victims of domestic violence who describe being tracked by their abusers through the use of GPS devices (Dvorak, 2012). Edward does not immediately confront Bella because she goes to a friend's house, but when she returns home Edward is waiting for her in her room. She notes his nonverbal behavior, "He stood against the wall across from me, in the shadow beside the open window. His face was hard and his posture tense. He glared at me wordlessly" (*Eclipse*, p. 140). After an extensive period of silence, with Bella attempting to make conversation, Edward, who is not allowed on the La Push reservation where she visited Jacob, says, "'Bella . . . Do you have *any* idea how close I came to crossing the line today? To breaking the treaty and coming after you?'" (p. 141). When Bella explains that she was not in danger, Edward rolls his eyes and tells Bella, "'You aren't exactly the best judge of what is or isn't dangerous,'" demonstrating his opinion of her and potentially undermining her confidence in her abilities to make such judgments. "He ground his teeth together. His hands were balled up in fists at his sides" (p. 141). Again, Edward's sense of superiority, his sense of knowing what is good for Bella and his sense that Bella is unable, or incapable, of making sound judgments in this regard comes through, as does the nonverbal cues that imply his anger and potentially dangerous behavior toward Bella. Moreover, Edward blames Bella for his potentially breaking the treaty his family has with the Quileute, another characteristic typical of abusers, who often blame their victims for the treatment they have doled out to them (Center for Relationship Abuse Awareness, 2010b; National Domestic Violence Hotline, n.d.).

Other characters in the stories, including Jacob, do understand that Edward's behavior is inappropriate. In yet another scene in *Eclipse*, Jake asks Bella to come to La Push for a bonfire party. She says, "'I'll ask,'" referring to Edward. Jake, replies, "'Is he your warden, now, too? You know, I saw this story on the news last week about controlling, abusive teenage relationships and—'"; Bella cuts him off at this point and refuses to listen (p. 224). Unfortunately this sends a message to readers that such controlling behavior is really not an issue with which they need to be concerned. The message is that controlling behavior is acceptable as long as your partner loves you in the way Edward loves Bella, as long as it is for one's protection. Edward's behavior is forgiven by many readers because it is portrayed as something that girls and women should dream about, because it demonstrates the depth of their partner's love.

Interestingly, Jacob criticizes Edward for his treatment of Bella but shows minimal remorse for his own forceful treatment of Bella. As discussed earlier, Jacob kisses Bella despite the fact that she does not consent and, in fact, even resists. But many fans forgive Jacob, just as they forgive Edward, because Jacob also loves Bella. Similarly, Stephenie Meyer also dismisses Jacob's inappropriate behaviors, explaining that they are due to his youth. She says, referring to the tactics Jacob uses to save Bella from marrying Edward and becoming a vampire, including forcing her to kiss him so that she will realize she loves him,

> Jacob couldn't live with himself if he didn't give saving Bella his best effort—he knows it's going to hurt when he loses, but he knows it would hurt worse if he didn't try. Does he do everything right? Heck, no! But he's sixteen and he's making it up as he goes along. Those who are upset by some of his tactics should consider his youth and the fact that he is, after all right. Bella is in love with him. (Meyer, n.d.e, para. 4).

Thus, although both Edward's and Jacob's behaviors can be perceived as exemplifying the control that typifies patriarchy, they are dismissed as inconsequential because of their protective motivations, just as is true of behavior typifying benevolent sexism, as discussed in the last chapter.

In addition to controlling whether Bella is "allowed" to see Jacob, Edward and the Cullens also control the amount of contact she has with Renesmee, her baby. This is illustrated as Bella is recovering from being injected with vampire venom and just about completely changed into a vampire. She can hear someone cautiously indicate to others to keep Renesmee away from Bella. Then later when she asks to see Renesmee Edward says, "'That's not really a good idea. . . . You don't want to put her in danger, do you?'" (*Breaking Dawn*, p. 399). The first time Bella does see Renesmee she is surrounded by Edward and his brothers. "Emmett and Jasper were right in front of me, shoulder to shoulder, hands ready. Edward gripped me from behind. . . . Even Carlisle and Esme moved to get Emmett's and Jasper's flanks" (p. 439). There is a similar scene the second time Bella sees her daughter in *Breaking Dawn*. She smells blood in Renesmee's bottle, and Jasper reacts, restraining Bella, "And then Renesmee was out of my arms, which were pinned behind my back. I didn't struggle . . . I just looked at Edward's frightened face. 'What did I do?'" (p. 464). Certainly, this restrictive behavior is due to concern that Bella, as a newborn vampire, will be unable to resist the smell of Renesmee's blood and, therefore, attack her. In other words, the Cullens, including Edward, prevent Bella's contact with her newborn out of concern for the baby. But consider the impact this type of reaction should have on Bella. It should destroy her confidence in her ability to be a good mother, to not attack her child, because she is a newborn vampire, theoretically with little control. Furthermore, these scenes exemplify the use of physical force to control Bella's behavior, the control of when Bella can interact with her own daughter, and the control of the decision-making process by men such as Edward and Jasper. But all these precautions were unnecessary because Bella had no problem resisting her need for blood around Renesmee, nor anywhere else for that matter. Certainly, the Cullens had no way of knowing that Bella would not attack her own child, but Bella, and Alice, did know. During Bella's first encounter with Renesmee, Alice stayed in place, saying, "'Oh, give her some credit. . . . She wasn't going to do anything. You'd want a closer look, too'" (p. 439). Again, the implication is that the Cullens (including Edward) think they know what Bella will do better than Bella herself.

It should be noted that many of these examples demonstrate characters resorting to physical force in order to control Bella. This is evident as Edward restrains Bella to prevent her from going to Jake, as Jasper inhibits her from approaching Renesmee, and as Edward rebuffs Bella's sexual advances. This physical restraint, a behavior specifically listed by the U.S. Department of Health and Human Services as abusive and controlling (Bragg, 2003), can be found in other aspects of Bella and Edward's relationship as well. In the blood-typing scene in *Twilight*, where Bella nearly passes out in biology class, Edward insists on driving her home even though she is resistant to the idea. As he is literally pulling her to his car, she thinks, "'He'd probably just drag me along anyway if I did'" resist (p. 103). As they approach his car she tells him to let her go and when he does she tells him, "'You are so *pushy*!'" She thinks about just running for her truck but he knows what she is thinking and tells her, "'I'll just drag you back'" (p. 104).

Edward also often enlists the aid of his family in order to physically restrict Bella's behavior. This is evident in the previously described scenes as Bella interacts with Renesmee, but there are additional scenes in which the Cullens enable Edward's controlling behaviors as well. In one scene in *Eclipse* Edward initially wants his brothers, Jasper and Emmett, and his sister Alice to watch over Bella while he is off hunting because Bella is being hunted by other vampires. Bella is displeased and tells him that she resents being "babysat" but Edward still insists on this supervision. In another scene where Bella is prevented from seeing Jake, Alice essentially kidnaps Bella when Edward needs to go away. The "kidnapping" is basically a sleepover party and so is not potentially dangerous, but Bella's wishes are again ignored. Edward paid Alice in the form of a Porsche so that she would look after Bella every time Edward is gone. Bella asks Alice, "'…don't you think this is just a little bit controlling? Just a tiny bit psychotic, maybe?'" (*Eclipse*, p. 146), clearly indicating her reluctance to accompany Alice. There is even debate as to whether Bella can use the telephone, and Bella must cancel plans with Jake who asks, "'Can't you have a life when he's gone?'" (p. 148). The fact is that the rest of the Cullens are accepting of Edward's controlling behavior, especially when they agree that Bella is in danger. Note that during this sleepover/kidnapping Rosalie is happy for an opportunity to talk to Bella, commenting, "'He so rarely leaves you alone'" (p. 153), referring to Edward. Her statement might imply some disapproval of Edward's overprotective nature, but she also tells Bella not to be too mad at Edward for keeping her locked up, excusing his behavior by telling Bella, "'It terrifies him to be away from you'" (*Eclipse*, p. 168). Such justification for Edward's controlling behavior just further normalizes it, sending readers inappropriate messages about its acceptability. Ultimately, Jake springs Bella from her imprisonment, referring to it as a "prison break" and Bella thinks to herself, "'It felt great to be free'" (pp. 170–171), indicating her clear reluctance to participate in this forced slumber party.

In sum, the *Twilight* series demonstrates extensive amounts of controlling behavior by both Edward and Jacob: They attempt to control her sexuality, withhold information from her, prevent her from seeing other friends, and they certainly use physical force and restraint in order to prevent or coerce her into certain behaviors. Consequently, both Edward's and Jacob's behavior is problematic. Although both characters are supernatural beings, they possess very human qualities and, therefore, readers can potentially see them as human role models. As noted in previous chapters, there is evidence that some readers do desire characteristics similar to those of the male *Twilight* protagonists in their human boyfriends (Behm-Morawitz, et al., 2010). Therefore, there is cause for concern that the *Twilight* novels are being used as templates for romantic relationships (Goodfriend, 2011). As such, readers can come away with the idea that controlling behavior is a sign of their partner's love, just as Edward's and Jacob's behaviors toward Bella are explained. These relationships are thought to be ideal, but similar relationships in real life would be considered abusive. While Edward ultimately becomes less controlling as his relationship with Bella develops and Jacob moves on to a new relationship after imprinting on Renesmee, in real-life human relationships, this is much less likely to happen because abusers do not readily relinquish control over their victims. Instead, they often escalate their control (Center for Relationship Abuse Awareness, 2010a).

Types of Abuse

The U.S. Department of Justice (2011) lists five types of abuse on its domestic violence Web site: physical, sexual, economic, psychological, and emotional. Physically abusive behaviors are those that can potentially result in bodily harm such as "hitting, slapping, shoving, grabbing, pinching, biting, and hair-pulling" (para. 2). Sexual abuse involves the use of force to engage in sexual behaviors, as in marital or date rape or treating one's partner in a sexually demeaning manner. It is these two types of abuse that most people think of as abuse, but, as noted, there are three other types of behaviors—considered abuse by experts and by the U.S. Department of Justice (2011)—that people are less likely to recognize as abuse. They include economic abuse, making a victim financially dependent on an abuser by maintaining total control over financial resources, such as money; psychological abuse, creating fear through such behaviors as intimidation, physical threats, and forced isolation from family and friends; and emotional abuse, destroying a person's self-worth and self-confidence through such acts as criticism, insults, and name-calling. This section points out examples of behaviors in the *Twilight* novels that are consistent with these types of abuse.

As just noted, the two most recognizable types of abuse are physical and sexual abuse, and there are examples consistent with both in the *Twilight* series that have already been discussed. For instance, there are numerous occassions throughout the novels where Edward physically restrains Bella, a behavior clearly listed as abusive on the Web site of U.S. Department of Health and Human Services describing basic information about domestic violence (Bragg, 2003). Similarly, there is a scene in *Breaking Dawn* in which Jacob not only grabs Bella and restrains her, but in which he shakes her, because he becomes upset as she discusses her and Edward's honeymoon plans. She describes the experience, "His enormous hands gripped the tops of my arms, wrapping all the way around, fingers overlapping. 'Ow, Jake! Let go!' He shook me. . . .'Jake—stop!'" (pp. 65–66). As is consistent with the definition of physical abuse Jacob's behavior could have potentially caused Bella physical injury, and clearly it does cause her pain. But it should additionally be noted that, as is common in abusive relationships, Bella continues her relationship with Jacob and with Edward despite their treatment of her. Victims of domestic violence often continue their relationships with their abusers for a variety of reasons: economic necessity, fear of retaliation if they leave, and so forth (Center for Relationship Abuse Awareness, 2010c). However, although these scenes exemplify physical abuse in many ways, they are often excused because they are portrayed as demonstrations of love and concern for Bella (Meyer, n.d.d; Meyer, 2008a). As such, these behaviors, which many others view as physically abusive, are normalized, encouraging readers to believe that they are a natural part of relationships between men and women. But behavior that controls another physically or sexually is not representative of healthy relationships. Instead, in this case it represents patriarchy.

There are also scenes in the *Twilight* series that are consistent with certain aspects of sexual abuse. As discussed earlier, Jacob does physically force Bella to kiss him in *Eclipse* despite her protests. What is especially disturbing about this scene is not just that Jacob realizes the inappropriateness of his behavior and that he still engages in it, but that Charlie, Bella's own father, a police officer, approves of Jacob's behavior and tells him so. He actually sides with Jake, not with his daughter, who broke her hand when she hit Jacob in response to the unwanted kiss! Later Charlie does say to Bella, "'No matter what side I'm on, if someone kisses you without your permission, you should be able to make your feelings clear without hurting yourself'" (pp. 362–363), but clearly these two sentiments are contradictory. Charlie cheers Jake's inappropriate behaviors on and then later indicates that Jake's behavior is unacceptable. Consequently, the novel sends mixed messages about how women should be treated and about what dating behaviors are appropriate.

The series has also been extensively criticized for its portrayal of Edward and Bella's first sexual experience on their honeymoon (Seifert, 2008; Wilson, 2011b). Edward, and later Bella, wants to remain abstinent until they are married. Initially, Edward's refusal to consent to Bella's sexual advances left her feeling rejected but she eventually adopted Edward's way of thinking, even though Edward was willing to renege on his original plan and make love to Bella while she is still human and before they are married. Edward's control of this experience is troubling, as is the fact that his behavior leaves Bella feeling rejected, but what is more problematic is the imagery used to depict the morning after Edward and Bella consummate their marriage: Readers discover that Bella is bruised extensively. She notices,

> There was stiffness, and a lot of soreness, too … but mostly there was the odd sensation that my bones all had become unhinged at the joints . . . It was not an unpleasant feeling. (*Breaking Dawn*, p. 88)

Edward tells Bella to look at herself and as she does she finds

> large purplish bruises were beginning to blossom across the pale skin of my arm. My eyes followed the trail they made up to my shoulder, and then down across my ribs. . . . I tried to remember this—to remember pain—but I

couldn't. I couldn't recall a moment when his hold had been too tight, his hands too hard against me. I only remembered wanting him to hold me tighter, and being pleased when he did. (p. 89)

Bella describes her bruising in more detail on page 95: "There was a faint shadow across one of my cheekbones, and my lips were a little swollen . . . The rest of me was decorated with patches of blue and purple." Edward apologizes profusely to Bella, and the book explains that the bruising is accidental, that it occurred because Edward, a vampire, is so much stronger than Bella, a human. Bella, despite all the damage to her body, is unconcerned, and when Edward expresses his regret, she gets angry with him for destroying the happiness she is experiencing about having finally made love. There is no indication that the behaviors that resulted in bruises or the bruises themselves hurt, although in real life an experience such as this would involve extensive pain on Bella's part. In fact, in later scenes Bella literally begs Edward to have more sex, and at one point she cries until they do, despite her bodily state. Consequently this scene sends confusing messages that indicate that as long as someone loves you as much as Edward loves Bella that bruises are acceptable. Certainly, Edward is genuinely sorry for the injuries to Bella, but his remorse is still consistent with real-life abusive experiences. It reflects the reconciliation stage of the abuse cycle (Walker, 1979), a pattern of behavior in abusive relationships in which there is a build-up of tension resulting in an abusive episode, apologies for the abuse (reconciliation), followed by a period of calm. An additional concern of the pairing of this violent imagery with sexually arousing imagery is that there is evidence that repeated pairing of such abusive imagery with sex can potentially produce classical conditioning effects whereby violent imagery can eventually produce sexual arousal on its own even if such imagery did not originally produce arousal (Harris & Barlett, 2009; Malamuth & Donnerstein, 1982). Consequently, scenes such as these encourage unhealthy sexual relationships and send unintentional messages about the legitimacy of these experiences.

The less recognizable forms of abuse include those that are economic, psychological, and emotional in nature. Although there are no specific scenes consistent with economic abuse, Bella does become financially dependent upon Edward as she does not show any inclination for developing a career or to participation in the labor force, as fully discussed earlier. Edward willingly shares his wealth with her but clearly *his* wealth becomes *hers*. There are, however, several scenes in the *Twilight* series that are consistent with psychological abuse, which involves intimidation and/or threats (U.S. Department of Justice, 2011): Edward's threatening behaviors and looks, which have already been discussed, can be considered psychologically abusive, but additionally, Jacob behaves in ways that can also be considered psychologically abusive to Bella, in particular through his threat of suicidal behavior. Recall, for example, the scene in *Eclipse* in which Jacob manipulates Bella by implying that he will try to get himself killed in the fight with the newborns who are hunting Bella if she does not indicate her love by kissing him. In fact, suicidal threats are not uncommon in abusive relationships (Center for Relationship Abuse Awareness, 2010b; National Domestic Violence Hotline, n.d.), and they are just one more way abusers control and manipulate their victims. Unfortunately, suicide is frequently discussed and glorified by the series. For example, in *New Moon* Edward and Bella watch a movie of Shakespeare's *Romeo and Juliet*. Edward tells Bella that he envies Romeo "the ease of suicide" (p. 18). He explains that he thought of committing suicide (as best he could) when he was afraid that Bella was going to die by the hands (fangs?) of another vampire in the *Twilight* novel. Suicide is further glorified in *Breaking Dawn* when Edward asks Jacob to kill him if Bella dies during her pregnancy. Throughout the series suicide is portrayed as though it is the ultimate demonstration of love. This glamorization of suicide is especially troubling, as again, the series is geared toward young people who can see suicide as romantic (Saedi, 2011). But suicide creates unfailing emotional trauma for those left behind and a loss of a life that could have realized great potential. And in the case of abusive relationships, it represents a form of psychological control.

Finally, while the above noted scenes represent psychologically abusive behavior, other scenes in the *Twilight* series are consistent with emotional abuse. As noted earlier in this chapter, there are numerous examples of belittling behavior, a behavior that represents this type of abuse (U.S. Department of Justice, 2011). Edward frequently insults and compliments Bella at the same time, implying in many cases Edward's sense of superiority and a certain amount of condescension. And while Bella does not seem negatively affected by Edward's criticism of her, in real life repetitive use of such behavior results in damage to a victim's self-esteem and self-confidence. In sum, a variety of scenes from the *Twilight* series describe behaviors that have characteristics similar to a variety of forms of abuse.

Stalking Behavior

Before concluding this discussion of types of abusive behaviors, one last behavior must be considered: stalking. The National Institute of Justice (2007) describes stalking as a crime of power and control, similar to the abusive patriarchal behaviors just discussed. Stalking is behavior that is directed toward a particular person that involves nonconsensual, repeated proximity to that person. It can include unwanted verbal or nonverbal communication that is threatening, harassing, or a combination thereof (Housel, 2009). It can also include nonconsensual observation of a victim or leaving the target unwanted presents (Tjaden & Thoennes, 1998). The *Twilight* novels, especially the first, do include instances of what could be called stalking behavior perpetrated by Edward. In *Twilight* Edward follows Bella to Port Angeles, where she has gone shopping with her friends. Bella is unaware that she is being followed until she finds herself in yet another potentially dangerous situation. She is lost and wandering around trying to find her friends from whom she is separated. She is then surrounded by would-be attackers, when Edward comes to her rescue. They go out to dinner afterward and Edward admits to Bella that he followed her in order to continue to watch over and protect her. Bella responds by being pleased by this attention. She thinks to herself, "'I wondered if it should bother me that he was following me; instead I felt a strange surge of pleasure'" (p. 174). Similarly, in another scene in *Twilight,* Edward sneaks into Bella's bedroom and watches her sleep. When she first realizes that he has been watching her she says, "'You spied on me?' But somehow I couldn't infuse my voice with the proper outrage. I was flattered" (p. 292). She indicates her embarrassment but Edward begs her to not be upset. Ultimately Bella encourages the behavior, with it becoming a nightly ritual for Edward to spend the night in Bella's room. There are a number of different types of stalkers including rejected stalkers, resentful stalkers, predatory stalkers, intimacy seekers, and incompetent suitors (Mullen, Pathe, Purcell, & Stuart, 1999). Edward most likely could be considered an intimacy seeker as evidenced by the fact that he is described as being solitary and lonely, as are most of these types of stalkers, and as evidenced by the fact that these types of stalkers are in love with their victims and want to establish a relationship with them. Intimacy stalkers often view their victims as soul mates and as the *Twilight* stories are primarily about Bella and Edward's love, such a classification is reasonable.

In any case, these scenes are troubling because they again depict potentially dangerous, threatening behavior as being acceptable, reasonable, and pleasurable, as demonstrative of love. They normalize behaviors representative of stalking, portraying them as romantic instead of the dangerous, intimidating behaviors they are in real life. Consequently, readers can potentially interpret such images and such behaviors as appropriate and perhaps desirable, especially because Bella feels flattered by the attention and readily accepts and encourages it. But stalking behavior is not acceptable; it is not reasonable. Even Edward refers to himself as a peeping tom and is disgusted by his own behavior, according to Meyer's draft of *Midnight Sun*. But while Edward's intrusive behavior is romanticized and encouraged by Bella, in real life similar behavior would be considered frightening criminal activity. In fact, stalking victims are at risk for physical and psychological harm. Data from the National Center for Victims of Crime (2011) indicate that stalking is one of the risk factors for murder in an abusive relationship. Data likewise indicate that stalking victims experience violence at the hands of the stalker 40% of the time. Because of their fear, stalking victims are also likely to experience anxiety, insomnia, depression, and posttraumatic stress disorder (PTSD). In order to protect themselves, victims often move, change their day-to-day activities, install call blocking or caller ID, and change their e-mail address. In other cases victims attempt to secure restraining orders, which, although often helpful in restoring a sense of security to those victimized, can also sometimes be difficult to obtain and enforce (Keilitz, Hannaford, & Efkeman, 1997).

Summary and Implications

Both domestic violence and stalking behavior are crimes of power and control. While Edward is the prototypical hero in romance novels, what is often not considered is that this type of protagonist displays characteristics that typify domestic abusers and that domestic abuse typifies the patriarchy. Both Edward and Jacob claim to love Bella and attempt to protect her, but they also display characteristics that are paternalistic and controlling and engage in behaviors that are judged as abusive by many (Goodfriend, 2011; Saedi, 2011; Wilson, 2011b). Unfortunately, many readers do not recognize these behaviors as typical of an abusive relationship. Many ignore the negative qualities of these characters, focusing only on the qualities that they view as attractive or viewing the abusive behavior as a sign of affection (Housel, 2009; McClimans & Wisnewski, 2009). Fans of the series often excuse Edward's patriarchal and patronizing behavior, as does Bella herself, because Edward loves Bella so much. But excusing such behavior or ignoring it in similar real-life situations can be dangerous as abuse tends to escalate, and because many real-life abusers do actually justify their behavior as expressions of love (Center for Relationship Abuse Awareness, 2010a). Of additional concern is the fact that the *Twilight* stories—and other similar novels—normalize these abusive qualities and behaviors, implying that they are natural aspects of heterosexual romantic relationships, that they are acceptable and appropriate representations of the depth of a partner's love. But the behaviors discussed in this chapter are not typical of healthy romantic relationships: It is not normal to break into another person's bedroom to watch them sleep, to follow them to another city without their knowledge, to prevent them from seeing their friends, or to enlist the aid of family members to control the behavior of a partner. It is not normal to feel threatened by one's partner, to be physically restrained, or to find your car disabled in order to prevent travel. These behaviors should not be glorified as expressions of love. They are expressions of control, of the patriarchy.

Given that romance novels such as those of the *Twilight* series can potentially create confusion about what behaviors constitute domestic violence, it is vitally important that readers have an accurate awareness of the characteristics of abusive relationships. This is especially true considering that the *Twilight* novels are marketed toward teens and tweens. As such, it is likewise imperative that parents are aware of the signs of abusive relationships. In fact, one study found that 15% of teens have reported being hit, slapped, or pushed by their relationship partner (National Center for Victims of Crime, 2011). Consequently, parents must be more observant of their children's relationship experiences than Charlie was of Bella's and certainly they must be more supportive of their children than Charlie was of Bella when she told him of Jacob kissing her without her consent! Discussion with children on what constitutes inappropriate or abusive behavior is vital. Fortunately, many parents, mothers especially, have used the *Twilight* novels as a means for beginning discussions with their daughters about a variety of topics, including relationship violence (Leogrande, 2010). However, given the fact that so many other readers dismiss the negative aspects of Jacob's and Edward's behavior, it is likely that a significant number of other readers do not have accurate information on the warning signs of abusive relationships.

Breaking Up Is Hard to Do

As a romance novel, much of the appeal of the *Twilight* series revolves around the enduring love relationship between Edward and Bella. As an illustration, note the positive reactions to the bond between the two main characters that many readers surveyed expressed: One 20-year-old reader noted, "I absolutely adore their relationship." Another stated, "I am jealous, I would love to have what they have. It is a very strong bond between two people that are just drawn to one another." Still another noted that Edward's relationship with Bella is "… pure love. He just wants her to be happy." And yet another remarked about Edward, "I like that he is completely committed to protecting those he loves." As noted in an earlier chapter, such reactions are typical to female readers of romance novels who sometimes use these types of scripts to fulfill emotional needs as they identify with a female protagonist who is romantically pursued by the male main characters (Juhasz, 1988; Radway, 1991). Romance novels allow the reader to vicariously experience a love relationship that they covet, thus replacing one that might be less satisfactory or absent.

Alternately, a significant number of readers view the relationship between Bella and Edward as unhealthy. One 21-year-old female survey respondent describes Bella's relationship with Edward as "…weird. I think it's ridiculous how much she needs him." Another 25-year-old woman describes it as "…screwed up. They are addicted to each other. Their relationship is too dependent upon each other." And still another respondent described it as "unstable." As noted in an earlier chapter, these less positive interpretations of the relationship between Edward and Bella are consistent with feminist perspectives on romance novels. Sterk (1986), for example, discusses the dysfunctional characteristics of relationships typically depicted in romance novels as the characters progress through the stages of first meeting to their ultimate happily-ever-after commitment to each other. As an illustration, Sterk notes that romance novels portray storylines that suggest that traditional sex stereotypes, where the man is dominant and the woman ultimately submits to him, are common. They also tend to contribute to myths implying that there is one man who is the perfect soulmate for each woman, that love is necessary to complete or fulfill us, and that love is necessary to experience the greatest happiness available to us. Additionally, and more pertinent to this discussion, Clasen (2010) suggests that the *Twilight* novels, in particular, encourage four myths of romantic love including the notion that there is such a thing as love at first sight, that love lasts forever, that romantic love relationships are the most important of all relationships, and that if someone loves us s/he will be able to read our mind and know what we need-want-mean with little to no communication. These myths, like those noted by Sterk, depict love relationships in unrealistic ways, and although readers might under-stand that such relationships are fictitious, their depictions can still influence readers, creating dissatisfaction when their own relation-ships cannot measure up to these unreasonable and unreachable standards (Clasen, 2010).

As such, it is evident that there are again two divergent views, this time of Bella and Edward's relationship, but as their relationship is discussed from a psychological perspective in this chapter, the view that emerges is more consistent with the latter, that is, it is unhealthy. In fact, Bella herself describes her initial attraction to Edward as "pathetic" and "unhealthy," in *Twilight* (p. 74). As the relationship between the two *Twilight* lovers is examined, the work of Karen Horney, psychoanalyst and notable personality theorist, is used to understand this latter perspective. Karen Horney was one of the first to critique Freud's psychoanalytic theory from a feminist perspective, and she is also known for developing her own theory of personality development, the psychoanalytic social theory, which emphasizes the influence of culture and the social world on mental health and illness, in contrast to Freud's sexual emphasis (Horney, 1945). Additionally, later in the chapter, the behavior of Bella, especially, is further exam-ined from a psychological perspective by discussing the symptoms of both depression and posttraumatic stress disorder (PTSD). As will be demonstrated, Bella's behavior can be described as maladjusted on occasion because she shows symptoms of each of these disorders, but it should also be noted that Edward too shows signs of maladjustment, that is, the characteristics he shares with domestic abusers discussed in the last chapter.

Horney's Psychoanalytic Social Theory

The strength of Horney's theory can be found in her description of the neurotic personality. She suggested that neurotic conflict can be initiated at any age, but it is especially common for it to begin in childhood because children are not always given the warm, loving, disciplined environment they need in order to grow into well-adjusted adults (Horney, 1937, 1950). Parents, sometimes because of a lack of understanding about what appropriate parenting is, and sometimes because they have issues of their own, often raise their children in environments that are too lax in discipline or that seem hostile, and because of this, children sometimes grow up feeling insecure and unloved. Horney labeled these uncomfortable feelings basic anxiety. Basic anxiety can result in unhealthy modes of interacting with others and other maladjusted behaviors. Consider, for example, authoritarian parents, who are very strict and demanding (Baumrind, 1991). They expect to be obeyed without question. They are also very nonresponsive to their children, that is, they are not very emotionally supportive toward them and do not readily demonstrate affection. Children raised with this type of parenting tend to have lower self-esteem and higher levels of depression in comparison to children of other types of parents. They also tend to have poorer social skills. Conversely, indulgent parents (Baumrind, 1991) are very responsive (warm) toward their children but do not discipline them. Children raised with this type of parenting are more likely to be immature, demanding, and dependent. They are also more likely to display problematic behaviors such as underage drinking and drug use. Thus, in both cases, poor parenting is associated with maladjustment in later life, just as Horney suggested that basic anxiety results from a lack of a warm, loving parental environment and results in neuroses later in life.

Bella's experiences with her parents can certainly be qualified as less than ideal. In fact, she seems to be the parent in her relationships with both her mother and father, rather than the child. She describes her mother, Renée, as loving, erratic, and harebrained in *Twilight* and notes that she often took care of her mother instead of vice versa. For example, Bella thinks to herself, "I would have taken better care of her," referring to her mother as she compares her ability to do so to her stepfather's (*Eclipse*, p. 45). Likewise, she explains to Edward that "'someone has to be the adult'" (*Twilight*, p. 106) as she describes her relationship with Renée to him. As is noted in chapter 2 of *Twilight*, Bella also takes care of her father after she moves to Forks. She takes charge of the cooking and food shopping after she moves in with her father at the beginning of the series. She is also frequently described as cleaning the house and doing laundry. Charlie, her father, does take care of Bella in some ways: He provides for her as chief of police in Forks and he buys her a truck to get around in. In another scene he put chains on her truck tires on an icy day to ensure her safety. But Bella is described as taking care of Charlie much more frequently than vice versa. Additionally, while these behaviors indicate that Charlie loves Bella, Charlie is also described as emotionally unavailable. In *Breaking Dawn*, after Bella and Edward are married and they are about to leave on their honeymoon, Bella approaches Charlie to say good-bye. "It was hard to talk about love with Charlie—we were so much alike, always reverting to trivial things to avoid embarrassing emotional displays" (p. 73). Ultimately they do tell each other that they love one another but readers can see how difficult it is for them and the implication is that such displays of affection have not been typical. In real life this difficulty in expressing love, this emotional distance, can be confusing to children, especially early on in childhood (Horney, 1937, 1950). This, combined with the fact that Bella seems to take care of both her parents, most likely led to feelings of insecurity and anxiety, according to Horney. And one can see Bella's insecurities throughout the *Twilight* novels. For example, she thinks she is clumsy and unattractive, and she often worries that Edward will leave her. Because neurotics' early (parental) relationships leave them feeling insecure about being loved, they tend to overvalue love and employ mechanisms that protect them from feeling unloved, from basic anxiety (Horney, 1937). While there are a variety of mechanisms or coping strategies we can use to combat basic anxiety, the behavior of neurotics tends to be rigid; that is, they tend to use the same strategies over and over instead of using a variety of strategies (Horney, 1950). These repetitive strategies appear to fulfill specific needs, which Horney referred to as neurotic needs.

Neurotic Needs

Behaviors we use to fulfill neurotic needs can be thought of as strategies that maladjusted people use to deal with the feelings of being lonely and unloved. They develop and linger because of early childhood experiences, specifically relationships with parents. Horney suggested that there are ten neurotic needs, as listed in the following table. However, only the first two will be extensively discussed because they are most relevant to the discussion of Bella and Edward's relationship.

Table 2. Horney's 10 Neurotic Needs.

Horney's 10 Neurotic Needs
The need for affection and approval **The need for a partner** **The need for power** **The need to exploit others** **The need for social recognition** **The need for personal admiration** **The need for personal achievement** **The need for self-sufficiency and independence** **The need for perfection** **The need to restrict life practices to within narrow borders**

Source: K. Horney. (1950). Neurosis and human growth: The struggle toward self-realization. New York, NY: Norton.

The first neurotic need that can be discussed as relevant to understanding Edward and Bella's relationship is the need for affection and approval. According to Horney (1950) neurotics who display this need attempt to please everyone because they, like other neurotics, overvalue love. They want everyone to like them and approve of them, regardless of their relationship to them. Thus, they try to gain others' approval even if they have limited interactions with them. They also attempt to live up to other people's expectations of them, even if those expectations do not match their own desires. As such, this type of person is not very assertive; they dread any hostility displayed toward them. Such a strategy is employed to combat basic anxiety because neurotics are trying to obtain the love and approval they feel they did not get as children from their parents. Certainly, there are numerous examples of Bella's overemphasis on love throughout the *Twilight* series. For example, Bella notes, "Once you cared about a person, it was impossible to be logical about them anymore" (*New Moon*, p. 304). She further explains, "Love is irrational . . . The more you loved someone, the less sense anything made" (p. 340). Other evidence of Bella's overemphasis on love can be found in *New Moon* as Charlie is talking to Alice about Bella's (over) reaction to Edward leaving her. He tells her, "'It's not normal, Alice . . . Not normal at all. Not like someone . . . left her, but like someone died.'" As Bella overhears this conversation she thinks to herself, "It *was* like someone had died—like *I* had died. Because it had been more than just losing the truest of true loves, as if that were not enough to kill anyone" (p. 398). Each of these thoughts suggests untrue and unhealthy assumptions about love relationships and illustrates that Bella places too much importance on love and her relationship with Edward. That is not to say that love is unimportant. It certainly is, and other personality theories have noted love as a basic human need (e.g., Maslow, 1970), but in this case, Bella's overemphasis on the experience of a loving relationship eclipses (pun intended!) all other experiences to the point that nothing else matters. This exemplifies the prototypical neurotic need for affection and approval that Horney discussed. Thus, it is normal, healthy even, for someone to love another deeply and to miss them when they cannot see them or if the relationship ends, but it is completely different to become debilitated to the point of being incapable of functioning after a breakup as Bella did.

Neurotics displaying this need for affection and approval also usually display the neurotic need for a partner. Those who display this need are the type of person who can never be without a partner. They move from one relationship to the next, looking for a long-term relationship with someone they can love and who will love them and solve all problems, because they see love as being the answer to all problems. Once they form a relationship they cling to it and are desperate to maintain it because they are afraid of being alone and are overly concerned about being abandoned. Unfortunately, this neediness often drives their partners away. Bella's unhealthy obsession with and emotional dependence upon Edward is apparent throughout all the novels. She has trouble functioning when he is not around. In one scene, Bella experiences "desolation" when she finds out that Edward is not in the school cafeteria that day. She informs the reader,

> With dwindling hope, my eyes scoured the rest of the cafeteria, hoping to find him alone, waiting for me. The place was nearly filled . . . but there was no sign of Edward or any of his family. Desolation hit me with crippling strength. . . .The rest of the day passed slowly, dismally. (*Twilight*, pp. 145–146)

On another school day Bella seems choked up because she must leave Edward to attend gym class. She notes, "My goodbye stuck in my throat" (*Twilight*, p. 220). She also later notes that since she had "come to Forks, it really seemed like my life was *about* him" (*Twilight*, p. 251), referring to Edward. And after Edward leaves her in *New Moon* Jake finds Bella curled up in a ball on the beach because she's been thinking about Edward. She couldn't walk or breathe (*New Moon*, p. 351). Clearly these scenes are indicative of a neurotic need for a partner and of its related maladjustment.

Bella's desperation to continue her relationship with Edward, which exemplifies the clinginess that typifies the neurotic need for a partner, is also evident as she indicates that she would follow Edward around, no matter what his behavior toward her. To illustrate, after Edward abandons Bella in *New Moon*, she rushes to his rescue at the end of the novel. During this rescue she considers being changed into a vampire and thinks, "'...Edward could run after his distractions all he wanted, and I could follow'" (*New Moon*, p. 437). It is unclear what these distractions are but one interpretation is that Bella is referring to other women. Bella further notes that "it did not matter if he did not want" her, referring to Edward's perceived feelings toward herself. "I would never want anything but him, no matter how long I lived" (p. 451). Still later in the novel, Bella, unconvinced that Edward loves her, is happy on the way home from Volterra because she can have a few hours more with Edward even if he will leave her again as she thinks he will do. Bella describes the scene, "I wrapped my arms around his neck—what was the worst he could do? Just push me away—and hugged myself closer to him" (p. 488). In this last scene, her physical clinginess symbolizes her emotional clinginess, but even more illustrative of her neediness is the fact that after she "saves" Edward by making him aware that she is still alive, it is her turn to be in mortal danger from the Volturi—but Bella doesn't mind. She feels "well" because she is with Edward again. She is happy to be with him despite the fact that he left her and despite the fact that she could be killed momentarily. She thinks, "'... I knew we were both in mortal danger. Still, in that instant, I felt *well*. Whole'" (p. 452). Such sentiments certainly demonstrate the overemphasis of a need for a partner, as Bella's need to be with Edward takes precedence over the peril imposed by the Volturi.

Further evidence of Bella's instability is also found after Edward leaves her in *New Moon* when Bella only shows an interest in living after she hears Edward's hallucinatory voice, a voice that is heard when she engages in risky, potentially dangerous behaviors. Indeed, in order to hear his voice, Bella purposefully tries to trigger this hallucination by placing herself in danger. The voice seems to allow her some semblance of a continued relationship with Edward even though he is no longer present. Similarly, Bella's use of fantasy as a coping mechanism to contend with her feelings of being unloved and rejected by Edward at the end of the novel is additional evidence of maladjustment. It allows her to ignore her fear of being abandoned by him again. As she considers how much she loves Edward and the misconception that he does not love her at the end of *New Moon*, Bella *pretends* that he does indeed feel the same way about her. She notes,

"... it was easy to pretend that he felt the same way. So that's what I did. I pretended, to make the moment sweeter" (p. 489). She also explains,

> ...it was so easy to fantasize that he wanted me. . . . Maybe the time apart had been enough that I didn't bore him for the moment. But it didn't matter. I was so much happier pretending. (p. 490)

Clearly all these scenes illustrate Bella's unhealthy need for affection and for a partner. Her desperation to maintain her relationship with Edward comes through as she indicates that she would do anything in order to do so. She utilizes maladjusted coping mechanisms, including fantasy and hallucinations, in order to alleviate her own feelings of being unloved, to alleviate her own feelings of insecurity. While everyone utilizes similar mechanisms (excluding hallucinations) to combat feelings of insecurity and anxiety, what distinguishes adjustment from maladjustment is the fact that neurotics use these strategies more frequently and more consistently than well-adjusted individuals. Neurotics attempt to fulfill very few needs, utilizing limited strategies to do so, to make themselves feel better, to make themselves feel loved, whereas people who are well adjusted use a variety of strategies (to fulfill a variety of needs) to make themselves feel secure. And as one can see, Bella continuously tries to fulfill just two needs—the need for affection and the need for a partner—but rarely feels the need to employ other mechanisms to combat basic anxiety.

Neurotic Trends

Horney suggested that these ten neurotic needs could be grouped together into three neurotic trends: the trends of moving against people, moving away from people, and moving toward people (Horney, 1945). The trend of moving against people includes the needs for power, social recognition, personal admiration, personal achievement, and to exploit others. The type of person who exhibits this trend is also referred to as the aggressive personality. They tend to treat others with anger and hostility. They want others to admire them and so tend to be achievement driven, often putting on a façade of omnipotence. They also are quite selfish about meeting their own needs and desires, often at the expense of others, and would not hesitate to use others in order to get what they want. The trend of moving away from others includes the needs for self-sufficiency and perfection. The type of person who exhibits this trend is also referred to as the detached personality. They withdraw from others, preferring instead to be self-sufficient and independent as a way of protecting themselves from possibly being hurt by others. Consequently, they form a minimal number of relationships and are often solitary beings.

The last trend, which is the one most evident in the *Twilight* series, and which will be more extensively discussed here, is the trend of moving toward people. It includes the two needs described in detail earlier: the need for affection and approval and the need for a partner, as well as the need to be inconspicuous (that is, to restrict life practices to narrow borders). The type of person who exhibits this trend is also referred to as the compliant personality. S/he has a fear of abandonment and so repetitively seeks out new partners and desperately tries to hang on to these partners, often becoming very needy and clingy, as noted earlier about the neurotic need for a partner. S/he believes that love and a constant relationship are the answers to all life's problems. Clearly, Bella falls into this category as indicated by numerous examples whereby she demonstrates the need for love and the need for a partner. Bella herself notes that she has an "addiction" to Edward (*Twilight*, p. 292), illustrating the clinginess that typifies the trend of moving toward people. Additionally, Bella's fear of abandonment is also evident in *Twilight* where she has a dream in which Edward walks away from her and leaves her in "blackness." She describes the dream,

> That was the first night I dreamed of Edward Cullen . . . I couldn't see his face, just his back as he walked away from me, leaving me in the blackness. No matter how fast I ran, I couldn't catch up to him; no matter how loud I called, he never turned. (pp. 67–68).

This scene, which clearly suggests that Bella is concerned that Edward will leave her, takes place just after Edward saves Bella from being crushed by a vehicle in the school parking lot and even before a romantic relationship between the two starts. Fear of abandonment is further exemplified as Bella begins to hyperventilate when Edward is indifferent to her after Jasper attacks her at her birthday party at the Cullens in *New Moon*. She imagines running away with Edward and panics again when she sees him. She is described as anxious when she receives the silent treatment from him. When Edward does ultimately leave Bella in *New Moon*, she begs him not to go and, similar to her dream, walks after him as he walks away from her. She gets lost in the woods and falls into a stupor saying over and over again, "'He's gone'" (pp. 74–76). Bella doesn't even respond to others afterward, even when she is found and carried back home by a member of a search party. She is described as "lifeless" for four months. Even Charlie, her father, is aware that her behavior is not normal and suggests that she see a therapist and move back in with her mother (and away from Forks, where everything reminds her of Edward). Still later when Bella saves Edward from the Volturi and she is pretending that he loves her, even though she truly does not believe it, she describes being with Edward as "heaven—right smack in the middle of hell" (p. 491) because of her fear that Edward will abandon her again.

This trend of moving toward people is further demonstrated by the fact that after Edward breaks up with Bella in *New Moon*, she begins another relationship with Jacob even though she is still in love with Edward and has not recovered from their breakup. This is typical of the compliant personality because such a trend includes the neurotic need for a partner and so, often, this type of person moves on to new relationships after another has just recently ended. Similar to her behavior with Edward, Bella becomes excessively dependent on Jake. After Jake (as a werewolf) rescues Bella from Laurent, a vampire who was about to feed on (and kill) Bella, Jacob ends contact with her but she does not know the reason why. She misses Jake terribly. She keeps on calling him even though it is evident that he does not want contact with her.

I'd half expected him to call on Monday. ... I called him Tuesday, but no one answered. ... On Wednesday I called every half hour until after eleven at night, desperate to hear the warmth of Jacob's voice. (*New Moon*, p. 253)

Weeks later, Bella goes to La Push and waits in front of Jake's house for him. Bella herself notes her desperation to talk to Jake and to continue her relationship with him. In fact at one point, Bella herself notes that she "wasn't handling alone well" (p. 228) after this extended period of time with no contact from him. Such desperation exemplifies the neurotic need for a partner, the neurotic need for affection and the compliant personality. Additionally, and similar to the discussion about neurotic needs, we again see that Bella's behavior is rigid in the sense that she employs only one trend to alleviate her basic anxiety. She initiates another relationship (with Jacob) after the one with Edward ended, and then she becomes overly dependent on him, just as she did with Edward. While Bella utilizes just this one trend of moving toward people, well-adjusted people tend to employ all three trends and are, therefore, more flexible in the ways they alleviate their basic anxiety.

Depression

Other evidence of dysfunction in Edward and Bella's relationship, and in Bella's behavior in particular, comes from the fact that Bella also shows signs of clinical depression in the series, especially in *New Moon* after Edward leaves her. According to the National Institute of Mental Health (NIMH, 2010) clinical depression is a mood disorder that goes beyond the occasional feelings of sadness that we all experience. In contrast to everyday types of depression, clinical depression is much more severe and lasts for an extensive period of time. Clinical depression has a number of symptoms that go beyond feelings of intense sadness. Certainly there are emotional symptoms that include feelings of sadness, but additionally, someone with clinical depression can feel anxious, empty, hopeless, or pessimistic. Sometimes they feel worthless or helpless. Other symptoms are more behavioral in nature. For example, some victims of depression are irritable and restless while others experience fatigue and less energy that can include a loss of interest in activities that used to be viewed as pleasurable. This can result in insomnia or excessive sleeping, respectively. Still other symptoms are cognitive in nature. People who are depressed often have difficulty with concentration, remembering, and making decisions. They sometimes have thoughts of suicide and can make suicide attempts. Finally, some depressive symptoms are physical and can include body aches, headaches, and digestive difficulties. Changed eating habits are also typical in depression resulting in either overeating or loss of appetite and subsequent weight gain or weight loss.

Depressive symptoms in Bella are evident as Charlie explains to Alice what Bella was like after Edward left her in *New Moon*. He describes her as "catatonic" for the first week. "'I thought I was going to have to hospitalize her. She wouldn't eat or drink, she wouldn't move'" (p. 396). He further describes Bella's behavior after she started functioning again,

> "She went back to school and work, she ate and slept and did her homework. … But she was … empty. Her eyes were blank … she wouldn't listen to music anymore; … She didn't read; … She was alone all the time. … It was night of the living dead around here. I still hear her screaming in her sleep." (pp. 396–397)

In this description there are examples of a wide variety of depressive symptoms: Describing Bella as catatonic, empty, blank, and as the living dead are all examples of emotional symptoms of the disease. The fact that Bella would not eat is an example of a physical symptom. Bella's inability to move is indicative of reduced energy typical of behavioral symptoms of depression. Other behavioral symptoms include the fact that she lost interest in activities that she once enjoyed, such as music and reading. And certainly Bella shows suicidal indications even though those are not described here by Charlie. They are, however, found later in *New Moon* as Bella begins to engage in escalating risky behavior once she starts interacting with Jacob: She approaches men she hopes are dangerous. She learns to ride a motorcycle and goes too fast, crashing the bike and hurting herself in the process. And ultimately she tries to cliff dive and almost drowns. In contradiction, some readers view Bella's risky behavior as adventurous and evidence of Bella's feminist nature. For example, one survey respondent who agreed that Bella is a feminist explained why. "She's strong in the movie. Feminism is the power of women and she shows it, especially in the bike scene," referring to when she learns to ride a motorcycle in the *New Moon* movie. But if one looks deeper at her adventurous behaviors to deconstruct them from a psychological perspective, they are not adventurous. They are self-destructive and can even be viewed as suicidal, as further explained in the next section.

Self-Destructive Behavior

Further maladjustment in the *Twilight* characters can be found in their self-destructive behaviors, of which there are numerous instances, some indicating suicidal tendencies. As discussed, the first of Bella's self-destructive behaviors is found after Edward has left her in *New Moon*. When Bella begins to function again months after being abandoned, she goes to Port Angeles with Jessica, a girl in her class. As they are walking through town, Bella approaches strange men at a bar even though Jessica is resistant and discourages her, the implication being that these men might be dangerous, similar to those from which Edward rescued Bella in the previous novel. At this point she hears Edward's voice in her head admonishing her, "'Bella stop this right now!'" (p. 111). In fact, Bella is disappointed that these men were not the same as those who attacked her the year before. She notes, "They were probably nice guys. Safe. I lost interest" (p. 114). As an aside, it should be noted that psychologists usually interpret hearing voices as a sign of a mental disorder, for example, schizophrenia or delusional depression, which is more likely in this case. Such experiences as hearing voices are labeled as hallucinations, that is, bodily sensations that are also not real. Hallucinations can include hearing voices as noted but can also include seeing, smelling, or feelings things that are also not real (National Institute of Health, 2011). Nevertheless, what is most relevant to this discussion is that Bella wants to place herself in danger and is disappointed when she is unsuccessful in doing so. In fact, Jessica asks Bella if she is suicidal, "'Are you crazy?' she whispered. 'Are you suicidal?'" (p. 110). Bella says she is not but this is not necessarily true. As we all know, just because someone says something does not mean that what they say is true, and actions speak louder than words.

Additional evidence of self-destructive behavior can be found as Bella considers breaking her promise to Edward to stay safe in response to Edward being unable to keep his promise to her, that when he left her, it would be as though he had never existed. She looks for ways to purposefully be "reckless" (*New Moon*, p. 125). She thinks, "I wanted to be stupid and reckless, and I wanted to break promises" (p. 127). As also noted, her next potentially dangerous action is acquiring two motorcycles and using her college fund to restore them to working order. She approaches Jacob to help her repair them and they both hide the new acquisitions from their fathers. Later, after the bikes are in working order, Bella is terrified about riding one but is still determined to do so. When she does, she hears Edward's voice in her mind again telling her that she is being "reckless and childish and idiotic" (p. 184). Startled by the voice she stalls the bike, which falls on top of her. In response Bella attempts to ride the motorcycle again, at which point Edward's voice asks Bella whether she really does want to kill herself, just as Jessica did when Bella approached the strange men outside a bar. Bella, who ultimately hits a tree and injures herself, reacts with a smile to the voice's question about her suicidal tendencies. Whether this smile is an affirmation or not, Bella does note after her crash, "I'd take whatever pain … without complaint" (p. 193) as long as she could continue to hear Edward's voice.

In an ultimate example of self-destructive behavior Bella agrees to go cliff diving with Jacob in order to hallucinate Edward's voice again. Clearly she understands that her behavior is not healthy and admits that she is "'addicted to the sound of [her] delusions '" (*New Moon*, p. 352). Even earlier than this admission, Bella admits to Jacob that she is maladjusted, using the word "pathetic"and "messed up" to describe herself, as well as Jacob (p. 349). Her cliff diving behavior further confirms her dysfunction: Rather than waiting for Jacob, Bella dives off the highest cliff even though lower ones are available and she has never dived before. She knows that this is dangerous. "I knew that this was the stupidest, most reckless thing I had done yet. The thought made me smile. The pain was already easing, as if my body knew that Edward's voice was just seconds away" (pp. 357–358). Bella jumps, hits the water, and almost drowns. In fact, she would have drowned if Jake had not saved her at the last minute. Potentially drowning, however, did not disturb Bella. She notes that she did not mind dying because her last image was of Edward. She describes herself as "content" and doesn't even try to save herself. She thinks, "'Why would I fight [to live] when I was so happy where I was? ... Happiness. It made the whole dying thing pretty bearable'" (p. 361). Consequently we find a third character, this time Charlie, wondering whether Bella is suicidal. He asks Bella, if she was trying to kill herself when he later discusses this incident with her in *New Moon* (p. 544). Bella again denies it but there can be no doubt as to her intention.

Even outside these dramatic self-destructive episodes, there are other examples of suicidal tendencies in both Bella and Edward. Bella says to Edward, "'I'd rather die than be with anyone but you'" (*New Moon*, p. 45), and although Edward tells Bella that she is being melodramatic, Edward is also suicidal on occasion. For example, in *Twilight* Edward tells Bella that he would have killed himself if James had killed her. Similarly, at the end of *New Moon*, Edward is about to expose himself as a vampire in order to be punished by the Volturi because he believes that Bella is dead. He assumes his punishment will be his destruction. And in *Breaking Dawn* he discusses the possibility of Jake killing him if Bella dies during her pregnancy with Renesmee. Edward tells Jacob, "'The moment Bella's heart stops beating, I will be begging for you to kill me.'" Jacob replies, "'You won't have to beg long,'" to which Edward responds, "'I'm very much counting on that'" (pp. 183–184). Such scenes are disturbing because they romanticize suicide. They imply that it is acceptable to consider suicide if one's heart is broken, and this is troubling considering that these novels are primarily marketed toward young adults.

Posttraumatic Stress Disorder

Finally, evidence of other types of dysfunction in the *Twilight* saga can also be found again in Bella's reaction to Edward leaving her at the beginning of *New Moon*. Her behavior is reminiscent of symptoms of posttraumatic stress disorder (PTSD). PTSD is a type of anxiety disorder that occurs after the experience of a particularly traumatic event. According to the National Institute of Mental Health (2009) the symptoms of PTSD can fall into three categories: symptoms in which reexperiencing takes place, avoidance symptoms, and symptoms of hyperarousal. Symptoms of reexperiencing involve the reliving of the traumatic event. They include such experiences as flashbacks and nightmares. Often the nightmares can change in nature, initially starting out as a reliving of the event, then progressing toward a mastery of the event, and then an emotional coping with the event. For example, a soldier injured in battle who lost a number of friends in the fight might initially dream of the battle again and again. Then as healing begins s/he might dream about winning the battle and escaping unharmed and about her/his fellow soldiers surviving. Finally, as the coping progresses, her/his nightmares might be about emotional reactions to the battle experience. The second set of symptoms, avoidance symptoms, involves behaviors that help the victim avoid thinking about the traumatic experience. They include behaviors that help the victim to feel safe, such as avoiding anything that might trigger remembering the event. A rape victim, for example, might avoid crowds if she were gang raped. Emotional reactions to the traumatic event, such as feeling emotionally numb or depressed are also typical of these types of symptoms. Finally, symptoms of hyperarousal are those that indicate a heightened state of tension and agitation. People with PTSD often feel jumpy, on edge. They are often easily startled and sometimes have trouble sleeping.

Certainly Bella has numerous traumatic experiences throughout the *Twilight* saga. She is almost accidentally killed by a vehicle, accosted by would-be rapists, and hunted by a myriad of vampires. Interestingly, it isn't these experiences that seem to result in extensive trauma. Rather, it is her break up with Edward. As noted earlier in this chapter, this is typical of the trend of moving toward others (the compliant personality), which includes the need for affection and the need for a partner, according to Horney (1945). But her reaction to this breakup can also be explained through an examination of the symptoms of PTSD. While Bella does not exhibit all categories of symptoms typical of PTSD, she does show some in response to Edward ending their relationship. Her depressive symptoms and her inability to function after their breakup have already been discussed. Charlie describes her going through the motions of life—eating, going to school, and so forth—without any affect, which is typical of the emotional numbness that is representative of the avoidance symp-

toms of PTSD. Another symptom that Bella displays that is characteristic of PTSD is a repetitive nightmare, which is typical of the reexperiencing category of symptoms of this disorder. For example, in *New
Moon*, after Edward leaves her, Bella tells the reader that she has
recurring nightmares from which she awakes screaming. Relatedly,
the nature of Bella's nightmares change after Bella begins to spend
time with Jacob, a sign that she is healing. "I lay still in bed, and tried
to shake off the dream. There had been a small difference last night,
and I concentrated on that" (p. 151). The nature of the dream itself
might not seem like progress toward getting past the trauma of
Edward leaving her but the fact that the dream changed at all is
evidence of healing.

Summary

Fans of the romance genre often admire the relationships depicted in
such stories, and especially the relationship between Edward and
Bella in the *Twilight* novels. But while there are certainly agreeable
qualities to Edward and Bella's relationship, there are also dysfunctional characteristics to it. Consequently, it is important to recognize
that behavior that is often perceived as normal or even admirable by
some can actually be dysfunctional when examined from a psychological perspective. The romance genre often provides unrealistic and
unhealthy depictions of love relationships, and reading such novels—
or seeing such movies—can contribute to distorted opinions about
love relationships. As has been repeatedly noted, we learn through
social learning, that is, the observation of behavior in real-life experiences and also by scenarios depicted in novels, movies, and television
programs (Behm-Morawitz, et al., 2010). Furthermore, there is extensive research evidence that the media influences adolescent perceptions of heterosexual romantic interactions (Brown, et al., 2006;
Galician, 2004; L'Engle, et al., 2006). Although some readers, and
author Stephenie Meyer herself, dismiss the possibility that reading
novels such as *Twilight* can influence the thinking processes of readers
(Meyer, n.d.a), in this case about the characteristics of the ideal
romantic heterosexual relationship, Behm-Morawitz, et al. (2010)
indicate that there is evidence to suggest that the saga is doing just

that. They note a variety of popular merchandise slogans that represent views of fans, each of which imply that Edward (and sometimes Jacob) is the ideal mate. For example, note the slogans, "Edward ruined it for mortal men" and "Forget a prince on a horse. I want a vampire in a Volvo" (Click, et al., 2010, p. 138). Unfortunately, the *Twilight* novels depict Bella's obsession with Edward merely as a sign of the depth of her love for him. They imply that her depression is evidence of her heartbreak, and they misrepresent her self-destructive behaviors as indications of her sense of adventure. But as one looks past the surface of these behaviors, from a psychological perspective it is evident that none of these behaviors are examples of adjustment. Instead, they illustrate dysfunctional behavior. Accordingly, because tweens and teens are forming ideas about what behaviors are appropriate for romantic relationships through the use of symbolic models such as the characters in *Twilight*, and because adults can also come away from romance novels with inaccurate perceptions of healthy love relationships, it is important to separate the normal and healthy aspects of the relationship between Bella and Edward (and Jacob) from the dysfunctional aspects, that is, it is beneficial to distinguish between these features so as to eliminate confusion about the attributes of a healthy love relationship, and that is what is discussed in the next chapter.

CHAPTER EIGHT

Dr. Jekyll or Mr. Hyde?

As discussed in the last couple chapters, and as indicated by others (Behm-Morawitz, et al., 2010), there are discrepant views on whether Bella's relationships with Edward and Jacob are healthy. Some readers focus on what they see as idealized love, especially between Edward and Bella; others focus on the couple's less desirable characteristics. Certainly, there are elements of truth in both perspectives, but which perspective is better supported? This chapter continues to explore whether the relationships depicted in the *Twilight* novels are healthy ones, further deconstructing the characters' individual behaviors and their roles in the love triangle among Edward, Bella, and Jacob. Additionally, the fairy tale feature of the saga is examined in order to determine whether that aspect of the storyline and its related relationship implications represent well-adjusted or maladjusted relationship characteristics.

The Love Triangle

Edward: Loving Hero or Controlling Abuser?

Both Edward's positive and negative qualities have been extensively discussed throughout this book, and these qualities are briefly summarized and evaluated here. To review, note that Edward is affluent, well-educated, plays piano expertly, composes music, speaks numerous languages, and has a loving extended family who (for the most part) readily accepts Bella into it, all of which are admirable characteristics (Housel, 2009; Aubrey, Walus, & Click, 2010). Additionally, as has been noted and is obvious, Edward loves Bella deeply. Fans cheering on Team Edward are appreciative of the strong emotional bond between Bella and Edward, as well as his other just mentioned appealing qualities. This is evident from statements of respondents surveyed for *Deconstructing* Twilight: One survey respondent, for example, said that Edward's best qualities were "how loving he is." Another listed "thoughtful, protective" as Edward's best characteristics. Still another noted, "He treats Bella with respect." And yet another remarked about Edward, "He listens to Bella well when she is talking about her life, asks her questions." But Edward also has a darker side. On this negative side, there is plentiful evidence of his controlling, paternalistic nature (McClimans & Wisnewski, 2009). Recall, for example, that his initial treatment of Bella was inconsistent and often antagonistic and hostile, that he often physically restrained her, that he attempted to control which friends she could see, and that he often insulted and talked in condescending ways to her. Additionally, he often made decisions for Bella without consulting her, going so far as to suggest that she be shared between Jacob and himself so that Jacob could father her children instead of Edward in an effort to save her life during her dangerous pregnancy. As indicated earlier, especially in chapter 6, much of this conduct is consistent with the beginning of an abusive relationship (Goodfriend, 2011). Housel (2009) calls the relationship between Bella and Edward "toxic" (p. 184) and suggests that movies such as those of the *Twilight* saga encourage teens to perceive some abusive relationships as "good." But, as also discussed in chapter 6, these qualities and behaviors are often overlooked in favor of the more attractive qualities just mentioned. As likewise noted, ignoring negative qualities such as these in real life can, in some cases, result in increasingly abusive and dangerous relationships (Center for Relationship Abuse Awareness, 2010a). In a real-life relationship similar to that of Bella and Edward's, there would be no doubt that Edward's controlling and potentially abusive characteristics would tip the scale in favor of judging Bella and Edward's relationship as unhealthy. His negative qualities would clearly outweigh his positive because of their dangerous potential. In other words, while some negative qualities must be overlooked in any relationship, as we all have flaws, certain characteristics, such as paternalistic, patriarchal, and abusive tendencies, cannot be ignored. The depth of Edward's love cannot outweigh behavior that is potentially abusive. Given that some readers use Bella and Edward's relationship as a template for real-life relationships (Behm-Morawitz, et al., 2010; Goodfriend, 2011) it is vitally important that this real-life cautionary determination be kept in mind. Thus, although it is safe to answer that Edward is both a loving hero and a controlling abuser in response to the question that marks the beginning of this section, it is necessary to point out that while his positive qualities should be admired, readers must be even more mindful of his negative qualities.

Jacob: Best Friend or Manipulative Boyfriend?

Like Edward, Jacob also has both positive and negative qualities. On the positive side, Meyer (n.d.c) describes Jacob as sweet, and fans, consistent with the author, admire him because of his love for Bella, his fun-loving nature, his protectiveness toward Bella, and his loyalty. One survey respondent noted about Jacob, "No matter how much he gets hurt he keeps coming back—never gives up on love" and that "he is the type of guy I would date." Another wrote that he is "respectful to everyone." And another noted that, "He is very forgiving and is always there for Bella whenever she needs him..." Other characteristics of Jacob that were used to describe his positive qualities were kind and dependable. To illustrate these qualities, note that in *New Moon*, after Edward leaves Bella and she is barely able to function, that it is Jacob who befriends her and supports her while she heals. More specifically, in one scene Bella laughs after seeing Jake and his friends and is surprised by feeling good afterward because she had been so despondent since Edward left. She thinks to herself, "'I was laughing, actually laughing, and there wasn't even anyone watching. I felt so weightless'" (*New Moon*, p. 141), referring to the fact that she was displaying genuine happiness as opposed to artificial reproductions of emotions meant to fool family and friends. Later in *New Moon* Bella herself says she is much healthier around Jacob since Edward left her (emotionally devastated). In fact, she calls Jacob her "personal sun" (p. 198) and describes him as "a perpetually happy person, and he carried that happiness with him like an aura, sharing it with whoever was near him. Like an earthbound sun ... No wonder I was so eager to see him" (p. 145). Also consistent with survey respondents, Bella describes Jake as "'[s]omeone who knew the real me and accepted her. Even as a monster'" (*Breaking Dawn*, p. 459). Jake's other positive characteristics include his flexibility and concern for Bella. For example, Jacob's easy-going nature is found as he lets Bella decide what to do when they get together. Jake further shows his dependability and concern for Bella when he tells her, "'I wanted you to know that I'm always here. I won't ever let you down … you can always count on me'" (*New Moon*, p. 218).

But only focusing on the constructive aspects of this character, ignoring potentially maladaptive behavior, is not beneficial to the formation of healthy relationship scripts or schemas. While Jacob demonstrates love and support to Bella on numerous occasions, his manipulative and forceful behaviors should not be overlooked. Jacob attempts to control Bella's behavior (physically and otherwise) just as Edward does. Likewise, Jacob's behaviors do sometimes border on being abusive. As discussed, he shakes Bella in *Breaking Dawn* after becoming upset with her during a discussion about her upcoming honeymoon with Edward. And in *Eclipse*, Jacob kisses Bella forcefully even though she resists. Additionally, in *Eclipse*, Jacob manipulates Bella into kissing him by telling her that he won't try to get himself killed in the fight with the newborn vampires who are stalking Bella if she would indicate her attraction to him. Thus, Jacob is Bella's best friend, but he should also be considered a manipulative boyfriend. Just like Edward, he has a darker side as well as a lighter one. The question is, do Jacob's positive qualities outweigh his negative qualities, thereby providing a healthy well-adjusted relationship with Bella? Or are his forceful and manipulative behaviors serious enough to negate his positive characteristics and contribute to another dysfunctional relationship with Bella? As will be argued later in this chapter, Jacob's relationship with Bella should be considered unhealthy, despite his many positive, supportive qualities, because of both the way he treats her and the way Bella treats him. But before Bella's treatment of Jacob and Edward is considered, reasons for the popularity of both Edward's and Jacob's characters, despite their numerous flaws, must be examined.

Edward's and Jacob's Appeal

Although evidence supporting the idea that Jacob's and Edward's relationships with Bella are unhealthy is extensive, positive interpretations of Edward and Bella's love relationship are not completely unwarranted. One can see why some fans of the *Twilight* series are attracted to both male main characters, Edward and Jacob, if they focus solely on the positive qualities of the characters and overlook their darker characteristics. Both Edward and Jacob appear to love Bella deeply and are not afraid to openly express their love toward her. They are protective of her and seem to be genuinely interested in her and her life experiences. In fact, Susan Douglas (2010), in her book, *Enlightened Sexism*, found similar qualities to appeal to teens and young women generally, not just to readers of the *Twilight* series. That is, male protagonists in the popular media who demonstrated emotional availability, who did not objectify women, and who did not use women purely to satisfy their own sexual needs were found to be attractive to female viewers. Housel's (2009) assessment of why Edward is so appealing is also consistent with these characteristics. She suggests that Edward is the "quintessential female fantasy" (p. 187) who does not use Bella sexually, and who loves Bella for herself instead of her body. Similar arguments could be made for Jacob, who, even though he expresses sexual interest in Bella, seems to genuinely like to spend time with her, as evidenced by their engaging in platonic activities (working on their motorcycles, going to parties in La Push) (Housel, 2009). Certainly wanting to be valued for who we are, and not just for being able to fulfill our partner's sexual urges, is a reasonable relationship need, and it is an especially interesting perspective given the ubiquitous presence of sex in our society and the excessive objectification of women in the media. In real life women are still seen as sex objects and valued for their attractiveness (Douglas, 2010), but in many ways Edward and Jacob in the *Twilight* novels treat Bella in the opposite way to which young women are accustomed to being treated by men in real life (and in the media), that is, they don't want to use Bella for sexual gratification only. Edward, in particular, wants to marry her and commit to her! Perhaps this reflects the idea that young women are tired of being objectified, of being used sexually. Perhaps fans of the series are satisfying their need for a deeper, genuine love relationship where they are valued for who they are instead of what they look like (and instead of the sex they can offer) because, so often, this is not what they experience in real life. If so, it is troubling that many fans are treating the male characters, and the actors who portray them, in exactly the way they do not want to be treated, that is, many fans objectify the actors who portray the Edward and Jacob characters, as indicated by the number of scenes in which Jacob, especially, is shirtless in the movies!

Clearly this discussion indicates that the *Twilight* series fulfills emotional needs for readers as many romance novels do (Radway, 1991). However, although the romance genre has this beneficial quality, it should again be noted that such novels also have problematic characteristics; for example, they often portray sex-typed love relationships (Sterk, 1986). And in some cases these relationships are paternalistic or abusive, thereby potentially creating unhealthy relationship scripts for tween and teen readers who have little experience with romantic relationships. Additionally, they provide unreasonable standards for relationships, standards that place an enormous amount of pressure on men to fulfill all their female partner's needs. One can see this as Edward repeatedly explains that all he wants is to make Bella happy and fulfill all her desires. Even Jacob notices Edward's overindulgent treatment of Bella as he tells Edward, "'Usually, you just give her everything she wants.'" (*Breaking Dawn*, p. 434). Certainly the happiness of romantic partners is a legitimate concern, but this standard of conduct, that is, fulfilling your partner's desires, can be taken to an unfair extreme. To be more specific, concern for the happiness of a partner, putting his or her needs before one's own at least part of the time, is behavior that typifies healthy attachments, and this is true for both males and females. But when this behavior becomes extreme, when one partner is expected to fulfill all the needs of the other, often at the expense of fulfilling his or her own needs, such behavior becomes dysfunctional. Thus, from a psychological perspective, expecting partners to be considerate, to listen when we talk, and to love us deeply are all reasonable expectations, but we cannot be the center of another's universe such that we expect our partners to anticipate all our needs and fulfill every whim. Such behavior is not healthy for women or for men because it is inequitable. It typifies the neurotic needs described by Horney and discussed previously. In sum, although romance novels such as those of the *Twilight* saga do fulfill emotional needs in readers and provide them with enjoyment, they do so at a cost, that being potentially providing unhealthy relationship prototypes that either encourage paternalistic, patriarchal behavior or unreasonable expectations.

Bella: Selfless or Selfish?

The previous sections have examined Edward's and Jacob's treatment of Bella. In this section Bella's behavior is considered, that is, her treatment of her two love interests, in order to determine whether her relationships with Edward and Jacob are healthy or dysfunctional. Again there are discrepant views of Bella. On the one hand, an extensive number of readers feel favorably toward Bella's character. Many surveyed saw her as independent, caring, honest, faithful, and strong. One survey respondent said about Bella, for example, she is "nice to most people. Would do anything for someone she loves." Another said, "She is a very good friend and she is loyal." And still another said, "She cares about her family." Further, many perceive Bella as selfless, especially given the fact that she is willing to risk her life in order to save the life of a loved one. At the end of *Twilight*, for example, she rushes to her mother's aid, thinking that the vampire James is going to harm her, only to find that she has been deceived and that her mother is safely elsewhere. In *New Moon* she risks her life to rescue Edward from the Volturi. Less dramatically, at the beginning of the series, selflessness is displayed when she gives up living with her mother and goes to live with her father, in order to allow her mother freedom to travel with her new husband. But those surveyed also noted that Bella's worst qualities are her insecurity, her inability to make up her mind (presumably about choosing between Edward and Jacob), her neediness, and her obsession with relationships, among other traits. Furthermore, while Bella is perceived as selfless by many readers, when one examines her behavior at a deeper level, it is evident that she makes a large number of selfish choices also. For example, she manipulates Edward into staying with her when the rest of the Cullen clan and the werewolves are fighting Victoria's army of newborns in *Eclipse* because she cannot cope with the possibility that

Edward will be killed in the battle. She also completely abandons her friends after Edward's departure in *New Moon*, preferring instead to isolate herself in order to nurse her emotional wounds; she does not consider how her self-inflicted isolation affects her friends, or her father for that matter. Similarly, she does not consider her father's reaction to the dangerous, in some cases life-threatening, behaviors in which she engages, the purposes of which are to hear Edward's voice. She does not consider the devastation that Charlie (or her mother or Jacob) would have experienced if her suicidal cliff diving attempt had been successful. Even if Bella's inconsiderate treatment of her friends and family were to be disregarded as being due to her mental state, there are other numerous examples of her self-centeredness, such as her thoughtless treatment of Jacob: Bella treats Jacob in hurtful ways despite knowing that she is wounding him because she wants her relationship with him, as well as with Edward, to continue. This is true regardless of the fact that neither male partner is comfortable with the love triangle, preferring instead to be in a relationship with Bella exclusively. Some might question both Edward's and Jacob's preference for a monogamous relationship with Bella considering that Edward does offer to "share" Bella with Jacob if she aborts her life-threatening pregnancy, and considering that Jacob does ponder this and present the idea to Bella rather than reject it outright. But in both cases the consideration is due to the desire to save Bella's life and, for Edward, to provide her an opportunity to have other children who would not threaten her life. Ultimately, Bella rejects this offer, as it is as distasteful to her, as it is to both Edward and Jacob, and because she does not want just any child; she loves and wants the one she is pregnant with, her and Edward's half-human, half-vampire child.

Although, Bella does not use Jake for his reproductive abilities, she does use him in other ways, extracting numerous benefits from her friendship with him without thought as to determining or fulfilling his needs. Instead, she repetitively wounds him emotionally. To illustrate, recall that Bella heals emotionally when she renews her friendship with Jacob after Edward leaves her in *New Moon*. She knows she is much healthier after beginning to interact with him than in the previous months. Specifically she thinks to herself, "'I felt much, much healthier around Jacob'" (p. 159). But throughout the series Bella resists the idea of becoming romantically involved with Jacob despite the fact that he repeatedly approaches Bella with the idea of taking Edward's place in her affections, and despite the fact that Bella shows indications that she is interested in Jacob romantically. In fact, Myers (2009) notes that Bella abandons Jacob even after he showed her extensive kindness and love after Edward abandoned *her*. Bella thinks, "'How was I ever going to fight the blurring lines in our relationship when I enjoyed being with him so much'" (*New Moon*, p. 210), referring to Jacob. Despite her resistance to the idea of beginning a romantic relationship with Jacob, their relationship does deepen in *New Moon* to the point that Bella does consider moving on with her life, forgetting about Edward and beginning again with Jacob. But as her relationship with Jacob intensifies, it isn't Jacob that she thinks of. Instead, Bella considers her own feelings and *Edward's* imagined thoughts on the matter of her beginning a relationship with Jacob. She contemplates, "'Wouldn't Edward ... want me to be as happy as was possible. ... He wouldn't begrudge me this...'" (p. 376), illustrating concern for her own needs and for Edward's opinion rather than Jacob's feelings. Instead of considering the desires of Jacob, who has been supportive and sympathetic toward her, Bella deliberates whether Edward, who wounded her deeply and left her, would approve of her becoming romantically involved with someone else because it alleviates her guilt about not remaining faithful to Edward despite his departure. She concludes that Edward would want her to be happy and to begin a relationship with Jacob. She imagines Edward's reaction in order to give herself permission to finally move on with her life, which she has been unable to do until this point. But just as she is about to commit to beginning a relationship with Jacob, Alice shows up, and the chain of events resulting in Bella traveling to Italy to save Edward from the Volturi begins, thereby preventing the possibility of a relationship with Jacob.

It is certainly Bella's prerogative to begin or not begin a relationship with Jacob. However, what is significant here is that Bella sends Jacob contradictory messages, that she refuses to choose between Jacob and Edward for an extensive period of time, and that she only considers what she desires without consideration of what Jacob (and Edward) might need. Consider the mixed messages she sends to Jacob throughout the series. She indicates that she loves him but then repetitively rejects him: In *Twilight* she flirts with him in order to extract information about Edward from him. In *New Moon* she spends extensive periods of time with him, resulting in her emotional healing, and then suddenly leaves to rescue and resume her relationship with Edward. In *Eclipse* she kisses Jacob even though she is engaged to Edward. In *Breaking Dawn*, Bella tells Jake that she loves him, even though she is married and has a baby on the way and even though she knows he is in love with her (p. 197). Leah explicitly spells this rejection out to Jake as she tells him in *Breaking Dawn*, "'She has never been the one for you, she has never chosen you'" (p. 210). And it is evident that Bella's treatment of Jacob hurts him. In *Eclipse*, for example, when Jacob overhears that Bella has agreed to marry Edward, he howls in pain after having changed into his wolf form, again clearly demonstrating his desire for Bella and his disappointment at not being her choice. He says in *Breaking Dawn*, "...it would be better—not less painful, but healthier—for me if Bella left" (p. 288), as he considers suggesting to the Cullens to take Bella and run away from the potential Volturi threat. Bella repeatedly uses Jacob to fulfill her own needs but never considers Jacob's needs, that is, that she should either choose him over Edward or end her relationship with Jacob because ending the relationship would be less painful for him than dealing with the uncertainty of Bella's choice or her repeated rejection of him.

Similarly, consider how this behavior must make Edward feel: Bella kisses Jacob even though she is engaged to Edward, and Edward is aware of her behavior. In fact, in *Eclipse* Jacob asks Edward whether he is at least a little jealous of Jacob as Jacob warms Bella in the tent in which they spend the night before the attack of Victoria's newborn vampire army. Jacob asks, "'The jealousy . . . it *has* to be eating at you'" referring to Edward. Edward replies, "'Of course it is ... it's even worse when she's away from me, with you, and I can't see her'" (pp. 495–496 of *Eclipse*). Thus, Bella's inability to let Jacob go also causes Edward an extensive amount of pain, and although she is aware of this fact, she still continues her insensitive behavior.

Stephenie Meyer excuses Bella's behavior. She says that Bella would never have continued her relationship with Jacob if she had realized that she was in love with him. Meyer explains that Bella's tragic flaw is

> a lack of self-knowledge; she never would have pursued her friendship with Jacob if she had realized how much more than friendship it really was. You don't give up your friends when you fall in love; however, you do give up your other romantic interests. If Bella had understood herself better, she could have saved everyone a lot of heartbreak. (Meyer, n.d.f, para. 4)

But consider Bella's thoughts about her relationship with Jacob as they are returning from the movies in *New Moon*. Bella thinks, "It was so wrong to encourage Jacob. Pure selfishness" (p. 216). Even though she feels that she cannot start a relationship with Jacob because of residual feelings for Edward, she indicates, "Yet I knew I wouldn't send him away, regardless. I needed him too much, and I was selfish. Maybe I could make my side more clear, so that he would know to leave me" (p. 217). While Bella might not be aware that she was falling in love with Jacob, she clearly understands that Jacob is romantically interested in her and that it would be better for him if she did not continue her relationship with him. Nevertheless, she continues the relationship because it is what *she* wants and needs and she continues it knowing that to do so is selfish on her part.

While Bella does ultimately choose Edward over Jacob in the series, to the delight of some readers and the dismay of others (Housel, 2009), she does so after an extensive period of inconsistent behavior. Her indecision lasts through the first three books of the four-book series, resulting in emotional pain for both Edward and Jacob and further indicating her self-centeredness. Housel (2009) also discusses Bella's negative characteristics, her selfish choices especially, which she refers to as narcissism, suggesting that they are typical of many in "Generation Me" or "GenMe," those born during the 1970s through the 1990s, as Bella is, and who are unrepentantly concerned only with the self. Housel notes that Bella's self-centeredness is evident in her relationships with others and, therefore, indicative of their maladaptive qualities. For example, Housel notes that in ultimately choosing Edward in the saga, she does not consider her father's wishes, she ignores her mother's concern, and she pushes Jacob away after he helps her heal psychologically, when Edward returns to her after having deserted her earlier in *New Moon*. While all this is true, Bella did have to choose between Edward and Jacob at some point in the series. It is unfortunate that her family and friends did not agree with her choice, but what is of greater concern, especially to this discussion is that Bella sends Jacob contradictory messages, that she refuses to choose between Jacob and Edward for an extensive period of time, and that she only considers what she desires without consideration of what Jacob and Edward might need. Thus, although Bella does engage in some selfless acts, she also engages in many selfish behaviors, especially within the context of her romantic relationships with Edward and Jacob, and these behaviors indicate problematic relational patterns.

Additionally, although Bella's treatment of Jacob and Edward is troublesome, as discussed earlier, Jacob's and Edward's treatment of Bella are also problematic. Furthermore, Jacob's continued interest in Bella despite her repeated rejection of his romantic interest is indicative of maladjustment. Overdependence on a partner is not healthy in a relationship. This is certainly true of Bella's overdependence on Edward, as noted earlier, but it is likewise true about Jacob's desperate attempts to lure Bella away from Edward despite her repetitive rejection of him.

The Good, the Bad, and the Supernatural

To summarize then, the love triangle consists of Bella, who is overly dependent and in love with Edward and who also loves Jacob but treats him as a "second choice." It also consists of Edward, who is passionately in love with Bella and has some positive qualities, but who also tends to be very controlling and potentially abusive. And there is Jacob, who has some positive qualities but who also can be manipulative and forceful on occasion and who is in love with Bella despite the fact that she consistently chooses Edward over him. Finally, there is the competition for Bella between Edward and Jacob, during which Edward suggests sharing Bella between the two of them in order to make her happy and in order to keep her safe. Thus, even though many readers of the series interpret the love relationships in the stories as ideal, the aforementioned problems in the love triangle indicate that the relationships are dysfunctional. And this dysfunction is acknowledged by these very characters, as well as their family and friends, throughout the series: Edward refers to himself as a "sick masochistic lion" early in the series (*Twilight*, p. 274). Bella describes her initial attraction to Edward as "pathetic" and "unhealthy" (*Twilight*, p. 74). Jacob asks Bella in *New Moon*, "'We're a pretty messed-up pair, aren't we?'" (p. 349), to which Bella agrees, resulting in them comforting themselves with the knowledge that they "'at least have each other.'" Additionally, numerous friends and family members are concerned about Bella's mental health and potentially suicidal behavior, especially after Edward leaves her in *New Moon*. Given this acknowledgment by the characters themselves, and given the just discussed maladaptive behavior, it is especially troubling that there is evidence that the *Twilight* saga is affecting readers' relationship expectations (Behm-Morawitz, et al., 2010) because using these fictional relationships as standards to which relationships should aspire only encourages maladjustment.

Fairy Tales

The novels of the *Twilight* series are based upon classics in literature: *Twilight* is based on Jane Austen's *Pride and Prejudice*. *New Moon* is based on William Shakespeare's *Romeo and Juliet*. *Eclipse* is based on Emily Bronte's *Wuthering Heights*, and *Breaking Dawn* is based on two of Shakespeare's plays, *Merchant of Venice* and *A Midsummer Night's Dream* (Kirk, 2009). However, in addition to sharing characteristics of these classic pieces, the series also demonstrates qualities of other classic literature: fairy tales (Wilson, 2011a). In fact, some have described the series as a fairy tale for (young) adults (Buttsworth, 2010), and there is considerable support for this claim as there are numerous fairy tale references in the novels. For example, in *New Moon* after Bella prevents Edward from committing suicide because he thinks she is dead, Bella is happy to be with him despite all the pain he has caused her and despite the fact that she thinks it is only for a few short hours. Although this storyline is reminiscent of *Romeo and Juliet*, note that Bella says her reunion with Edward is like a "fairy tale" (p. 488). In fact, at the end of *New Moon* Bella notes, "The fairy tale was back on. Prince returned, bad spell broken" (p. 550). The fairy tale imagery and its subsequent implicit messages also continue in *Eclipse*, as Edward refers to Bella as "Sleeping Beauty" (p. 69). And in *Breaking Dawn* Bella describes the house she receives as a gift for her 19th birthday as "something from a fairy tale" (p. 479) and as a "miniature castle" (p. 480). Finally, and even more illustrative, the last chapter in the series is titled "The Happily Ever After" (p. 742). But it isn't just Bella that describes her life in fairy tale terms. Rosalie does also as she describes her story of becoming a vampire to Bella, whereby she was to marry the most eligible bachelor from the town in which she lived as a human. She says he "'...seemed to be everything *I'd* dreamed of. The fairy tale prince, come to make me a princess'" (*Eclipse*, p. 157). Given the numerous fairy tale references in the series, it is important to deconstruct both explicit and implicit messages found in fairy tale romance novels in order to determine the relationship expectations that can develop from them through the social learning process. As has been discussed throughout this book, the depiction of characters and relationships in novels, movies, and other media is of importance because those depictions allow for observational learning that influences the development of schemas and the construction of ideas about, and prototypes representing, what is thought to be appropriate behavior for men and women (Bussey & Bandura, 1999), in this case, when they are involved in relationships with each other. They help to determine relationship scripts.

One of the messages that can be implied from such fairy tale storylines is that some men fall into the Prince Charming category and others do not, with the additional insinuation being that it is preferable for women to marry a Prince Charming than an ordinary man. The above noted scenes clearly indicate that Bella thinks that Edward is her Prince Charming, but it is unclear what characteristics a man needs to possess in order to be considered royalty. Why is Edward Bella's prince but not Jacob? As discussed, they both share similar qualities that female fans find attractive: Both Edward and Jacob love Bella deeply. Both are attractive. Both are protective of, and rescue, Bella. Both possess supernatural powers, and ultimately readers determine that Bella is in love with both. But although they differ in a number of other characteristics, Edward and Jacob vary especially in one significant way: their financial portfolio. Some have suggested that the reason Edward ultimately becomes Bella's Prince Charming instead of Jacob is because Edward is affluent and better educated in comparison to Jacob (MacLean, 2012; Wilson, 2011a). Buttsworth (2010) in particular discusses the *Twilight* novels as adult fairy tales and compares Bella, whom she refers to as CinderBella, to other fairy tale princesses. She suggests the novels are so popular because they are fairy tales that depict the American dream of upward financial and social mobility. She notes that for women the American dream is often achieved through marriage, that is, women marry men who are affluent or who have the potential to become more affluent in time, which allows them to move up the socioeconomic ladder. While many fans would adamantly deny that Bella marries Edward for his money, given the arguments presented here and the comparison of Edward's and Jacob's behaviors, it is certainly a possibility, even if Bella is unaware of the reason behind her choice. As noted, Bella often lacks self-knowledge, as author, Stephenie Meyer indicates (Meyer, n.d.f). This possibility is further supported by the marital motivations indicated by other characters in the novels. Consider Rosalie's description of her Prince Charming whom, she reports, was the richest bachelor in her human town, thereby implying that money was a consideration for Rosalie's marital choice. Furthermore, acquiring economic stability through marriage is also typical of the female protagonists in romance novels generally (MacLean, 2012), a genre in which the *Twilight* series can certainly be classified. To illustrate, note Austen's *Pride and Prejudice*, on which *Twilight* is based: Elizabeth Bennet marries Darcy, who is clearly described as a wealthy man in this grandmother of romance novels, just as Bella marries into the affluent Cullen clan. Unfortunately this fairy tale emphasis on materialistic goals for girls and women does not necessarily result in the happily-ever-after that is also a focus of such stories: Rosalie was raped by her Prince Charming and his friends and left for dead. And in the real world, financial security does not necessarily mean that emotional needs are met. Similarly, this emphasis on affluence and materialism, as the female protagonist marries a wealthy prince in these fairy tale romances, is likewise problematic because it presents a sexual double standard whereby men provide the affluence and women aspire to that affluence through marriage. It supports the work-family dichotomy, encouraging women to become homemakers who are financially dependent upon their breadwinner Prince Charmings. As discussed extensively in chapter 4, readers are rarely provided role models that depict competent career women, and even less likely to be provided role models of competent career women who are also wives and mothers, that is, competent career women who have also found their Prince Charmings (Barner, 1999; Brown, 1998; Jennings, et al., 1980; Lauzen, et al., 2008). Instead of financially self-sufficient women, readers are presented with princesses—often in need of rescue—who happily agree to marry and be financially dependent upon their princes, and such implicit messages can potentially affect female adolescent career aspirations. While the explicit messages of fairy tales suggest that finding a prince will lead to happily-ever-after, their implicit message suggests that such happiness is achieved by becoming financially dependent upon that prince. In other words fairy tales can contribute to gender stereotypic roles for men and women. Furthermore, as also noted in chapter 4, it is difficult to grow, develop, and reach potential if one abandons his/her ambitions in order to live vicariously through a mate. Humanistic psychologists have long emphasized the achievement of purposeful and meaningful life ambitions, including careers, as means to mental health and happiness (Maslow, 1970; May, 1969, 1981; Rogers, 1959, 1961, 1980).

Beyond potentially affecting adolescent career aspirations and creating confusion about what qualities a man needs to possess in order to be considered Prince Charming, fairy tale themes are problematic because the qualities that are often associated with Prince Charming, such as physical attractiveness, financial security, and the ability to rescue damsels in distress, are often extraordinarily stringent and idealistic. Such depictions can leave the reader with a message that suggests that anything other than a love relationship with a larger-than-life, superhero Prince Charming is unfavorable and unwanted. The standards by which a man is judged an eligible suitor worthy of a woman's interest are demanding and unrealistic, and because of this men, in general, will have difficulty in meeting them. Even Jacob, who loves Bella, who rescues her from harm, who is attractive, and who has supernatural powers cannot be placed into this Prince Charming category! Consider Bella's mind frame as she contemplates kissing Jacob in *New Moon*. She compares him to Edward, thinking, "The prince was never coming back to kiss me awake from my enchanted sleep. I was not a princess, after all. So what was the fairy-tale protocol for *other* kisses? The mundane kind that didn't break any spells?" (p. 411). Bella thinks that kissing and starting a relationship with a man who is handsome, strong, and caring will be commonplace and disappointing because this particular man does not meet her standards for Prince Charming—whatever those might be! Stephenie Meyer suggests that Bella feels this way because she has only been in love one other time, with Edward, and that that experience is now her standard for judging other relationships. Meyer states,

> ...Bella does not fall in love with Jacob in *Eclipse*. Bella falls in love with Jacob in *New Moon*. I think it's easy to understand why this fact doesn't occur to her. Bella has only fallen in love one time, and it was a very sudden, dramatic, sweep-you-off-your-feet, change-your-world, magical, passionate, all-consuming thing (see: *Twilight*). Can you blame her for not recognizing a much more subtle kind of falling-in-love? (Meyer, n.d.f, para. 5)

But again consider that the *Twilight* series has been marketed as young adult novels and that, therefore, a significant portion, but not all, of its readership falls into the tween and teen age range. Consequently, a significant portion of its readership also has not had extensive dating experience and so can potentially use the romances depicted in the *Twilight* series as relationship scripts (Behm-Morawitz, et al., 2010). Unfortunately, one of the implicit messages in the stories is that anything less than the ideal relationship prototype that Bella has with Edward is "settling for second best." This is evident in merchandise slogans, such as "Edward ruined it for mortal men" written on them (Click, et al., 2010, p. 138). Consequently, real men, who cannot begin to measure up to these standards, will become frustrated trying, and women who are judging men by these standards will find those men lacking.

In sum, fairy tale themes can lead to inaccurate perceptions about what behaviors constitute healthy relationships. They can influence the construction of relationship ideals that can ultimately lead to disappointment because the standards by which a relationship is judged are so high, idealistic, and unrealistic. Such storylines not only imply that unhealthy standards should be used to determine the eligibility of a potential mate, they also suggest that girls and women need not aspire to financial independence because once they marry their prince, he will provide for them. Furthermore, simplistic depictions of fairy tale relationships in which a princess falls in love with a handsome prince (who has rescued her from peril) and then ultimately marries him and lives happily ever after are misleading. They do not allow for the complex understanding of adult romantic relationships that is necessary for the development of healthy love attachments. That is not to say that such stories should not be written and enjoyed, but it is necessary to be aware of the problems and misconceptions of the storylines, such as those of the *Twilight* series spelled out here because the *Twilight* saga does seem to be influencing readers' expectations about romantic relationship characteristics (Behm-Morawitz, et al., 2010), as does other media (Brown, et al., 2004; L'Engle, et al., 2006). Additionally, because fairy tale themes are so repetitive in romance novels and elsewhere (Buttsworth, 2010), it becomes difficult (although not impossible) to question that view of relationships and imagine a different one, as was similarly noted in an earlier chapter discussing repetitive damsel-in-distress themes. Consider similar fairy tale themes with which the public is bombarded from birth: Jasmine from *Aladdin*, Cinderella, Sleeping Beauty, Snow White, Rapunzel, Belle from *Beauty and the Beast*, and more adult versions of the theme such as that in the movie *Pretty Woman* (Buttsworth, 2010). Such repetition makes it difficult for young people to conceive of nontraditional, well-adjusted relationships because these storylines are sex-typed and often portray dysfunctional relationships. As such, these repetitive fairy tale themes can contribute to the development of maladaptive relationships and interfere with the development of well-adjusted relationships. Consequently, it is necessary to provide a variety of relationship scenarios that allow tweens and teens (and adults) enjoyment, as well as allow them to choose among a variety of relationship scripts.

Characteristics of Healthy Relationships

Thus far, the unhealthy aspects of the relationships portrayed in the *Twilight* series have been discussed, but what are the characteristics of healthy love relationships and how do the relationships in the *Twilight* saga hold up when examined from this perspective? While definitions of genuine love relationships vary, according to Erich Fromm (1981), notable psychologist whose writings on love are often quoted, genuine love relationships involve more than just an emotional attachment for another individual. They include a sense of responsibility for the partner, as well as respect for them and knowledge of them. Additionally, Fromm suggests that a healthy love relationship allows both partners to maintain their sense of individuality and uniqueness in the relationship. It could be argued that Edward and Jacob meet some of the criteria for a healthy love relationship according to Fromm's definition: They certainly love Bella deeply and both have a sense of responsibility for her safety and happiness. Likewise, they both do make an effort to get to know Bella on a personal level, as is exemplified by Edward asking her a multitude of questions about herself in the *Twilight* novel once they begin to build their relationship. But while some would argue that they also respect Bella, others could argue that they do not, considering Jacob's forceful and manipulative behaviors, and considering Edward's controlling behaviors, his lack of confidence in Bella's ability to take care of herself, and his belittling of her, all discussed in earlier chapters. More important, Bella especially, but Edward as well, have difficulty maintaining their individuality. A similar argument was made in chapter 7 as Horney's theory was discussed: It was noted that neediness, whereby a partner has difficulty functioning without the other, and the overvaluing of love are characteristics of dysfunctional love relationships (Horney, 1937, 1950). Such behaviors do not demonstrate that individuals love each other deeply and genuinely. Rather they demonstrate a codependence, and as demonstrated in the last chapter, such behaviors exemplify Bella's relationships with both Edward and Jacob.

In addition to Fromm's observations, mental health care professionals have noted other characteristics as indicative of healthy love relationships. Thus, psychologists and other researchers have studied relationships, gathering data on characteristics of happy, long-lasting relationships and found the characteristics noted in the accompanying topic box as being important to the maintenance of a well-adjusted love relationship (Allen, 2009). They include affection, respect, support, separate identities, good communication skills, equity, and trust and honesty. How do Bella's relationships with Edward and Jacob stand up when considering these relationship characteristics? Fromm's notions of affection, respect, support, and separate identities as characteristics of healthy love relationships have just been discussed, but what about the remainder of the listed characteristics, including good communication, trust and honesty, and equity?

As indicated, one of the features found to be indicative of a functional relationship is that both partners have good communication skills (Fincham, 2004). Again, like so many behaviors displayed by the primary characters in the *Twilight* series, there are inconsistent views

Table 3. Characteristics of a Healthy Relationship.

Characteristics of a Healthy Relationship	
Affection **Respect** **Support** **Separate Identities**	**Good Communication** **Fairness/Equality** **Trust/Honesty**

Source: Allen. (2009). University of Washington, Seattle Hall Health Primary Care Center.

on whether Bella, Edward, and Jacob can be considered good communicators. Bella and Edward's communication patterns, in particular, should specifically be examined because theirs is often considered an ideal relationship by fans, and upon inspection, it is evident that there are certainly scenes where Bella and Edward discuss their differences. For example, in the series, Bella discusses with Edward why she wants to be turned into a vampire, as well as her need to see Jacob. They also discuss sexual abstinence until marriage and their feelings about marriage in general, all indicators of good communication in their relationship. But there are also glaring gaps in communication: Edward repeatedly withholds information from Bella when he leaves her at the beginning of *New Moon*, and when he doesn't tell her that Victoria is hunting her in *Eclipse*. Withholding information, and poor communication in general, can contribute to conflict in relationships, as it sometimes does in Bella and Edward's relationship. But conflict can develop in even the healthiest of relationships, and, therefore, it is also important to note that good communication between partners also requires competence in conflict resolution, a skill that is also indicative of healthy relationships (Bradbury, Rogge, & Lawrence, 2001). To his credit, Edward's conflict resolution skills do develop and improve during the series, as he negotiates discrepancies between his and Bella's needs and desires. McClimans and Wisnewski (2009) note that although he is woefully unskilled initially in the series, Edward eventually learns to compromise with Bella. But while there is better communication toward the end of the series, Edward still tries to withhold information from Bella, for example, about Renesmee and the concern that because she is growing so rapidly she might die an at early age. He also does not tell her immediately that Jacob has imprinted upon Renesmee. In sum, then, although there are some indicators of adequate communication between Bella and Edward, there are numerous other indicators that Edward, especially, is lacking in these vital skills, and this deficiency contributes to dysfunction in the relationship.

Trust and honesty are also vital to healthy love relationships (Rempel, Ross, & Holmes, 2001). Unfortunately, although the relationships in the *Twilight* series are often perceived as healthy, there are numerous examples of dishonesty in the saga, many of which have already been discussed: Both Jacob and Edward withhold information from Bella, and both manipulate her on occasion. Edward does not tell Bella that Victoria is hunting her in *Eclipse*, and Jacob manipulates Bella into thinking that he will try to get himself killed in the fight with the newborn vampires in that same novel. Certainly Bella is also not completely honest with either of her love interests either. In *New Moon*, she never tells Jacob the reason she wants to engage in dangerous activities (her motorcycle riding and cliff diving) is because she wants to hear Edward's voice. Also, she kisses Jacob in

Eclipse when she is engaged to Edward. Thus, although the relationships depicted in *Twilight*, Edward and Bella's especially, are often interpreted as ideal, they are sadly lacking in honesty, a basic characteristic vital to relationship health.

Finally, equity and fairness are also characteristic of healthy relationships and, as noted in previous chapters, feminists have especially discussed equality as vital, noting that inequality represents dysfunction that can ultimately undermine relationships (McClimans & Wisnewski, 2009). Equality in relationships can be assessed in many ways. In earlier chapters the imbalance between Bella's damsel-in-distress role and Edward's rescuer role was explored. Bella commented on being uncomfortable with relationship disparity in her being repeatedly cast as "Lois Lane" and Edward being repeatedly cast as "Superman." In fact, as described in an earlier chapter, after Bella is changed into a vampire, when she feels powerful and, therefore, her relationship with Edward is more equitable, she expresses great joy in the feeling. Likewise, equal influence in the decision-making process can also be representative of healthy love relationships (Planned Parenthood, 2011), but Edward has a tendency to make the majority of the decisions for himself and Bella, especially at the beginning of their relationship. Given these considerations, it would be difficult to describe Edward and Bella's relationship as equitable, especially at the beginning of the series.

Although power in Edward and Bella's relationship is unbalanced throughout much of the series, with Edward possessing more than Bella, it should be noted that Bella frequently tries to assert herself in Edward's presence. Bella attempts to maintain control over her own body, repetitively asking Edward to change her into a vampire despite his resistance to do so. She struggles to maintain her relationship with Jacob despite Edward's attempts to prevent her from doing so. And she initiates sexual contact with Edward, originally resisting Edward's persistence that they marry first. Bella does ultimately become a vampire and does maintain her relationship with Jacob although she does ultimately come to agree with Edward's position that they marry before consummating their relationship. As such, her assertiveness sometimes pays off, and sometimes does not. Such efforts parallel those of many women, who, in real life, pursue gender equity only to have those efforts succeed in some cases and have them thwarted in others. Thus, in some ways, Bella's behavior can be viewed as illustrative of women's struggle for equality (Wilson, 2011a), and the fact that Bella becomes a supernatural hero at the end of the series can be viewed as a hopeful message for the women's movement that women will persevere. Nonetheless, Bella attempts to equalize her partnership with Edward while still engaging in traditional behaviors (marriage, motherhood), rather than nontraditional ones. While the series indicates that Bella desires equality, she does not take the steps that real women would need to take in order to equalize a romantic partnership in the human world (e.g., being less dependent on romantic partners, becoming career oriented).

Summary

In sum, although many fans of the series perceive the relationships in the *Twilight* novels as standards to which they should aspire and envy, it is evident that they also demonstrate numerous unhealthy qualities of which readers also need to be aware. While Bella does demonstrate deep affection for Edward and Jacob, and vice versa, her inconsistent and self-serving treatment of Jacob and her inability to fully commit to Edward does not conform to healthy relationship characteristics. Likewise, Edward's controlling and belittling treatment of Bella demonstrate maladaptive relationship patterns as do Jacob's forceful and manipulative behaviors. Although the main characters in the novels do demonstrate some behaviors indicative of genuine love relationships, such as affection, a sense of responsibility toward each other, and knowledge of their partners, their relationships do not allow for maintaining their individuality and do not always demonstrate good communication skills, equality, or honesty. Consequently, using these relationships as models for real-life relationships is not conducive to the development of healthy romantic attachments. Similarly, the *Twilight* saga's fairy tale theme can likewise create maladaptive relationship scripts, some of which encourage traditional gender roles, disproportionate interest in material possessions, and excessive relationship standards.

CHAPTER NINE

Integrating the Views

Discrepant Views on the *Twilight* Saga

Romance novels describe the development of passionate relationships, relating multiple obstacles to the maturation of love affairs on the road to happily-ever-after. As many literary analysts note, these types of novels seem to fulfill certain emotional needs in women who are the primary readers of this genre (Radway, 1991; MacLean, 2012). Feminist critics of the genre, however, often dismiss it as being patriarchal and sexist, noting that this type of novel often depicts men in dominant roles and women in ultimately submissive roles, although the female protagonist is often depicted as resisting the male protagonist's dominance (Sterk, 1986). Thus, although the romance genre is a favorite among millions, its depiction of traditional, if not sexist, gender roles is problematic because such depictions encourage the societal maintenance of these sex-typed roles through the process of social learning. Consequently, there are two sides to a debate revolving around the legitimacy of the romance genre, with both sides unable to see the validity of the other's views (Mann, 2009; Myers, 2009). The *Twilight* novels exemplify this debate; their storylines can be classified as belonging to the romance genre, specifically geared toward young adults (Martens, 2010; Granger, 2010; Meyer, n.d.a). Certainly, they are tremendously popular, having sold millions of books in a variety of languages in numerous countries, countless amounts of merchandise representing the characters and storylines, and a seemingly endless number of movie tickets, DVDs, and blue-ray discs from the associated movie franchise (Click, et al., 2010). But while the stories are well loved by millions, they are also routinely criticized for their sex-typed portrayals of the characters and the seemingly patriarchal relationship between Edward and

Bella and, less frequently, the relationship between Jacob and Bella (Housel, 2009; McClimans & Wisnewski, 2009; Wilson, 2011a). Just as is true of other romance novels, the main male characters are domineering (Sterk, 1986), and Bella, who occasionally attempts to resist their dominance, is ultimately portrayed as submissive until the very end of the saga. Consequently, Twihards, as fans of the series are called, promote it tirelessly, and the "haters" as Stephenie Meyer (n.d.a) calls those who are not positive in their evaluation of the stories (or the antifans as Sheffield & Merlo, 2010, call them), endlessly argue their problematic themes.

Explaining the Discrepant Views

Schemas

These two opposing views can be understood through the use of schemas. (See chapter 5 for additional discussion of schemas.) Recall that a schema is a lens through which we see the world. It is a hypothetical cognitive structure that we utilize in processing and understanding our experiences (Bartlett, 1932; Alba & Hasher, 1983). We all have a variety of schemas, some of which are similar to those of other people. However, even if two people use similar schemas to understand the world, chances are that they will not be identical, varying in their structure and components, and not everyone has the same schemas. For example, two people might have a schema for trees but the prototype that comes to mind for one person might be a maple tree and for another a white spruce. Similarly, one person might use gender schemas to understand the world but others might not (Bem, 1981). Recall again that someone who is gender schematic, typically a person who exhibits traditional sex-typed behavior, that is, a masculine male or a feminine female, sees the world through gender-related terms. They are likely to notice if a woman is dressed in a way that emphasizes the curves of her figure or if a man seems to be physically strong. Other people, who are not gender schematic, might not care about these characteristics, nor will they notice them because they are not relevant to whatever other schema they utilize to understand the world. It makes sense, then, that different people have different interpretations of the *Twilight* novels because different people have different schemas and utilize them to understand their experiences of reading these novels or seeing these movies. Thus, readers who see the books as typifying an ideal love relationship focus on different aspects of the stories than do those who see the stories as sex-typed and sexist because they are utilizing different schema to interpret the stories. Fans, for example, might focus on the love between Bella and Edward or the action between the vampires and werewolves. Critics might focus on the writing style or the traditional gender role depictions. In fact, there is some evidence that fans of the series focus on the story, whereas critics of the series focus on the characters who are often found to be unlikeable by nonfans, especially because of the traditional gender roles they depict (Ames, 2010). As such, Ames and Behm-Morawitz, et al. (2010) suggest that critics of the series cannot get past the traditional gender role depictions enough to enjoy the story. The gender roles are too distracting and troubling to them to be able to focus on the story in the novels. Consequently, the discrepancy in evaluating the *Twilight* series is dependent upon what aspect of the story a reader focuses on: character (Is Bella perceived as strong or weak? Is Edward perceived as protective or controlling? Is Jacob perceived as supportive or abusive?), storyline (Is the saga seen as a romance, a vampire story, or an action series?), or gender roles (Are the gender roles depicted perceived as traditional or nontraditional?). This schema explanation of the divergent views of the *Twilight* saga is consistent with findings from a study conducted by Behm-Morawitz, et al. (2010) who found that feminist identity and stage of life were important factors in determining interpretations of the saga. Specifically, these researchers found that readers who identified themselves as feminist were less immersed in the books and were less likely than other readers to desire a romantic relationship like that between Edward and Bella, presumably because they are "distracted by the conservative gender politics of the series" (p. 152). In other words, feminists in this study most likely used different schemas (gender schemas) to understand the series in comparison to those research participants who did not identify themselves as feminists.

Furthermore, the fact that some readers view the series as feminist while others see it as sex-typed can also be explained through the use of schemas. Readers embracing both views might have gender schemas, but the ideas of which those schemas consist are different, such as in the tree example. Additionally, recall that schemas influence what we notice, encode, and remember (Conway & Ross, 1984; Fiske, 1993; Wyer & Srull, 1994). We notice behaviors, events, and so forth that are consistent with our schemas, encode those experiences that are consistent with our schemas, and recall memories that are consistent with our schemas. It follows, then, that readers who interpret the series favorably do so because the schemas they utilize to interpret the works cause them to notice only the positive aspects of the characters and storylines and consequently those aspects of the stories are what is encoded into their memories and then later recalled. Likewise, those readers who view the series as sex-typed notice only those traditional aspects of the series and characters and encode that facet of the stories, subsequently only remembering that feature. Understanding these different views of the *Twilight* series through schemas is consistent with Wilson's (2011a) analysis of the novels, which suggests that they are written in an amenable way that allows for multiple interpretations.

Social Cognition

In addition to schema theory, psychology can further explain these discrepant views of the novels through the use of other concepts. For example, one of the areas of study in psychology is cognition, the study of how we think. Accordingly, examining cognitive processes allows for a better understanding of the development and maintenance of divergent thoughts on the *Twilight* series. One fact of cognition is that, at any one moment, we are bombarded with innumerable stimuli that we need to process. Think of the experience of walking down a street in a busy city like New York or Chicago. As you walk down the street you will need to understand which direction to walk in, but you will also need to process information about thousands of other pedestrians, as well as traffic lights and vehicular traffic. Additionally, you will be exposed to store windows with merchandise, countless advertisements, and noise from people, cars, radios, horns, and so on. That is a lot of stimuli to process! Consequently, we employ tactics that allow us to draw conclusions about this massive amount of data we need to process, without processing it all. In other words, we use shortcuts that help us to determine what information to pay attention to and process, and what information we should ignore. These tactics are referred to as heuristics and they are often used automatically, without us necessarily being aware that we are using them (Kahneman & Tversky, 1972, 1973, 1984; Nisbett & Ross, 1980). Stereotyping is a heuristic of sorts. When we draw conclusions about a person based upon what they look like or what clothing they are wearing, we are drawing those conclusions by processing a small amount of information about that person, that is, their appearance. Stereotypes allow us to draw conclusions about a person quickly without taking the effort needed to process multiple interactions with that person in order to determine their character. Regrettably, stereotypes are often negative and in many cases inaccurate. In fact, while heuristics, in general, are relatively accurate most of the time, that is, the conclusions we draw based on the small amount of information we process tend to be true (Kleinmuntz, 1985; Paquette & Kida, 1988; Nisbett & Ross, 1980), the repeated use of heuristics can result in cognitive errors (Arkes, 1991; Dawes, 1988). In other words, we sometimes draw inaccurate conclusions when we use these heuristics or cognitive shortcuts because our thinking process is faulty. These errors result in biases, such as prejudice and inaccurate preconceived ideas, or fallacies, such as myths and erroneous beliefs. These cognitive processes are examined more fully in the next section in order to further understand how differential perspectives on the *Twilight* series can develop.

Priming

One example that explains how our cognitive processes can explain the development of very different evaluations of the *Twilight* stories is priming. *Priming* is the process of having ideas planted in our minds that we then use at a later time to make decisions or process information (Higgins, Rhodes, & Jones, 1977). The prototypical example of this is medical student syndrome (Libby, 2003), which is the common phenomenon of medical students reading about symptoms associated with rare diseases and then believing that they have one of these diseases because they have similar symptoms, even though it is unlikely. Priming can occur for any number of reasons. It can result because of a discussion we had with someone, because of something we read, because of an advertisement we saw, or a newscast we heard. An example more pertinent to this discussion, and that demonstrates this, is when potential readers of the *Twilight* saga, who have not read the series at all, hear about it being sex-typed, sexist, and antifeminist. Then, when they read the novels for the first time, they are more likely to notice those aspects of the series, more so than if they had not heard those interpretations of the novels to begin with. Subsequently, they are also more likely to evaluate the novels as sexist. Similarly, if someone hears fans of the series sing its praises, those who read the novels for the first time are more likely to evaluate them positively. Consequently, different views of the series are, in part, determined by whom we interact with (fans or nonfans) and by our ideology (feminist or nonfeminist) and even our stage in life, as Behm-Morawitz, et al. (2010) found, because each of these factors determines what ideas we have been most recently exposed to and, therefore, primed to remember and use in cognitive processes.

Base Rate Fallacy

A second cognitive process that also allows for a better understanding of how readers develop their attitudes about the *Twilight* series is the base rate fallacy. The base rate fallacy is a matter of ignoring statistical evidence (Slovic, 2000). In our cognitive processing we tend to ignore statistical data, preferring instead to pay attention to salient examples to confirm our ideas and opinions. As an illustration, consider that there are some who choose not to pay attention to the data that suggests that smoking can contribute to heart and lung disease. The majority of people who smoke will later develop diseases such as lung cancer, emphysema, or heart disease (Centers for Disease Control and Prevention, 2011), but some still believe that smoking is not harmful to one's health because, for example, their uncle smoked two packs a day for 70 years and lived healthily into his 90s. Those that use these exceptions to the rule, these outstanding examples that are opposite to the majority of outcomes, are neglecting the data that suggests that this is unlikely. There will always be exceptions to the rule, but when people use these exceptions and neglect to pay attention to data in order to prove their points, they fall victim to this error in thinking, called the *base rate fallacy*.

The contrasting views regarding whether Bella and the *Twilight* novels are feminist in nature or not can be explained through the use of the base rate fallacy. In fact, this was already partially discussed in an earlier chapter when the process psychologists use to measure gender roles was explained, that is, through such scales as the Bem Sex Role Inventory (BSRI) (Bem, 1974). In order to determine gender role orientation with the BSRI, levels of both masculinity and femininity are measured. In order to qualify as feminine (or androgynous) a person needs to score high in femininity. It is not enough to act feminine only occasionally. Likewise, a person needs a certain amount of masculine traits to be considered masculine. In examining readers' perceptions of Bella, one can see that some pay attention to parts of the stories that suggest that Bella is a feminist (e.g., because she is instrumental in saving the Cullens at the end of the series) but then neglect the extensive data that suggests that there are far more scenes of Bella behaving traditionally than nontraditionally. Thus, these readers are paying attention to more prominent and noticeable aspects of the stories, whereas readers who see Bella as being traditional are paying attention to statistical evidence in order to draw their conclusions.

Confirmation Bias

Another example of illogical cognitive processes is confirmation bias, the process of seeking out examples or data that confirm our ideas (Snyder & Swann, 1978). In other words, we have a tendency to look for evidence that our conclusions or ideas are correct and we tend to ignore evidence contrary to our beliefs. Thus, if we belong to the Democratic (political) Party we might read articles in magazines that confirm our notions about how the government should be run. Similarly, if we are Tea Party followers we might watch news programs that affirm our ideas. With regards to the *Twilight* series this means that if we evaluate the series favorably, if, for example, we perceive Bella and the series as feminist in nature, we look for information that confirms that notion, such as discussing the books or movies with friends who also hold that view or by reading and posting to blogs that are consistent with that view. Similarly, if we have interpreted the stories as traditional and perhaps sexist, then we attempt to confirm those opinions by discussing them with others who hold the same opinions, and by reading articles, blogs, and so on that also confirm those opinions. Consequently, we surround ourselves with information that allows us to confirm our views, in this case about the saga, and in turn, does not allow us to consider alternate views. Similarly, because we tend to befriend individuals with attitudes similar to our own (Byrne, 1971), it is relatively easy to find support for our opinions.

Theory Perseverance

Similar to the concept of confirmation bias is theory perseverance. This is a cognitive error that allows us to continue holding opinions even though data contrary to those views has been presented (Gallup Poll Editors, 2002). In the case of the *Twilight* series, and as similarly noted in the discussion about how schemas affect our thinking, theory perseverance is demonstrated if someone evaluates the saga as being feminist and s/he continues to evaluate it as feminist, even if evidence opposing that view is presented to him/her. Similarly, if a reader views the series as sex-typed, theory perseverance is demonstrated if s/he continues to evaluate it as sex-typed, even if evidence suggesting that it is not is presented. It should be noted, however, that it is possible to change one's thinking once exposed to alternate views, but it is not as likely to happen as continuing to maintain one's original perspective.

In sum, there are discrepant views on the *Twilight* series because its readers have different thinking processes. Interpretation of the series as feminist or nonfeminist is determined by the schemas utilized to understand the world—and in this case the saga—by what ideas readers have been primed with, and by whether readers pay attention to statistical data about the behaviors depicted in the stories. Relatedly, whether readers' perceptions of the stories can be altered is determined by the extent to which they are influenced by the confirmation bias and the need to preserve their theories on the tales.

Integrating the Views

In addition to understanding why there has been such extensive and divisive debate about the *Twilight* saga, it is also important to note that neither side of the debate acknowledges that the key to resolving this difference of opinion comes from acknowledging the validity of each view. As in any argument or debate, each side has legitimate points but we often act as though only one side does. Thus, it is important for critics of the genre to acknowledge that many women—young and old—enjoy romance novels, the *Twilight* series in particular. Unfortunately, some critics of the series have dismissed the novels and movies without reading or seeing them. And some readers have dismissed the stories out of hand without presenting legitimate reasons for doing so. But it is important to acknowledge that these novels seem to fulfill certain psychological needs for many women. Dismissing the legitimacy of this experience is tantamount to dismissing a significant number of women's experiences as being illegitimate.

At the same time it is also important for fans of the genre to acknowledge that there are legitimate reasons for concern about such stories. Specifically, in the case of the *Twilight* series, even if readers enjoy the series it is vital for them to acknowledge that there is ample evidence of sex-typed and maladjusted behaviors portrayed by the characters, and that such portrayals are problematic from a social learning perspective because the traditional gender role depictions in the novels can influence the gender role development of the young adult market, for whom the books are written. Likewise, from a psychological perspective, depicting unhealthy behavior and relationships in a way that suggests that dysfunctional behaviors are normal and acceptable can create confusion about their appropriateness.

Just as it is unfortunate that critics have unjustly dismissed the series, it is also unfortunate that some fans of the series have suggested that criticism of it comes from a "rhetoric of superiority" (Click, et al., 2010; Sheffield & Merlo, 2010), implying that criticism against the series is unfounded. Certainly in the case of criticism that is baseless, this is true, that is, dismissing the series without having read the novels or without presenting grounds for the criticism is unwarranted. On the other hand, suggesting that all criticism of the series comes from a need to feel superior to fans of the series is also unwarranted, as is the suggestion that some readers of the series respond negatively to it because they don't understand the underlying meaning contained in the stories (Granger, 2010). Such suggestions are offensive to those who do not respond in the same way to the series as fans and comes from the same sense of superiority of which critics have been accused. That is, dismissing criticism of the series out of hand, without considering the criticism or the reasons for the criticism, is akin to dismissing the series without having read the novels. Surely such dismissal does not allow for the consideration of the legitimacy of the criticism. And there definitely are legitimate reasons for criticism of the series, many of which have been extensively explained and supported with research in *Deconstructing* Twilight. In conclusion, whether you are a fan of the series or not, it is hoped that *Deconstructing* Twilight has given you new ideas to think about and new perspectives on the series.

References

100 most popular baby names of 2010. (n.d.). *Babycenter*. Retrieved March 16, 2011, from http://www.babycenter.com/top-baby-names-2010

Adams, G., & Akbar, A. (2009, November 24). The world's richest bloody franchise. *The Independent*. Retrieved from http://www.independent.co.uk/arts-entertainment/books/features/twilight-the-worlds-richest-bloody-franchise-1826440.html

Adler, A. (1927). *Understanding human nature.* (W. B. Wolfe, Trans.). New York, NY: Fawcett. (Original work published 1921)

Adler, A. (1939). *Social interest.* New York, NY: Putnam.

Adler, A. (1964). *Social interest: A challenge to mankind.* New York, NY: Capricorn. (Original work published 1936)

Adler, A. (1972). *The neurotic constitution: Outline of a comparative individualistic psychology and psychotherapy.* (Bernard Gluek & John E. Lin., Trans.). Freeport, NY: Books for Libraries. (Original work published 1930)

Alba, J. W., & Hasher, L. (1983). Is memory schematic? *Psychological Bulletin, 93,* 203–231.

Allen, N. (2009). *Healthy vs. unhealthy relationships.* University of Washington, Seattle Hall Health Primary Care Center. Retrieved July 29, 2011, from http://depts.washington.edu/hhpccweb/article-detail.php?ArticleID=376&ClinicID=13

Ames, M. (2010). *Twilight* follows tradition: Analyzing "biting" critiques of vampire narratives for their portrayals of gender and sexuality. In M. A. Click, J. S. Aubrey, & E. Behm-Morawitz (Eds.), *Bitten by* Twilight: *Youth culture, media, & the vampire franchise* (pp. 37–53). New York, NY: Peter Lang.

APA Psychologically Healthy Workplace Program. (2011). *Work life balance.* Retrieved January 21, 2011, from http://www.phwa.org/resources/creatingahealthyworkplace/worklifebalance/

Arendell, T. (2000). Conceiving and investigating motherhood: The decade's scholarship. *Journal of Marriage and Family, 62,* 1192–1207.

Arkes, H. R. (1991). Costs and benefits of judgment errors: Implications for debiasing. *Psychological Bulletin, 110,* 486–498.

Ashcraft, D. M. (1998). Introduction to women's studies and feminist theories. In D. M. Ashcraft, (Ed.), *Women's work: A survey of scholarship by and about women* (pp. 1–17). Binghamton, NY: Haworth.

Atkin, C., & Miller, M. (1975, April). *The effects of television advertising on children: Experimental evidence.* Paper presented at the annual meeting of the International Communication Association, Chicago, IL.

Aubrey, J. S., Walus, S., & Click, M. A. (2010). *Twilight* and the production of the 21st century teen idol. In M. A. Click, J. S. Aubrey, & E. Behm-Morawitz (Eds.), *Bitten by* Twilight: *Youth culture, media, & the vampire franchise* (pp. 225–241). New York, NY: Peter Lang.

Bandura, A., Ross, D., & Ross, S. (1961). Transmission of aggression through imitation of aggressive models. *Journal of Abnormal and Social Psychology, 63,* 575–582.

Barner, M. R. (1999). Sex-role stereotyping in FCC-mandated children's educational television. *Journal of Broadcasting and Electronic Media, 43*(4), 551–564.

Barnett, R. C., & Hyde, J. S. (2001). Women, men, work and family: An expansionist theory. *American Psychologist, 56,* 781–796.

Bartlett, F. (1932). *Remembering: A study in experimental and social psychology.* Cambridge, England: Cambridge University Press.

Baumgardner, J., & Richards, A. (2000). *Manifesta: Young women, feminism and the future.* New York, NY: Farrar, Straus & Giroux.

Baumrind, D. (1991). The influence of parenting style on adolescent competence and substance use. *Journal of Early Adolescence, 11*(1), 56–95.

Behm-Morawitz, E., Click, M. A., & Aubrey, J. S. (2010). Relating to *Twilight*: Fans responses to love and romance in the vampire franchise. In M. A. Click, J. S. Aubrey, & E. Behm-Morawitz (Eds.), *Bitten by* Twilight: *Youth culture, media, & the vampire franchise* (pp. 137–154). New York, NY: Peter Lang.

Belkin, L. (2003, October 6). The opt-out revolution. *New York Times.* Retrieved from http://www.nytimes.com/2003/10/26/magazine/26WOMEN.html

Bellafante, G. (1998, June 29). Feminism: It's all about me! *Time.* Retrieved from http://www.time.com/time/printout/0,8816,988616,00.html

Bem, S. L. (1974). The measurement of psychological androgyny. *Journal of Consulting and Clinical Psychology, 42,* 155–162.

Bem, S. L. (1981). Gender schema theory: A cognitive account of sex-typing. *Psychological Review, 88,* 354–364.

Bergman, B., Ahmad, F., & Stewart, D. E. (2003). Physician health, stress and gender at a university hospital. *Journal of Psychosomatic Research, 54,* 171–178.

Bernstein, G., & Triger, Z. H. (2011). Overparenting. *UC Davis Law Review, 44*(4), 1221–1279. Retrieved from http://ssrn.com/abstract=1588246

Bly, L. (2010, June 29). Travelers enter the "Twilight" zone in Forks, Wash. *USA Today.* Retrieved from http://travel.usatoday.com/destinations/2010-06-24-forks-la-push-twilight-tourism_N.htm

Boston Women's Health Book Collective. (2005). *Our bodies, ourselves* (4th ed.). New York, NY: Touchstone.

Bradbury, T., Rogge, R., & Lawrence, E. (2001). Reconsidering the role of conflict in marriage. In A. Booth, A. C. Crouter, & M. Clements (Eds.), *Couples in conflict* (pp. 59–81). Mahwah, NJ: Erlbaum.

Bragg, H. L. (2003). *Child protection in families experiencing domestic violence.* Washington, DC: U.S. Department of Health and Human Services. Retrieved April 23, 2012, from

http://www.childwelfare.gov/pubs/usermanuals/domesticviolence/

Brescoll, V. L., & Uhlmann, E. L. (2005). Attitudes toward traditional and nontraditional parents. *Psychology of Women Quarterly, 29*, 436–445.

Brown, B. A. (1998). Gender stereotypes in advertising on children's television in the 1990's: A cross-national analysis. *Journal of Advertising, 27*(1), 83–96.

Brown, J. D., L'Engle, K. L., Pardun, C. J., Guo, G., Kenneavy, K., & Jackson, C. (2006). Sexy media matter: Exposure to sexual content in music, movies, television, and magazines predicts black and white adolescents' sexual behavior. *Pediatrics, 117*, 1018–1027.

Bushman, B. J., & Huesmann, L. R. (2001). Effects of televised violence on aggression. In D. G. Singer & J. L. Singer (Eds.), *Handbook of children and the media* (pp. 223–224). Thousand Oaks, CA: Sage.

Bussey, K., & Bandura, A. (1999). Social cognitive theory of gender development and differentiation. *Psychological Review, 106*, 676–713.

Bustillos, M. (2012). Romance novels: The last great bastion of underground writing. *The Awl*. Retrieved February 21, 2012, from

http://theawl.com/2012/02/romance-novels

Buttsworth, S. (2010). CinderBella: *Twilight*, fairy tales, and the twenty-first century American dream. In N. R. Reagin (Ed.), Twilight *and history* (pp. 47–69). Hoboken, NJ: Wiley.

Byrne, D. (1971). *The attraction paradigm*. New York, NY: Academic.

Caplan, P. J. (2000). *The new don't blame mother: Mending the mother-daughter relationship*. New York, NY: Routledge.

Casad, B. J. (2008). Issue and trends in work-family integration. In A. Marcus-Newhall, D. R. Halpern, & S. J. Tan (Eds.), *The changing realities of work and family: A multidisciplinary approach* (pp. 277–292). Malden, MA: Blackwell.

Cawthorne, A. (2008, October). *The straight facts on women in poverty*. Washington, DC: Center for American Progress.

Ceballo, R., Lansford, J. E., Abbey, A., & Stewart, A. J. (2004). Gaining a child: Comparing the experiences of biological parents, adoptive parents, and stepparents. *Family Relations, 53*, 38–48.

Center for Relationship Abuse Awareness. (2010a). *What is relationship abuse?* Retrieved August 22, 2011, from

http://stoprelationshipabuse.org/educated/what-is-relationship-abus/

Center for Relationship Abuse Awareness. (2010b). *Warning signs of abuse*. Retrieved August 22, 2011, from

http://stoprelationshipabuse.org/educated/warning-signs-of-abuse/

Center for Relationship Abuse Awareness. (2010c). *Barriers to leaving an abusive relationship*. Retrieved April 25, 2012, from

http://stoprelationshipabuse.org/educated/barriers-to-leaving-an-abusive-relationship/

Centers for Disease Control and Prevention. (2011, March). *Health effects of smoking*. Retrieved August 23, 2011, from

http://www.cdc.gov/tobacco/data_statistics/fact_sheets/health_effects/effects_cig_smoking/

Clasen, T. (2010). Taking a bite out of love: The myth of romantic love in the *Twilight* series. In M. A. Click, J. S. Aubrey, & E. Behm-Morawitz (Eds.), *Bitten by* Twilight: *Youth culture, media, & the vampire franchise* (pp. 119–134). New York, NY: Peter Lang.

Click, M. A., Aubrey, J. S., & Behm-Morawitz, E. (2010). Introduction. In M. A. Click, J. S. Aubrey, & E. Behm-Morawitz (Eds.), *Bitten by* Twilight: *Youth culture, media, & the vampire franchise* (pp. 1–17). New York, NY: Peter Lang.

Cohen, S. (2011, September 15). Mother of all museums. *New York Post*. Retrieved from
http://www.nypost/p/entertainment/mother_of_all_museums_5VxRDcFsy68g
ADBdn7p7YP/0

Conway, M., & Ross, M. (1984). Getting what you want by revising what you had. *Journal of Personality and Social Psychology, 47*, 738–748.

Costain, A. N. (2003). Paving the way: The work of the women's movement. In R. P. Watson & A. Gordon (Eds.), *Anticipating madame president*. Boulder, CO: Lynn Rienner.

Crosby, F. J., & Sabattini, L. (2006). Family and work balance. In J. Worell & C. D. Goodheart (Eds.), *Handbook of girls' and women's psychological health: Gender and well-being across the life span* (pp. 350–358). New York, NY: Oxford University Press.

Cuddy, A. J. C., Fiske, S. T., & Glick, P. (2004). When professionals become mothers, warmth doesn't cut the ice. *Journal of Social Issues, 60*(4), 701–718.

Cusk, R. (2002). *A life's work: On becoming a mother*. New York, NY: Picador.

D'Arcy, J. (2011, September 6). D. C. parents choosing to home-school their children. *Washington Post*. Retrieved from
http://www.washingtonpost.com/lifestyle/dc-parents-choosing-to-home-school-their-children/2011/08/24/gIQAwIFi7J_story.html

Darley, J. M., & Latané, B. (1968). Bystander intervention in emergencies: Diffusion of responsibility. *Journal of Personality and Social Psychology, 8*, 377–383.

Dawes, R. M. (1988). *Rational choice in an uncertain world*. San Diego, CA: Harcourt Brace Jovanovich.

de las Fuentes, C., Baron, A., & Vasquez, M. J. (2003). Teaching Latino psychology. In P. Bronstein & K. Quina (Eds.), *Teaching gender and multicultural awareness* (pp. 207–220). Washington, DC: American Psychological Association.

Diekman, A. B., & Murnen, S. K. (2004). Learning to be little women and little men: The inequitable gender equality of nonsexist children's literature. *Sex Roles, 50*, 373–385.

Dixon, J. (1999). *The romantic fiction of Mills & Boon: 1909–90s*. London: Routledge.

Douglas, S. (2010). *Enlightened sexism: The seductive message that feminism's work is done*. New York, NY: Henry Holt.

Douglas, S., & Michaels, M. (2004). *The mommy myth: The idealization of motherhood and how it has undermined all women*. New York, NY: Free Press.

Dvorak, P. (2012, March 4). All the ways to abuse women. *Pittsburgh Post Gazette*, B1, B4.

Ekman, P., & Friesen, W. V. (1974). Detecting deception from the body or face. *Journal for Personality and Social Psychology, 29,* 288–298.

Erikson, E. H. (1950). *Childhood and society.* New York, NY: Norton.

Erikson, E. (1968). *Identity, youth and crisis.* New York, NY: Norton.

Etaugh, C. (1993). Women in the middle and later years. In F. Denmark & M. Paludi (Eds.), *Psychology of women: A handbook of issues and theories* (pp. 213–246). Westport, CT: Greenwood Press.

Evans, J. (1995). *Feminist theory today: An introduction to second-wave feminism.* London: Sage.

Ex, C., & Janssens, J. (2000). Young females' images of motherhood. *Sex Roles, 43,* 865–890.

Faludi, S. (1991). *Backlash: The undeclared war against American women.* New York, NY: Anchor.

Feeny, J. A., Hohaus, L., Noller, P., & Alexander, R. P. (2001). *Becoming parents: Exploring the bonds between mothers, fathers, and their infants.* New York, NY: Cambridge University Press.

Felker-Jones, B. (2009). *Touched by a vampire: Discovering the hidden messages in the* Twilight *saga.* Colorado Springs, CO: Multnomah.

Fincham, F. D. (2004). Communication in marriage. In A. L. Vangelisti (Ed.), *Handbook of family communication* (pp. 83–103). Mahwah, NJ: Erlbaum.

Firestone, S. (1993). The case for feminist revolution. In A. Minas (Ed.), *Gender basics: Feminist perspectives on men and women* (pp. 285–290). Belmont, CA: Wadsworth.

Fiske, S. T. (1993). Social cognition and social perception. In L. W. Porter & M. R. Rosenzweig (Eds.), *Annual review of psychology* (Vol. 44, pp. 155–194). Palo Alto, CA: Annual Reviews.

Fleming, A. S., Berry, M. F., Horn, S., Ramirez, B. C., Ruckelshaus, J. S., & Saltzman, M. (1982, January). *Under the rule of thumb: Battered women and the administration of justice. A Report of the United States Commission on Civil rights.* Washington, DC: U.S. Commission on Civil Rights.

Fokkema, T. (2002). Combining a job and children: Contrasting the health of married and divorced women in the Netherlands. *Social Science and Medicine, 54,* 741–752.

Freud, S. (1963). Introductory lectures on psychoanalysis. In J. Strachey (Ed. & Trans.), *The standard edition of the complete psychological works of Sigmund Freud* (Vols. 15 & 16). London: Hogarth Press.

Friedan, B. (1963). *The feminine mystique.* New York, NY: W. W. Norton.

Fromm, E. (1955). *The sane society.* New York, NY: Rinehart.

Fromm, E. (1981). *On disobedience and other essays.* New York, NY: Seabury.

Fuligni, A. S., & Brooks-Gunn, J. (2002). Meeting the challenges of new parenthood: Responsibilities, advice, and perceptions. In N. Halfon, K. T. McLearn, & M. A. Schuster (Eds.), *Childrearing in America: Challenges facing parents with young children* (pp. 83–116). New York, NY: Cambridge University Press.

Gager, C. T., McLanahan, S. S., & Glei, D. A. (2002). Preparing for parenthood: Who's ready, who's not? In N. Halfon, K. T. McLearn, & M. A. Schuster (Eds.), *Childrearing in America: Challenges facing parents with young children* (pp. 50–80). New York, NY: Cambridge University Press.

Galician, M. (2004). *Sex, love and romance in the mass media*. Mahwah, NJ: Erlbaum.

Gallup Poll Editors. (2002). *Gallup Poll of the Islamic world: Subscriber report*. Princeton, NJ: Gallup.

Ganong, L. H., & Coleman, M. (1995). The content of mother stereotypes. *Sex Roles, 32*, 495–512.

Geis, F. L., Brown, V., Jennings, J., & Porter, N. (1984). TV commercials as achievement scripts for women. *Sex Roles, 10*, 513–525.

Gibbs, N. (2009, November 20). The growing backlash against overparenting. *Time Magazine*. Retrieved from

http://www.time.com/time/magazine/article/0,9171,1940697,00.html

Glass von der Osten, K. (2010). Like other American families, only not: The Cullens and the "ideal" family in American history. In N. R. Reagin (Ed.), Twilight *and history* (pp. 182–203). Hoboken, NJ: Wiley.

Glick, P., & Fiske, S. T. (1996). The ambivalent sexism inventory: Differentiating hostile and benevolent sexism. *Journal of Personality and Social Psychology, 23*, 1323–1334.

Glick, P., & Fiske, S. T. (1997). Hostile and benevolent sexism: Measuring ambivalent sexist attitudes toward women. *Psychology of Women Quarterly, 21*, 119–135.

Glick, P., & Fiske, S. T. (2001). An ambivalent alliance: Hostile and benevolent sexism as complementary justifications of gender inequality. *American Psychologist, 56*, 109–118.

Goldner, M. (1994). *Accounting for race and class variation in the disjuncture between feminist identity and feminist beliefs: The place of negative labels and social movements*. Paper presented at the annual meeting of the American Sociological Association, Los Angeles, CA.

Goodfriend, W. (2011, November). Relationship violence in *Twilight*. *Psychology Today*. Retrieved from: http://www.psychologytoday.com/blog/the-psychology-movies/201111/relationship-violence-in-twilight

Granger, J. (2010). *Spotlight: A close-up look at the artistry and meaning of Stephenie Meyer's* Twilight *saga*. Allentown, PA: Zossima.

Gravett, S. L. (2010). *From* Twilight *to* Breaking Dawn: *Religious themes in the* Twilight *saga*. St. Louis, MO: Chalice.

Harpaz, B. J. (2012, May 10). *Time* cover shows mom breastfeeding 3-year-old. *ABC News*. Retrieved from http://abcnews.go.com/Health/wireStory/time-cover-shows-mom-breastfeeding-year-16322651

Harris, R. J., & Barlett, C. P. (2009). Effects of sex in the media. In J. Bryant & M. B. Oliver (Eds.), *Media effects: Advances in theory and research* (3rd. ed., pp. 304–324). New York, NY: Routledge.

Hastorf, A., & Cantril, H. (1954). They saw a game: A case study. *Journal of Abnormal and Social Psychology, 49*, 129–134.

Hays, S. (1996). *The cultural contradictions of motherhood*. New Haven, CT: Yale University.

Heymann, J., Earle, A., & Hayes, J. (2007). *The work, family, and equity index: How does the United States measure up?* Boston: The Institute for Health and Social Policy. Retrieved January 10, 2011, from www.mcgill.ca/files/ihsp/WFEIFinal2007.pdf

Higgins, E. T., Rhodes, C. R., & Jones, C. R. (1977). Category accessibility and impression formation. *Journal of Experimental Social Psychology, 13*, 141–154.

Hofer, B. K., & Moore, A. S. (2010). *The iConnected parent: Staying close to your kids in college (and beyond) while letting them grow up*. New York, NY: Free Press.

Hoffnung, M. (1995). Motherhood: Contemporary conflict for women. In J. Freeman (Ed.), *Women: A feminist perspective* (pp. 162–181). Mountain View, CA: Mayfield.

Horney, K. (1937). *The neurotic personality of our times*. New York, NY: Norton.

Horney, K. (1945). *Our inner conflicts: A constructive theory of neurosis*. New York, NY: Norton.

Horney, K. (1950). *Neurosis and human growth: The struggle toward self-realization*. New York, NY: Norton.

Housel, R. (2009). The "real" danger: Fact vs. fiction for the girl audience. In R. Housel & J. J. Wisnewski (Eds.), Twilight *and philosophy: Vampires, vegetarians, and the pursuit of immortality* (pp. 177–190). Hoboken, NJ: Wiley Blackwell.

Housel, R., & Wisnewski, J. J. (Eds.). (2009). Twilight *and philosophy: Vampires, vegetarians, and the pursuit of immortality*. Hoboken, NJ: Wiley Blackwell.

Hurtado, A. (2003). *Voicing Chicana feminisms: Young women speak out on sexuality and identity*. New York, NY: New York University Press.

Huston, T. L., & Holmes, E. K. (2004). Becoming parents. In A. L. Vengelisti (Ed.), *Handbook of family communication* (pp. 105–133). Mahwah, NJ: Erlbaum.

Hyde, J. S. (2007). *Half the human experience: The psychology of women*. New York, NY: Houghton Mifflin.

I put glitter on my boyfriend so he sparkles like Edward Cullen. (n.d.). Retrieved August 21, 2011, from
http://www.facebook.com/group.php?gid=62986840525

Jacobs, K. (2004). Gender issues in young adult literature. *Indiana Libraries, 23*(2), 19–24.

Jacobson, C. K., & Heaton, T. B. (1991, Summer). Voluntary childlessness among American men and women in the late 1980s. *Social Biology, 38*(1–2), 79–93.

Jennings, J., Geis, F. L., & Brown, V. (1980). Influence of television commercials on women's self-confidence and independent judgment. *Journal of Personality and Social Psychology, 38*, 203–210.

Johnston, D. D., & Swanson, D. H. (2002, November). *Defining mother: The experience of mothering ideologies by work status*. Paper presented at the annual meeting of the National Communications Association, New Orleans, LA.

Johnston, D. D., & Swanson, D. H. (2003). Undermining mothers: A content analysis ofthe representation of mothers in magazines. *Mass Communication & Society, 6*, 243–265.

Johnston, D. D., & Swanson, D. H. (2007). Cognitive acrobatics in the construction of worker-mother identity. *Sex Roles, 57,* 447–450.

Johnston, D. D., & Swanson, D. H. (2008). Where are the mommies? A content analysis of women's magazines. In L. B. Arnold (Ed.), *Family communication: Theory and research* (pp. 395–403). Boston, MA: Pearson.

Johnston-Robledo, I. (2000). From post-partum depress to the empty nest syndrome: The motherhood mystique revisited. In J. C. Chrisler, C. Golden, & P. D. Rozee (Eds.), *Lectures on the psychology of women* (pp. 129–148). Boston, MA: McGraw-Hill.

Jones, E. E., Rock, L., Shaver, K. G., Goethals, G. R., & Ward, L. M. (1968). Pattern of performance and ability attribution: An unexpected primacy effect. *Journal of Personality and Social Psychology, 10,* 317–340.

Juhasz, S. (1988). Text to grow on: Reading women's romance fiction. *Tulsa Studies in Women's Literature, 7,* 239–259.

Jung, C. G. (1969). *The archetypes and the collective unconscious* (R. F. C. Hull, Trans.) (2nd ed.). Princeton, NJ: Princeton University Press.

Kahneman, D., & Tversky, A. (1972). Subjective probability: A judgment of representativeness. *Cognitive Psychology, 3,* 430–454.

Kahneman, D., & Tversky, A. (1973). On the psychology of prediction. *Psychological Review, 80,* 237–251.

Kahneman, D., & Tversky, A. (1984). Choices, values and frames. *American Psychologist, 39,* 341–350.

Kanner, M., & Anderson, K. J. (2010). The myth of the man-hating feminist. In M. A. Paludi (Ed.), *Feminism and women's rights worldwide: Vol. 1* (pp. 1–26). Santa Barbara, CA: Praeger.

Keilitz, S. L., Hannaford, P. L., & Efkeman, H. S. (1997). *Civil protection orders: The benefits and limitations for victims of domestic abuse.* (Report #-201). Williamsburg, VA: National Center for State Courts Research.

Keuhn, M. F. (1998). Gender and communication: The influence of gender on language and communication. In D. M. Ashcraft (Ed.), *Women's work: A survey of scholarship by and about women* (pp. 237–255). Binghamton, NY: Haworth.

Kirk, C. A. (2009, May 24). Stephenie Meyer's 'classical inspirations' for '*Twilight*' saga. *Examiner.com.* Retrieved from
http://www.examiner.com/article/stephenie-meyer-s-classical-inspirations-for-twilight-saga

Kleinmuntz, D. (1985). Cognitive heuristics and feedback in a dynamic decision environment. *Management Science, 31,* 680–702.

Klumb, P. L., & Lambert, T. (2004). Women, work, and well-being 1950–2000: A review and methodological critique. *Social Science and Medicine, 58,* 1007–1024.

Lassiter, M. (2010, May 7). Isabella reigns as new queen of baby names—takes top spot on Social Security's Most Popular Baby Names List. *Social Security Online.* Retrieved March 16, 2011, from
http://www.socialsecurity.gov/pressoffice/pr/baby-names2009-pr.htm

Lauzen, M. M., Dozier, D. M., & Horan, N. (2008). Constructing gender stereotypes through social roles in prime-time television. *Journal of Broadcasting & Electronic Media, 52*, 200–214.

Lee, J. A. (1973). *The colors of love: An exploration of the ways of loving*. Don Mills, ON: Shoe String Press.

Lee, J. A. (1988). Love-styles. In R. J. Sternberg & M. L. Barnes (Eds.), *The psychology of love* (pp. 38-67). New Haven, CT: Yale University Press.

L'Engle, K. L., Brown, J. D., & Kenneavy, K. (2006). The mass media are an important context for adolescent's sexual behavior. *Journal of Adolescent Health, 38*, 186–192.

Leogrande, C. (2010). My mother, myself: Mother-daughter bonding via the *Twilight* saga. In M. A. Click, J. S. Aubrey, & E. Behm-Morawitz (Eds.), *Bitten by* Twilight: *Youth culture, media, & the vampire franchise* (pp. 155–171). New York, NY: Peter Lang.

Leupp, K. M. (2011, August). *Even supermoms get the blues: Employment, gender attitudes and depression*. Paper presented at the 106th Annual Meeting of the American Sociological Association in Las Vegas, NV.

Libby, F. (2003, November). Medical student syndrome. *Psychologist, 16*(11), 602.

Luscombe, B. (2010, October 18). Week-on, week-off parenting: Does it work? *Time Magazine*. Retrieved from

http://www.time.com/time/magazine/article/0,9171,2024208,00.html

MacLean, S. (2012, April, 20). *Real heroines rip their own bodices*. Keynote address at the fifth annual Pennsylvania State University, Behrend College Gender Conference, Erie, PA.

Malamuth, N. M., & Donnerstein, E. (1982). The effects of aggressive-pornographic mass media stimuli. In L. Berkowitz (Ed.), *Advances of experimental social psychology* (Vol. 15, pp. 103–136). New York, NY: Academic.

Mamapalooza. (2011). *About*. Retrieved September 27, 2011, from http://mamapalooza.com/about

Mann, B. (2009). Vampire love: The second sex negotiates the twenty-first century. In R. Housel & J. J. Wisnewski (Eds.), Twilight *and philosophy: Vampires, vegetarians, and the pursuit of immortality* (pp. 131–145). Hoboken, NJ: Wiley Blackwell.

Marano, H. E. (2004, November). A nation of wimps. *Psychology Today, 37*, 58–103. Retrieved from http://www.psychologytoday.com/articles/pto-20041112-000010.html

Martens, M. (2010). Consumed by *Twilight*: The commodification of young adult literature. In M. A. Click, J. S. Aubrey, & E. Behm-Morawitz (Eds.), *Bitten by* Twilight: *Youth culture, media, & the vampire franchise* (pp. 243–260). New York, NY: Peter Lang.

Maslow, A. (1954). *Motivation and personality*. New York, NY: Harper & Row.

Maslow, A. H. (1970). *Motivation and personality* (2nd ed.). New York, NY: Harper & Row.

May, R. (1969). *Love and will*. New York, NY: Norton.

May, R. (1981). *Freedom and destiny*. New York, NY: Norton.

McClimans, L., & Wisnewski, J. J. (2009). Undead patriarchy and the possibility of love. In R. Housel & J. J. Wisnewski (Eds.), Twilight *and philosophy: Vampires, vegetarians, and the pursuit of immortality* (pp. 163–175). Hoboken, NJ: Wiley Blackwell.

McKinley, J. (2010, May 7). A name for newborns thanks to vampires. *The New York Times.* Retreived from

http://www.nytimes.com/2010/05/08/us/08names.html?_r=1&ref=books

McMahon, J. L. (2009). Twilight of an idol: Our fatal attraction to vampires. In R. Housel & J. J. Wisnewski (Eds.), Twilight *and philosophy: Vampires, vegetarians, and the pursuit of immortality* (pp. 193–208). Hoboken, NJ: Wiley Blackwell.

Megan, C. E. (2000, November). Childless by choice. *Ms. Magazine*, pp. 43–46.

Melender, H. (2002). Experiences of fears associated with pregnancy and childbirth: A study of 329 pregnant women. *Birth, 29*, 101–111.

Meyer, S. (2005). *Twilight.* New York, NY: Little, Brown.

Meyer, S. (2006). *New moon.* New York, NY: Little, Brown.

Meyer, S. (2006a, April 18). Personal correspondence 9. *The* Twilight *lexicon.* Retrieved March 6, 2012, from http://www.twilightlexicon.com/?p=81

Meyer, S. (2006b, March 11). Personal correspondence 4. *The* Twilight *lexicon.* Retrieved March 6, 2012, from http://www.twilightlexicon.com/?p=37

Meyer, S. (2006c, March 11). Personal correspondence 1. *The* Twilight *lexicon.* Retrieved March 11, 2012, from http://www.twilightlexicon.com/?p=34

Meyer, S. (2006d, March 19). Personal correspondence 6. *The* Twilight *lexicon.* Retrieved March 6, 2012, from

http://www.twilightlexicon.com/2006/03/19/personal-correspondence-6/

Meyer, S. (2007, February 13). The Q & A session in Spain with the member of Crepusculo. *The* Twilight *lexicon.* Retrieved March 6, 2012, from http://www.twilightlexicon.com/?p=277

Meyer, S. (2007). *Eclipse.* New York: Little, Brown.

Meyer, S. (2008). *Breaking dawn.* New York, NY: Little, Brown.

Meyer S. (2008a). *Midnight Sun.* Retrieved April 25, 2012, from http://www.stepheniemeyer.com/midnightsun.html

Meyer, S. (n.d.a). *Frequently asked questions:* Breaking Dawn. *Is Bella an antifeminist heroine?* Retrieved August 21, 2011, from

http://www.stepheniemeyer.com/bd_faq.html

Meyer, S. (n.d.b). *Frequently asked questions:* Breaking Dawn. *What is the most pivotal plot development that happens in* Eclipse? Retrieved August 21, 2011, from http://www.stepheniemeyer.com/ecl_faq.html

Meyer, S. (n.d.c). *The story behind the writing of* New Moon. Retrieved March 16, 2012, from http://StephenieMeyer.com/nm_thestory.html

Meyer, S. (n.d.d). *Being Jacob Black.* Retrieved April 25, 2012, from http://stepheniemeyer.com/nm_extras.html

Meyer, S. (n.d.e). *What are the characters biggest mistakes in* Eclipse, *their tragic flaws?* Retrieved April 25, 2012, from http://stepheniemeyer.com/ecl_faq.html

Meyer, S. (n.d.f). *Frequently asked questions:* Eclipse. Retrieved May 7, 2010, from http://www.stepheniemeyer.com/ecl_faq.html

Miller, L. (2008, July 30). Touched by a vampire. *Salon.* Retrieved from http://www.salon.com/books/review/2008/07/30/Twilight/index.html

Morran, C. (2010, April 15). *Twilight's* Carlisle Cullen named wealthiest fictional character. *Consumerist.* Retrieved from http://con.st/10004603

Moskowitz, C. (2010, September 13). Vampire books like *Twilight* may be altering teen minds. *Live Science.* Retrieved from http://www.livescience.com/10752-vampire-books-twilight-altering-teen-minds.html

Mueller, K. A., & Yoder, J. D. (1997). Gendered norms for family size, employment and occupation: Are there personal costs for violating them? *Sex Roles, 36,* 207–220.

Mullen, P. E., Pathé, M., Purcell, R., & Stuart, G. W. (1999). A study of stalkers. *American Journal of Psychiatry, 156,* 1244–1249.

Myers, A. E. (2009). Edward Cullen and Bella Swan: Byronic and feminist heroes … or not. In R. Housel & J. J. Wisnewski (Eds.), Twilight *and philosophy: Vampires, vegetarians, and the pursuit of immortality* (pp. 147–162). Hoboken, NJ: Wiley Blackwell.

National Center for Victims of Crime. (2011). *Stalking.* Retrieved July 9, 2011, from http://www.ncvc.org/ncvc/main.aspx?dbName=DocumentViewer&DocumentID=38720

National Domestic Violence Hotline. (n.d.). *Is this abuse?* Retrieved January 19, 2011, from http://www.thehotline.org/is-this-abuse/am-i-being-abused-2/

National Institute of Child Health and Human Development. (2001). Nonmaternal care and family factors in early development. *Applied Developmental Psychology, 22,* 457–492.

National Institute of Child Health and Human Development. (2004). Type of child care and children's development at 54 months. *Early Childhood Research Quarterly, 19,* 203–230.

National Institute of Child Health and Human Development. (2005). *Child care and child development: Results from the NICHD study of early child care and youth development.* New York, NY: Guildford.

National Institute of Child Health and Human Development. (2006). Child-care effect sizes for the NICHD study of early child care and youth development. *American Psychologist, 61,* 99–116.

National Institute of Health. (2011). *Hallucinations.* Retrieved July 6, 2011, from http://www.nlm.nih.gov/medlineplus/ency/article/003258.htm

National Institute of Justice. (2007). *Stalking.* Retrieved January 24, 2011, from http://www.ojp.usdoj.gov/nij/topics/crime/stalking/welcome.htm

National Institute of Mental Health. (2009). *Post-Traumatic Stress Disorder (PTSD).* Retrieved March 29, 2011, from http://www.nimh.nih.gov/health/topics/post-traumatic-stress-disorder-ptsd/index.shtml

National Institute of Mental Health. (2010). *Depression.* Retrieved April 1, 2011, from http://www.nimh.nih.gov/health/publications/depression/complete-index.shtml

National Poverty Center. (2011). *Poverty in the United States: Frequently asked questions.* Ann Arbor, MI: Author. Retrieved August 21, 2011, from http://www.npc.umich.edu/poverty/

Newcomb, N. S. (2007). Developmental psychology meets the mommy wars. *Journal of Applied Developmental Psychology, 28,* 553–555.

Nisbett, R. E., & Ross, L. (1980). *Human inference: Strategies and shortcomings of social judgment.* Englewood Cliffs, NJ: Prentice Hall.

Oakley, A. (1974). *The sociology of housework.* New York, NY: Pantheon.

Ould, P. (1998). Women and sociology: How the structure of society affects women. In D. M. Ashcraft (Ed.), *Women's work: A survey of scholarship by and about women* (pp. 135–165). Binghamton, NY: Haworth.

Paquette, L., & Kida, T. (1988). The effect of decision strategy and task complexity on decision performance. *Organizational Behavior and Human Decision Processes, 41,* 128–142.

Pew Research Center. (2007, July 12). Fewer mothers prefer full-time work. Washington, DC: Author. Retrieved January 10, 2011, from http://pewresearch.org/pubs/536/working-women

Philipp, D. A., & Carr, M. L. (2001). Normal and medically complicated pregnancies. In N. L. Stotland & D. E. Stewart (Eds.), *Psychological aspects of women's healthcare: The interface between psychiatry and obstetrics and gynecology* (2nd ed.) (pp. 13–32). Washington, DC: American Psychiatric Publishing.

Piaget, J. (1952). *The origins of intelligence in children.* New York, NY: International Universities Press.

Planned Parenthood. (2011). *Is your relationship good for you?* Retrieved July 29, 2011, from http://www.plannedparenthood.org/health-topics/relationships/your-relationship-good-you-19922.htm

Quindlen, A. (2005, February 21). The good enough mother. *Newsweek,* pp. 50–51.

Radway, J. A. (1991). *Reading the romance: Women, patriarchy, and popular literature.* Chapel Hill, NC: University of North Carolina Press.

Reagin, N. R. (Ed.). (2010). Twilight *and history.* Hoboken, NJ: John Wiley & Sons.

Rempel, J. K., Ross, M., & Holmes, J. G. (2001). Trust and communicated attributions in close relationships. *Journal of Personality and Social Psychology, 81,* 57–64.

Rich, A. (1993). Compulsory heterosexuality and lesbian experience. In L. Richardson & V. Taylor (Eds.), *Feminist Frontiers III* (pp. 158–179). New York, NY: McGraw-Hill.

Riggs, J. M. (2001, April). *Who's going to care for the children? College students' expectations for future employment and family roles.* Paper presented at the annual meeting of the Eastern Psychological Association, Washington, DC.

Riggs, J. M. (2005). Impressions of mothers and fathers on the periphery of child care. *Psychology of Women Quarterly, 29,* 58–62.

Rockler-Gladen, N. (2008). *Stereotypes about feminism: Myths about those bra-burning feminists rebuked.* Retrieved September 15, 2010, from http://www.suite101.com/content/stereotypes-about-feminism-a51504

Rogers, C. (1959). A theory of therapy, personality, and interpersonal relationships, as developed in the client-centered framework. In S. Koch (Ed.), *Psychology: A study of a science:* Vol. 3. New York, NY: McGraw Hill.

Rogers, C. (1961). *On becoming a person: A therapist's view of psychotherapy.* London: Constable.

Rogers, C. (1980). *A way of being.* Boston, MA: Houghton Mifflin.

Romance Writers of America. (2011). About the romance genre. Romance literature statistics: Industry statistics. Retrieved May 21, 2012, from http://www.rwa.org/cs/the_romance_genre/romance_literature_statistics/industry_statistics

Romance Writers of America. (2012). *Romance literature statistics: Industry statistics.* Retrieved April 28, 2012, from

http://www.rwa.org/cs/the_romance_genre/romance_literature_statistics/industry_statistics

Rosen, R. (2000). *The world split open: How the modern women's movement changed America.* New York, NY: Viking.

Rotter, J. (1982). *The development and applications of social learning theory: Selected papers.* New York, NY: Praeger.

Russo N. F. (1979). Overview: Sex roles, fertility, and the motherhood mandate. *Psychology of Women Quarterly, 4,* 7–15.

Saedi, G. A. (2011, November 4). The trouble with twihard teens. *Psychology Today.* Retrieved from http://www.psychologytoday.com/blog/millennial-media/201111/the-trouble-twihard-tweens

Schwebel, D. C., Brezausek, C. M., Ramey, S. L., & Ramey, C. T. (2004). Interactions between child behavior patterns and parenting: Implications for children's unintentional injury risk. *Journal of Pediatric Psychology, 29*(2), 93–104.

Seifert, C. (2008, December 17). Bite me! (or don't): Stephenie Meyer's vampire-infested *Twilight* series has created a new YA genre: Abstinence porn. *Bitch Magazine.* Retrieved from http://bitchmagazine.org/article/bite-me-or-dont

Seltzer, S. (2008). *Twilight*: Sexual longing in an abstinence-only world. *Huffington Post.* Retrieved from http://www.huffingtonpost.com/sarah-seltzer/twilight-sexual-longing-i_b_117927.html

Sheffield, J., & Merlo, E. (2010). Biting back: *Twilight* anti-fandom and the rhetoric of superiority. In M. A. Click, J. S. Aubrey, & E. Behm-Morawitz (Eds.), *Bitten by Twilight: Youth culture, media, & the vampire franchise* (pp. 207-220). New York, NY: Peter Lang.

Siering, C. (2010, July 1). Bella's eclipsed role in *Twilight* lacks fangs. *Ms. Magazine.* Retrieved from http://msmagazine.com/blog/blog/2010/07/01/bellas-eclipsed-role-in-twilight-lacks-fangs/

Signorielli, N. (1989). Television and conceptions about sex roles: Maintaining conventionality and the status quo. *Sex Roles, 21,* 341–360.

Slovic, P. (2000). *The perception of risk.* London: Earthscan.

Snyder, M., & Swann, W. B., Jr. (1978). Hypothesis-testing processes in social interaction. *Journal of Personality and Social Psychology, 36*, 1202–1212.

Sterk, H. M. (1986). *Functioning fictions: The adjustment rhetoric of silhouette romance novels.* Iowa City, IA: University of Iowa Press.

Stern, D., & Bruschweiler-Stern, N. (1998). *The birth of a mother.* New York, NY: Basic Books.

Sternberg, R. J. (1986). A triangular theory of love. *Psychological Review, 93,* 119-135.

Strauss, V. (2010, September 4). How *Twilight,* other dark fiction affect teen brains. *Washington Post.* Retrieved from http://voices.washingtonpost.com/answer-sheet/literature/experts-probe-how-twilight-and.html

Thompson, J. F., Roberts, C. L., Currie, M., & Ellwood, D. A. (2002). Prevalence and persistence of health problems after childbirth: Associations with parity and method of birth. *Birth, 29,* 83–94.

Tjaden, P., & Thoennes, N. (1998). *Stalking in America: Findings from the National Violence Against Women Survey.* Washington, DC: U.S. Department of Justice, National Institute of Justice.

Tobin, A. M. (2006, October 3). "Copycat effect" may explain cluster. *Toronto Star,* p. A7.

Today my girlfriend dumped me saying she wanted someone more like her Edward. (2010). *FMyLife.* Retrieved August, 21, 2011, from http://vampirescafe.com/today-my-girlfriend-dumped-me-proclaiming-she-wanted-someone-more-like-her-edward/

Toscano, M. M. (2010). Mormon morality and immortality in Stephenie Meyer's *Twilight* series. In M. A. Click, J. S. Aubrey, & E. Behm-Morawitz (Eds.), *Bitten by Twilight: Youth culture, media, & the vampire franchise* (pp. 21-36). New York, NY: Peter Lang.

Twenge, J. M. (2006). *Generation me: Why today's young Americans are more confident, assertive, entitled—and more miserable than ever before.* New York, NY: Free Press.

U.S. Bureau of Labor Statistics. (2011a, March 24). *Employment characteristics of families.* News release. Report number USDL-11-0396. Washington, DC: U.S. Department of Labor. Retrieved March 7, 2012, from http://www.bls.gov/news.release/famee.t04.htm

U.S. Bureau of Labor Statistics. (2011b, June 22). *American time use survey.* Retrieved August 21, 2011, from http://www.bls.gov/news.release/atus.t01.htm

U.S. Census Bureau. (2009a, April 21). *Facts for features: Father's Day June 21, 2009.* Report number CB09-FF.10. Washington, DC: U.S. Department of Commerce. Retrieved January 10, 2011, from www.census.gov/newsroom/releases/pdf/cb09-ff10.pdf

U.S. Census Bureau. (2009b, May 10). *Facts for features: Mother's Day May 10, 2009.* Report number CB09-FF.09. Washington, DC: U.S. Department of Commerce. Retrieved January 10, 2011, from www.census.gov/newsroom/releases/pdf/cb09-ff09.pdf

U.S. Department of Justice. (2011, May). *About domestic violence.* Retrieved August 22, 2011, from http://www.ovw.usdoj.gov/domviolence.htm

Walker, L. E. (1979). *The battered woman.* New York, NY: Harper & Row.

Warner, J. (2005). *Perfect madness: Motherhood in the age of anxiety.* New York, NY: Riverhead Books.

Warren, E., & Tyagi, A. W. (2003). *The two-income trap.* New York, NY: Basic Books.

Weintraub, S. (2010, August 3). The *Twilight* saga: *Breaking Dawn Part 2* gets released November 16, 2012. *Collider.com.* Retrieved from http://www.collider.com/2010/08/03/the-twilight-saga-breaking-dawn-part-2-release-date-november-16-2012-release-date

Williams, J. (2010). *Reshaping the work-family debate: Why men and class matter.* Cambridge, MA: Harvard University Press.

Wilson, N. (2011a). *Seduced by* Twilight: *The allure and contradictory messages of the popular saga.* Jefferson, NC: McFarland & Co.

Wilson, N. (2011b, November 16). Breaking Dawn: Part I—*The morning after—will there be bruises and feathers?* Retrieved April 22, 2012, from http://seducedbytwilight.wordpress.com

Wyer, R. S. Jr., & Srull, T. K. (Eds.). (1994). *Handbook of social cognition* (2nd ed.) (Vol. 1). Mahwah Hillsdale, NJ: Erlbaum.

Yen, H. (2010, January 15). *Census finds more stay-at-home dads.* Retrieved January 10, 2011, from http://www.manufacturing.net/News-Census-Finds-More-Stay-At-Home-Dads-011510.aspx

Yoder, J. D., Christopher, J., & Holmes, J. (2008). Are television commercials still achievement scripts for women? *Psychology of Women Quarterly, 32*(3), 303–311.

Zach, N. (2009). Bella Swan and Sarah Palin: All the old myths are not true. In R. Housel & J. J. Wisnewski (Eds.), Twilight *and philosophy: Vampires, vegetarians, and the pursuit of immortality* (pp. 121–129). Hoboken, NJ: Blackwell Wiley.

Index